GO, GIRL, GO!

The Women's Revolution in Music

By James L. Dickerson

SCHIRMER
TRADE
BOOKS

SCHIRMER TRADE BOOKS

New York / London / Paris / Sydney / Tokyo / Berlin / Copenhagen / Madrid

To Allie and Mattie,
without whom this book could not have been written,
and to their devoted mother, Mardi.

Schirmer Trade Books
A Division of Music Sales Corporation, New York

Exclusive Distributors:
Music Sales Corporation
257 Park Avenue South, New York, NY 10010 USA
Music Sales Limited
8/9 Firth Street, London W1D 3JB England
Music Sales Pty. Limited
120 Rothschild Street, Rosebery, Sydney, NSW 2018, Australia

Order No. SCH 10155
International Standard Book Number: 0-8256-7316-X

Printed in the United States of America

Cover Design: Phil Gambrill

Library of Congress Cataloging-in-Publication Data

Dickerson, James.
  Go, girl, go! : the women's revolution in music / By James L. Dickerson.
    p. cm.
  Includes bibliographical references and index.
  ISBN 0-8256-7316-X (hardcover : alk. paper)
  1. Feminism and music. 2. Women musicians—United States. 3. Popular music—United States—History and criticism. I. Title.

ML82.D528 2005
782.4216'3'0820973—dc22
                    2004016825

CONTENTS

Music Books by James L. Dickerson

Goin' Back to Memphis: A Century of Blues, Rock 'n' Roll, and Glorious Soul

That's Alright, Elvis: The Untold Story of Elvis' First Guitarist and Manager, Scotty Moore (with Scotty Moore)

The Dixie Chicks: Down-Home and Backstage

Faith Hill: Piece of My Heart

Colonel Tom Parker: The Curious Life of Elvis Presley's Eccentric Manager

Just for a Thrill: Lil Hardin Armstrong, First Lady of Jazz

The Fabulous Vaughan Brothers: Jimmie and Stevie Ray

ABOUT THE AUTHOR

The author of eighteen non-fiction books and over 2,000 magazine and newspaper articles, James L. Dickerson has been the dominant voice in the South for twenty-five years on matters related to popular culture and music.

Born and raised at the intersection of Highways 61 and 82, the heralded blues "crossroads" of the Mississippi Delta, Dickerson attended the University of Mississippi, where he played keyboards and sax in a series of well-known Southern bands, including the Dynamics, the Roadrunners, and the Strokers. After leaving college, Dickerson put his sax and keyboards aside to write for a living. His first magazine article, an interview with singer Bobbie Gentry, was published in 1967.

After becoming a regular contributor to the book pages of the *Baltimore Sun* and the *Toronto Star* in the early 1970s, Dickerson began writing full-time in 1977 when he joined the staff of the Pulitzer Prize-winning *Delta Democrat-Times* in Greenville, Mississippi. In the years that followed, he worked as a reporter, editorial writer, and editor for several newspapers, including the *Greenwood (Miss.) Commonwealth*, the *Jackson Daily News* in Jackson, Mississippi, and *The Commercial Appeal*, the largest-circulation newspaper in the mid-South.

In 1986 the author left *The Commercial Appeal* to edit and publish a pop-culture magazine, *Nine-O-One Network*. At the time *Nine-O-One Network* magazine suspended publication in 1988, it was sold on newsstands in all fifty states and was the third largest circulation music magazine in the United States. Also during this time, Dickerson served as the executive producer and co-owner of Pulsebeat-Voice of the Heartland, a radio syndication that offered a weekly blues program and a weekly country program to a network of 100 stations that stretched from New York to the Yukon.

For the past several years, Dickerson has worked as a freelance writer, book editor, and photographer. His work has appeared in numerous national and regional magazines, including *Mid-South Magazine*, *CoverStory*, *BookPage*, *Good Housekeeping*, *Omni*, *Glamour*, and *Penthouse*, to name a few.

Dickerson, who makes his home in Jackson, Mississippi, is the author of several critically acclaimed music books, including: *Goin' Back to Memphis*; *That's Alright, Elvis*; *Dixie Chicks: Down-Home and Backstage*; *Faith Hill: Piece of My Heart*; *Colonel Tom Parker: The Curious Life of Elvis Presley's Eccentric Manager*; *Just for a Thrill: Lil Hardin Armstrong, First Lady of Jazz*; and *The Fabulous Vaughan Brothers: Jimmie and Stevie Ray Vaughan*.

ACKNOWLEDGEMENTS

I would like to thank the following people for helping me with this book: Ed Frank at the Mississippi Valley Collection at the University of Memphis, the Jean and Alexander Heard Library at Vanderbilt University, the Public Library of Nashville and Davidson County, John Bakke at the University of Memphis, Deana Carter, Pat Benatar, Kathy Mattea, Pam Lewis, Sandy Neese, Frances Preston, Terri Clark, Sheila Lewis, Tiffany, Abra Moore, Shelia Shipley Biddy, Marilyn Arthur, Twana Burns, Renee Bell, the late Estelle Axton, Tracey Edmonds, Anita Mandell, Shania Twain; my editor at Schirmer, Andrea Rotondo; Alison Wofford at Schirmer; and my agent for this project, Alison Picard.

CREDITS

Managing Editor: Andrea M. Rotondo, Copyeditor: Andrea Beach, Proofreader: Barbara Schultz, Cover Design: Phil Gambril, Production Director: Dan Earley, Interior Design: Mary Belibasakis, Publicity Coordinator: Alison Wofford

INTRODUCTION

By any measure, 1996 was a landmark year in American music. It was the year female solo artists, for the first time in history, out-charted their male counterparts on the Top Twenty charts. Never, since the modern era began (defined as 1954, the year Elvis Presley made his first recordings), had more women than men charted on the Top Twenty. In most years between 1954 and 1995, male solo artists recorded 75% of the hit records on the charts. For four decades, women artists were almost an afterthought for record companies and radio program directors.

From 1954 to 1959, women could take credit for only 29% of the hits on the Top Twenty. Only three women—Kay Starr, Gogi Grant, and actress Debbie Reynolds—scored Number One hits. Actually, that early showing by women, during what is today considered an ultra-conservative period, would remain the strongest for over twenty years. For the next two decades, women would make their worst showing of the modern era, despite the reputation of the 1960s and 1970s as liberal, freewheeling eras of feminist self-fulfillment.

In truth, the 1960s and 1970s were disastrous years for female recording artists. All the talk about advancement for women was just that: Talk. From 1960 to 1969, only seventy-one women made the Top Twenty, compared to 221 men. That gave men a 76% to 24% edge over women. The next decade was even worse. From 1970 to 1979, sixty-two women made the Top Twenty, but so did 208 men, giving them 77% of the total.

It was not until the 1980s that the charts reflected a trend in favor of women. From 1980 to 1989, seventy-three women, or 31% of the total, made the charts. It was the best decade ever for women, but 31% hardly seemed like a victorious number. An analysis of the chart positions from 1954 to 1989, based on gender, leaves room for no interpretation other than that American popular music was the sole preserve of male recording artists.

All that changed—forever, some say—in 1996. Chart totals show that of the twenty-three solo recording artists who made the Top Twenty in 1996, fourteen were women. That gave the women a 61% to 39% margin over their male counterparts. The women who brought about the historic transition were:

Tori Amos
Toni Braxton

Mariah Carey
Tracy Chapman
Sheryl Crow
Celine Dion
Janet Jackson
Madonna
Natalie Merchant
Alanis Morissette
Joan Osborne
Leann Rimes
Shania Twain
Wynonna

The two women most dominant on the charts for the entire year were Canadians Shania Twain and Alanis Morissette. Their music was similar in that both expressed more aggressive viewpoints toward males than had previously been acceptable for the pop charts. They differed in that Shania was playful, almost teasing, in her approach, while Alanis seemed to struggle to contain her sometimes perplexing rage toward the opposite sex.

The male list was notable in that, of the nine men who made the Top Twenty in 1996, five—Alan Jackson, Garth Brooks, George Strait, Vince Gill, and Tim McGraw—were country artists (considered gender-friendly by women CD buyers) and only one—Sting—came close to fitting the traditional male pop/rocker mold. Simply put, 1996 was the worst showing ever for traditional male rock/pop recording artists. All year, only one male pop/rocker was able to crack the Top Twenty. For women, it was the musical equivalent of the crumbling of the Berlin Wall. What happened, and why?

Before the mid-1950s, women had enjoyed modest success with blues, jazz, and as frontispieces for big bands of the swing era. Hollywood movies gave women another outlet. Yet despite the emergence of high-profile women during the first half of the century—women such as Billie Holiday, Lil Hardin Armstrong, Alberta Hunter, Judy Garland, and others—their cut of the financial pie was minuscule compared to the generous helping dished out to male competitors.

Gender-based statistics for the first half of the century are scant, but in 1980 two academic researchers, Peter Hesbacher and Bruce Anderson, did a gender-focused survey, the results of which were published in *Popular Music and Society*. Their analysis of *Billboard's* popularity charts from 1940 to 1958 found that female solo artists made up 30% of the Number One hits charted during that period. For his book, *All of This*

Music Belongs to the Nation, Kenneth J. Bindas looked at the gender breakdowns for the WPA's Federal Music Project in the 1930s. He found that the project, which hired musicians, conductors, and composers, never gave women more than 16% of the positions available. To summarize attitudes toward women in music for that time period, Bindas chose an article from *Etude* magazine titled "What Great Music Owes to Women." The article concluded that "behind every great male composer, a woman contributed to his art by being his lover, friend, cook, and maid servant."

For most of the first half of the century, music was basically a feminine domain at the lowest rungs. For every man achieving success as a composer or instrumentalist, there were hundreds of women teaching music in low-paying jobs. Male music teachers were often perceived as gender-confused. Not until the 1940s did public perceptions about music begin to change. Responsible for that, to a large degree, were Frank Sinatra and Bing Crosby, who demonstrated that there was big money in music. Crosby didn't generate the large crowds of enthusiastic females that Sinatra did, but he transformed his stylized crooning into a multi-million-dollar movie career. So did Sinatra, who became the first sex symbol associated with popular music.

Watching from a distance, with great interest, was a man who transformed the music industry with his theory of gender-based marketing. Tom Parker, who later picked up the honorary title of "Colonel" from a Louisiana governor, took the Crosby-Sinatra phenomenon and bumped its threshold up several notches with an unknown Mississippi-born truck driver named Elvis Presley. No one knows for certain the gender breakdown for record sales prior to the modern era, but for the nearly half-century since Presley topped the charts with "Heartbreak Hotel," women have purchased most of the records, cassettes, and CDs sold in America.

The enormously successful marketing theory developed by Parker and executives at RCA Records was based on selling Presley's *sex appeal* to female record buyers, the largest segment of record buyers, and the *lyrical content* of the music to male record buyers. With the exception of ballads such as "Love Me Tender," there was nothing in the lyrical content of Presley's songs with which women could identify. What they could identify with was the way he looked and the way he moved on stage. It is interesting that "Heartbreak Hotel," Presley's first Number One hit for RCA, was written by a woman, Mae Axton. For the most part, male record buyers identified with the aggressive testosterone rhythms of the music and lyrics that put women in their place.

For forty years, that philosophy dominated the music industry. Women purchased most of the music, but men pulled the behind-the-scenes strings that determined what was offered. That formula of good-looking males with songs that offered tough love to women was never seriously challenged until the 1980s, when Madonna used rebellious sex appeal and strong lyrics to build her predominately female audience. Even so, Madonna's sex appeal was based on what men wanted to see in women. She was rebellious, but in a way that expressed male sexual fantasies about women. It was a bold departure, but it was not the stuff of which revolutions are made.

What were needed to actualize the revolution were female artists who could flip the Parker-RCA strategy and use the same marketing dynamics to their advantage. Not until 1996 did all the pieces fall into place. By then there was no shortage of women in executive positions at the record labels. Women had been filling those positions at a steady pace for the past decade.

The women who won the battles of 1996 all had two things in common: They had sex appeal, and their songs had content that women liked. Just take a look at the revolution's chart leaders: Shania Twain, Mariah Carey, Toni Braxton, Sheryl Crow, Janet Jackson, Alanis Morissette, and Madonna. All are Elvis-like in the appeal they make to men, and all connect with women at a deeper level, with messages that address the issues of ordinary life.

The women who captured the charts and hearts of America in 1996 were all media-savvy entertainers who understood that imagery, whether expressed in print photos or on television, was critical to their success. Their images, sometimes haunting, sometimes seductive, sometimes daring, were splashed across the media until they were recognizable by consumers who got to know their faces, even if they didn't know their music. Stardom is a measurement of what is received by the public, not what is offered by the artist. Stardom is always in the eyes of the beholder.

While the public is familiar with the names and faces of the women who made history in 1996, they are not familiar with the women in the trenches who made the revolution possible. Was it a fluke that women outsold their male competitors in 1996 for the first time in history? Was it some sort of gender-based fate? Was it luck?

If you examine the bigger picture, it is hard to escape the conclusion that the revolution of 1996 was the inevitable by-product of a lot of ambitious, goal-directed women who had been working for years behind the scenes of the music industry. For every female recording artist who scored in the Top Twenty, there were other unseen, unheralded women developing strategies, and pulling strings, all harmonizing to chants of, "Go, girl, go!"

1 The Early Years: 1900-1953

All revolutions begin with a single provocateur, a strong-willed individual, a fearless leader, whose foresight and courage give expression and energy to others. For the women's revolution in music, that individual was Lil Hardin Armstrong.

Growing up in Memphis, Tennessee, in the first decade of the twentieth century, Lil Hardin was subjected to a dizzying array of contradictions. At the time of her birth in 1898, slavery had only been abolished in the South for 33 years. Her grandmother, who lived in the household with her, had been a slave on a Mississippi plantation, and dinner-table conversation often centered on the evils of human bondage. For Lil, slavery was not an abstract historical concept, or some distant blemish on the national psyche; it was the cold, hard reality of her grandmother's life.

Such dire representations of man's inhumanity to man could easily have dampened Lil's spirit, but that was not the case. Lil's soul burned with the promise of freedom; a promise that was expressed with music. From a very early age, she showed an interest in the organ that graced the living room of the boarding house where her family lived.

Lil showed such promise on the keyboard that her mother, Dempsey, who worked in domestic service for a white family, took on extra work so that she could pay for Lil's after-school music lessons. Dempsey didn't envision her sacrifice paying off in financial terms. She was preparing Lil for stardom in that most sacrosanct of African-American institutions: The church. Dempsey wanted Lil to do the Lord's work—hallelujah!— by playing the music that uplifted the congregation's spirits and carried them on to glory.

Dempsey's plan had only one weakness. As the business axiom dictates, success often is based on three principles: Location, location, location. Unfortunately for Dempsey's dream, they lived only a couple of blocks off of Beale Street at a time when W.C. Handy was composing a new type of music there called the blues.

By 1910, when Lil was 12, Handy and his band regularly marched up and down the streets of Memphis, playing a mixture of Mississippi Delta folk music and European harmonics—Handy was a classically trained trumpet player—immortalized two years later with "Memphis Blues." Beale Street rocked every night with the sounds of Handy's blues, Delta folk music, and a second, new style of playing called jazz that had made its way upriver from New Orleans.

What Dempsey heard on Beale Street horrified her because she considered it the "devil's music." Those feelings had nothing to do with the way the music sounded. It had everything to do with the stories, true stories, she heard about the young girls that were lured to Beale Street by the bright lights and promises of pretty new clothes, only to discover that their only financial assets were their bodies. So many young women were flocking to Memphis at the turn of the last century that the city was forced to create a women's protection agency to deal with the problems associated with their arrival.

The ironic thing about that was that because sex was such a valuable commodity on Beale Street, women were afforded a level of protection not seen in any other city in America. Beale Street gained a national reputation as the safest place in the country for female performers: Not only were women protected from the perils of the street, they were given equal status with male performers. Blues singer Alberta Hunter got her start there, though she later denied it. So did guitarist Memphis Minnie.

None of that mattered to Lil Hardin. She was much too young to understand the dangers that her gender attracted when the sun went down and the prostitutes, drug dealers, and con artists hit the street. All she knew was that the music she heard in her neighborhood set her soul on fire. How could such wonderful music be evil? Lil was smart enough not to advertise her interest in the music, and whenever Dempsey railed about the devil's music, Lil simply nodded her approval and kept her thoughts to herself.

By the time Lil was nine, her skills on the organ were such that she landed a position as the organist for her Sunday school class at the Lebanon Baptist Church. Her favorite hymn was "Onward Christian Soldiers," and she played it at every opportunity. Unfortunately for her career as a church organist, she added jazz and blues riffs to the song. This rebellion delighted her classmates, but ultimately attracted the wrath of her pastor, who agreed with Dempsey that blues and jazz were the devil's music.

Lil had many disagreements with her mother over the music.

"It's only music," Lil argued.

"No," Dempsey fumed. "It's Satan's handiwork!"

That generational tug-of-war went on between Lil and her mother for years. Finally, when Lil turned seventeen, Dempsey decided that she needed to do something desperate to save her daughter from the perils of Beale Street. Her solution was to send her to Fisk University in Nashville, an all-black school founded for the express purpose of educating the sons and daughters of former slaves. There, Dempsey felt, Lil would get a good Christian education and learn to become a lady.

Going off to college was a rarity for girls of any age at that time in Memphis, and it was nothing short of astonishing that Dempsey was able to raise enough money to send her only child to a private school. There were only three other students from Memphis in Lil's class, and two of them were males. Lil took as many music courses as she could at Fisk, expanding her horizons, but she never lost interest in blues and jazz.

In 1917, when she returned to Memphis after her first year at Fisk, she purchased the sheet music to Handy's "St. Louis Blues," a song that was popular with young people all across America. Dempsey found the sheet music. It was the final straw. She gave Lil a sound beating with a broomstick, packed up all their belongings, and left the city that bluesman Sleepy John Estes once called "the center of all evil in the known universe."

Dempsey and Lil took the train to Chicago, where they hoped to build a new life. Unknown to Dempsey, Chicago had a thriving jazz scene that attracted the best of the New Orleans players, all hoping for a better payday. Chicago and Memphis were more alike than Dempsey realized, in that both were riddled with crime and political corruption, and both had unresolved racial problems. The main way the two cities differed, though, was that Chicago nightclubs did not have a protective attitude toward women.

As a result, women musicians in Chicago were a rarity. Women were allowed to front bands as singers, or as glorified hostesses, but they were not allowed to have equal status with men as musicians. Lil Hardin was destined to change all that, although in the beginning she seemed an unlikely candidate for leadership. At nineteen, she looked more like fourteen. Diminutive in stature and not especially well developed in her hips or bust, she had a slender, girlish appearance that camouflaged her age and experience.

Lil continued her music education in Chicago, not with structured lessons, but with sheet music purchased on a regular basis. Her second summer in Chicago, when she would have been twenty, she strolled into Jones Music Store on South State Street and asked the "demonstrator" if he would play a particular piece of sheet music for her. (In those days, music stores kept demonstrators on duty as sales aides.) The demonstrator did as she requested, but Lil let it be known that she was disappointed in the way he played the music. She asked if she could give it a try. The demonstrator, who thought Lil was much younger than she was, was so impressed with her playing ability that he offered her an "after school" job.

It was while Lil was working at the music store that she met legendary ragtime pianist Jelly Roll Morton, who stopped by the store one day to visit friends. "He was standing up by the door, and he was looking and people were playing, so he didn't say a word, just sat down," Lil later recalled. "I paid no attention to him at first. I didn't know who he was, you know. There were so many people there. So he sat down and he started a playing—oh, boy, oh, boy—and I started jumping up. The place was rockin' and the people were jumping up, keeping up with him, and I was jumpin' higher than anybody."

Lil's brush with greatness that day had a profound impact on her. She realized then that playing in a jazz band was what she wanted most in life. Unfortunately, she had few options. With only two types of musical entertainment available in the city—ragtime and symphonic music for white residents, and low-down blues and jazz for African Americans—Lil had no choice, really, and was further limited because the only female performers welcomed in black nightclubs were singers such as Memphis-born Alberta Hunter. At that time, Hunter was performing in South Side clubs that catered mostly to prostitutes and pimps. Women were welcome there as prostitutes, or as escorts for male customers, but not as musicians.

Lil didn't know it when she took the job at the music store, but the owner, Mrs. Jennie Jones, also booked talent for South Side nightclubs. When Lil learned that her boss was influential with the city's jazz performers, she begged for a booking. Mrs. Jones was so impressed by Lil's talent—attracting customers by sitting in the store window and playing the piano for hours at a time—that she agreed to do what she could to find her work as a musician.

The obstacles were formidable. Not many bands had arrangements for pianos, and fewer still had any interest in hiring a woman. It looked bleak for Lil, until Lawrence Duhe strolled into the store looking for work for his New Orleans Creole Jazz Band. Lil was there that day, and she certainly knew who he was. His band was the first New Orleans jazz band to make a splash in Chicago. She also knew that Duhe had created a stir by hiring a group of female singers.

Jones booked the band at a West Side Chinese restaurant. After the first night or two, they realized that they needed a piano player to perform the requests received from the restaurant's sophisticated clientele. Mrs. Jones promptly sent them a piano player, but he played Chicago style, and the band needed someone who could handle their New Orleans style of jazz. Lil had never been to New Orleans, nor was she familiar with New Orleans style arrangements, but Mrs. Jones sent her anyway, correctly guessing that Lil's extraordinary talents for improvisation would enable her to blend right in.

When Lil arrived at the restaurant for the audition, she asked Duhe what number they would play first and in what key. Duhe was horrified. None of them could read music.

"I don't know what key," he answered. "When you hear two knocks, just start playing."

Two knocks later, Lil jumped into the song and played all over the keyboard, allowing her keen ear to guide her fingers to the correct key. Several songs later, Duhe told her that she had the job, to which one of the band members, thinking that she was much younger than twenty, responded, "Oh, they will put us under the jail."

Lil was an enormous success. When patrons asked her name, she told them that she was called "Hot Miss Lil." Indeed she was. There was something about her high, neon-sweating energy that drew all eyes to the piano, even though she dressed like a man and had a schoolmarm primness about her.

Lil was an overnight sensation at the age of twenty. This woman, who had never in her life been into a nightclub on the arm of a man—indeed, had never really even dated a man—was the talk of the town. The New Orleans Creole Jazz Band made the rounds of the most popular nightclubs in Chicago, with "Hot Miss Lil" matching the men in the band note for note, a feat that made her quite an attraction with the public.

Despite the band's success, Duhe had a difficult time keeping everyone together. Players came and went with alarming frequency. After going through a string of trumpet players, he imported a cornet player from New Orleans named King Oliver. Quiet and unassuming at first, Oliver grew more aggressive with time, eventually becoming critical of the other players, creating so much dissension that Duhe finally got fed up and quit his own band, leaving the New Orleans Creole Jazz Band in Oliver's manipulative hands.

Lil, too, left the band, taking a job as the house pianist at the Dreamland Ballroom. There she backed guest performers such as Alberta Hunter, who was attracted to Lil's beauty and her aggressive piano style. About Lil, Hunter once said: "All you had to do—we knew nothing about arrangements, keys, nothing—all you had to do was sing something like 'Make Me Love You.' And she would [be] gone. She could play anything in this world and could play awhile. She was marvelous."

Lil eventually rejoined the New Orleans Creole Jazz Band, after King Oliver made her feel indispensable to their cause—as indeed she was. It was during her second stint with the band that Oliver decided to bring in a second-chair cornet player, a whiz from New Orleans named Louis Armstrong. Lil hated him at first sight. His hair was too long, with bangs that hung down over his forehead, and his clothes were obviously refugees from a second-hand store. On top of that, he weighed in at 226 pounds. Lil thought Oliver had lost his mind. Later, when asked to describe her first reaction to Louis, the word that gathered the most resonance was "disgusted."

Louis felt differently. Married at the time, he immediately fell in love with Lil and wasted no time pursuing her affections. It was a tough sell. By then she had married and had established herself as a major star. Louis was a dud as a charmer and he fared even worse as a conversationalist. The only potent weapon he had in his arsenal was his talent— and he used that to his advantage.

Lil fell in love with his playing long before she fell in love with him. That love crossed the line to romance on the night Freddie Keppard, the famous trumpet player, strolled up to the bandstand in between numbers and asked Louis for his horn. Keppard blew his best stuff; then he handed the trumpet back to Louis. Lil leaned over and whispered to Louis, "Now go get him!"

Louis turned loose with the best trumpet playing Lil had ever heard. Devastated by Louis's skill, Keppard slipped out the back door and never again asked to borrow Louis's horn. Lil fell in love with Louis on the spot. Not long after that, she separated from her husband and Louis separated from his wife. They started dating, and became black Chicago's most visible power couple.

"She used to tell me her troubles concerning her married life, and I would tell her mine," Louis later recalled. "It seemed as though we felt so sorry for each other we decided out of a clear skies [sic] to get together for good."

Lil and Louis were married on February 5, 1924. Not long after they were married, Lil told Louis that she did not wish to be married to a second trumpet. Stunned, Louis asked what she meant. Lil explained that she felt he was too talented to play behind a trumpet player who had less talent.

"I can't play first. Joe's [Oliver] playing first."

"That's why you have to quit."

"I can't quit Mr. Joe. Mr. Joe sent for me and I can't quit him."

"Well, it's Mr. Joe or me!"

Louis chose wisely and never looked back. Lil took charge of his career—put together a band for him, arranged bookings—and encouraged Louis to make his first recordings. In November 1925, she arranged for Louis to record a series of songs for Okeh Records. She helped him put together a recording band that included herself on piano, and she named the group Louis Armstrong and the Hot Fives, a derivative of her own "Hot Miss Lil" title.

By then, Lil had become a prolific songwriter, and knew the value of original songs. She took three of her tunes to the session: "My Heart," "My Heart Will Always Lead Me Back to You," and "(Yes) I'm in the Barrel." Louis took one of his own songs, "Gut Bucket Blues." Most historians consider the work that came out of that session to be the first jazz songs ever recorded.

From that point on, Louis's career skyrocketed. Lil continued to write songs for him—"King of the Zulus," "Lonesome Blues," "Jazz Lips," and "Struttin' With Some Barbecue," a masterpiece that brought Louis much success—and she continued to play in sessions with him, but as his fame increased their marriage suffered.

Eventually, Lil and Louis divorced, although they stayed in contact. Lil went on to have a solid career of her own as a band leader, prolific songwriter, and clothing designer, but she never came close to achieving the same level of fame as Louis. Her contributions to American music were largely relegated to footnote status, even though her songs continued to be recorded by artists such as Frank Sinatra, Ray Charles, Willie Nelson, Billie Holiday, and Peggy Lee.

When Lil Hardin Armstrong began her career, she had no female role models, white or black, to draw on for inspiration. She made it up as she went along, listening to an inner voice that always seemed to keep her on track. At that time, women could front bands or make records, but they could not influence the direction of music with their songs or their business savvy. Women performers of that era were put in the same category as prostitutes. Indeed, some female performers of that era, including Memphis Minnie and Billie Holiday, did work as prostitutes.

◆◇◆◇◆◇◆◇◆◇◆◇◆◇◆◇◆

Memphis Minnie, who grew up in tiny Walls, Mississippi, began her performance career with the Ringling Brothers circus, which taught her how to use her adolescent sexuality to attract male customers. By the time she started working in Memphis nightclubs, she had a reputation among other musicians as a violence-prone hothead who turned tricks when necessary to supplement her income. "They tell me she shot one old man's arms off, down in Mississippi," bluesman Johnny Shines told authors Paul and Beth Garon. "Shot his arm off, or cut it off with a hatchet, something. Some say shot, some say cut. Minnie was a hellraiser, I know that!"

Minnie was a major figure on Beale Street throughout the 1920s, and after the release of her first record in 1929, she dominated the national blues scene with classic recordings such as "Bumble Bee" and "I'm Talking About You." What set her apart from other female blues artists was her extraordinary talent on the guitar, an instrument that was not then associated with female performers. Indeed, perhaps because of its hourglass shape and phallic neck design, it was considered a *man's* instrument, one that women were discouraged from playing, for fear of appearing salacious.

Minnie had a profound influence on female attitudes toward the guitar, but the music she loved ultimately did not return that love. She spent her final days in poverty, confined to a wheelchair, paralyzed, unable to speak, weeping over the unkindness that life had bestowed upon her. Alone and forgotten at the time of her death, she was buried in an unmarked grave.

Billie Holiday, born Eleanora Fagan in 1915, began her life in Baltimore much as Memphis Minnie ended hers: In extreme poverty. The daughter of a jazz guitarist who toured with Fletcher Henderson's band, she was abandoned by her father at an early age and was raised primarily by her mother. She dropped out of school in the fifth grade and found a job in a brothel, where the madam paid her to run errands and wash the toilets. While she was working in the brothel, she heard her first jazz record, a song called "West End Blues," written by King Oliver and recorded by Louis Armstrong. She was shocked that Armstrong could evoke such "beautiful feelings" without singing actual words. Years later, she admitted that she copied her vocal style from Armstrong's singing and playing, even to the point of lifting his music note for note for her phrasing. It was during those years, when she was desperate for money, that she was arrested for prostitution, even though she was still a minor.

When Billie and her mother moved to Harlem, she applied for a job as a dancer at a speakeasy and was told that there were no openings. So she auditioned as a jazz and blues singer instead. The club owner was knocked out by her voice and offered her a job. Over the next several years, she made the rounds of the Harlem nightclubs, slowly building a reputation as a jazz singer. Not until 1933 did she attract the attention of producer John Hammond, who told friends that she was the best singer he had ever heard. Hammond got her studio work with two of the most successful big-band leaders of the day—Benny Goodman and Duke

Ellington—and helped her launch a recording career that led to some of the best jazz records ever made.

In 1935, while fronting Count Basie's band, she was told that she was too light-skinned to perform out on the road with black bands. People might mistake her for a white woman, and that would mean big trouble. Those were sensitive times racially, so she took the advice to "go white" and auditioned for Artie Shaw's band, becoming the first black vocalist to travel with a white orchestra. She soon became the highest paid entertainer in New York, a small consolation considering that, despite her star status, she still had to enter nightclubs, hotels, and restaurants through the back entrance.

After Billie Holiday formed a recording partnership with saxophonist Lester Young, she released a series of records, including "This Year's Kisses" and "Mean to Me," that established her as a major artist. She found stardom very stressful, however. Not only was she faced with the demands of delivering a perfect performance each time she stepped out into the spotlight, she was routinely attacked by racists who were envious of her success. In 1939, she released a record titled "Strange Fruit," a moving song about lynching. She followed that success with "God Bless the Child" and "Gloomy Sunday," songs that expressed the growing inner turmoil she felt.

Perplexed by a troubled world that seemed to offer no sanctuary, she retreated into heroin addiction and spent most of the 1940s in a drug-induced haze. Despite her personal problems, her celebrity grew. "When you saw her, it was just so different than any other person you'd seen onstage singing," recalled baseball great Buck O'Neill. "The way she would sell a song—anybody else could sing that song, and when Lady Day [the nickname given to her by Lester Young] sang it, it was a different song altogether."

By the late 1940s, Billie was arrested so many times for drug offenses that she was barred from performing in New York nightclubs. Frustrated by her legal troubles and her faltering voice, she added alcoholism to her list of personal demons. By the late 1950s, with her weight down to only 100 pounds, she often had to be led on stage, where she stood and rolled her head when she sang, spit trickling down her chin.

On May 30, 1959, she collapsed and was taken to Knickerbocker Hospital in New York. Doctors smelled alcohol on her breath and found needle tracks on her arms, so they transferred her to a public hospital where she could be treated for addiction.

When Billie was tracked down by her personal physician, he found her on an unattended stretcher in a hallway. Eleven days after she was admitted to the hospital, nurses found traces of cocaine in her room and called the police. Although Billie was barely conscious, police officers fingerprinted her and photographed her for a mug shot. Before she could be transferred to the Women's House of Detention, she lapsed into a coma and died, leaving an estate worth only $1,345.36.

Paralleling Billie Holiday's slide from grace was the rise and fall of Judy Garland, who began her career in the movies at the age of fourteen with a role in 1936's *Every Sunday,* starring Deanna Durbin. Subsequently, she was paired with established child star Mickey Rooney in a succession of films in the Andy Hardy series. Movie executives knew they had a star on their hands, but they didn't realize how big a star until she sang "Dear Mr. Gable" in her third film, *Broadway Melody of 1938.* That led to a role in 1939's *The Wizard of Oz,* in which she sang "Somewhere Over the Rainbow," the song that made her a major movie star and launched her career as a recording artist.

Garland released nearly 100 singles and over a dozen albums, one of which, *Judy at Carnegie Hall* (1961), received five Grammy awards, including album of the year. Throughout the 1940s, her recording career was dictated by her movie career, since studios wanted to pair hit songs with hit movies, but she was eventually able to stand alone as a recording artist. Perceived by some as white America's answer to Billie Holiday, Alberta Hunter, and Bessie Smith, Garland was considered one of the greatest entertainers of her day, a troublesome distinction that almost certainly contributed to her Billie Holiday-like attraction to alcohol and drugs. By the time she died at age forty-seven of an overdose of barbiturates, she had attempted suicide several times.

America had peculiar requirements of female recording artists during the first half of the twentieth century. It wasn't enough to have superior voices, or even stunning looks. The qualities that the public found irresistible clustered around the self-destructive personas radiating from desperate lives made torturous by public displays of promiscuity, drug addiction, and violence. Audiences flocked to see them with the same perverse attraction they usually reserved for train wrecks or hotel fires.

Billie Holiday and Judy Garland always knew that they were loved. Indeed, they thrived on the daily reminders of public adoration that they received. But their worst fear was to be adored for all the wrong reasons. In the end, that fear was what hurt them the most.

◆◇◆◇◆◇◆◇◆◇◆◇◆◇◆◇◆◇◆

What Lil Hardin Armstrong began on a high moral plane in the 1920s ran into trouble in the 1930s and 1940s, as the pressures of success in a man's world and the unceasing degradation of racism evolved into an emotional torture chamber for women aspiring to a high level of success in the music industry. What was needed to take up the slack in Lil's Revolution was a woman, preferably a photogenic white woman, with a voice that could be convincing in either blues or jazz—and, most important, nerves of steel!

Born Norma Egstrom on May 26, 1920, Peggy Lee was raised in a small North Dakota farm town by parents of Norwegian and Swedish heritage. Blonde and attractive, she seemed an unlikely person to ever achieve fame as a jazz singer. Her first-generation American parents loved music, but not the gritty sounds emanating from Chicago and New Orleans during the Jazz Age. Peggy was encouraged to participate in her school glee club and her church choir, but no one ever considered singing as a potential occupation for her—at least not until she was eight, when she announced to the world that she wanted to be in show business when she grew up. As evidence of her determination, she learned the popular songs of the day, such as "Moonglow" and "In My Solitude."

Peggy was so convincing in her argument that soon everyone believed that she was destined for stardom. While still a pre-teen, she performed with Doc Haines and his orchestra, who always introduced her as their "little Hollywood girl." Soon she landed her own radio show, for which she was paid five dollars a night and all the food she could eat in the restaurant that sponsored her show. That led to a performance on WDAY in Fargo, the most important radio station in that part of the state. Before the show began, the announcer pulled her aside and told her that she needed to change her name. Norma Egstrom just didn't have the right resonance for radio, he insisted. He suggested that she call herself Peggy Lee, and she did.

Almost immediately after her high school graduation, eighteen-year-old Peggy gathered her life savings (eighteen dollars) and a railroad pass that belonged to her father (he worked for the railroad) and struck out for Hollywood to share a boarding house room with a family friend. Unfortunately, Hollywood did not give her the greeting she expected. The only work she could find was as a short-order cook and waitress. When that job played out, she got work as a barker at a local carnival, where she urged passers-by to "hit the wino with the baseball." It was one of those booths in which a down-on-his-luck transient sat on a perch above a tank of water and waited for the baseball throw that would send him tumbling into the tank. While working at the carnival, two guitarists who were nephews of one of the concessionaires heard Peggy sing. They talked her into hitchhiking back to Hollywood to audition at a popular nightclub named the Jade.

On the way to the audition, her flimsy shoes fell apart and she walked into the nightclub barefoot to sing for the master of ceremonies. He hired her that day. Peggy thought she had hit the big time, although her two-dollars-a-night salary was not enough to enable her to buy the Chinese fare offered in the nightclub. Instead, she frequented the street vendor outside, where she purchased foot-long hot dogs for only ten cents.

Everything went well at the Jade, until one night when the owner invited her to sit at the table with him and a man she had never seen before. The man offered to give her a lift home after work, and since he seemed to be a friend of her boss, she accepted. Once they left the parking lot, she noticed he was driving in the wrong direction. When she pointed that out to him, he said he was hungry and wanted her to join him for a late dinner. She protested, but he assured her it would be all right.

Peggy's heart sank when they pulled up outside a shabby-looking nightclub. Inside, they joined several women and two men, who made it a point to sit on either side of Peggy in the booth. "The man on my left tried to make a little conversation, but I was too frightened to talk and too busy praying," she later wrote in her autobiography. "We both watched Sam [the man who brought her there] getting drunker by the minute, which this man seemed to think was a little unusual. Suddenly he whispered to me, 'I'm going to get you out of here. Follow me, stick close.'

"We scooted out of the booth, and Sam suddenly loomed up in front of my friend. There was a terrible fight, and, fortunately for me, my new friend won. The next minute we were rushing out of the club and running for the car.

"When we were safely out of the area and he was breathing a little more easily, he said, 'Look you don't know what you just got away from, but I'm going to tell you. I don't know why I should do this, but you remind me of my little sister. You, young lady, were headed for white slavery, and nobody would have heard from you again. Nobody.'"

Many years later, when she ran into her rescuer again at a function at her daughter's school, Peggy asked him why he had been so mysterious that evening. He answered, "I was a G-man."

Not long after her rescue from her would-be abductor, she had to be rescued from a riptide while swimming in the ocean. She almost drowned. She wrote her sisters about the incident, and they arranged for her old high school boyfriend to drive out to Hollywood and bring her back to North Dakota. Peggy was so angry, not just at her ex-boyfriend and her sisters, but at herself as well for failing, that she barely spoke on the long drive back.

As it turned out, her return to North Dakota was the first step that led to her big break. She quickly found work at radio station WDAY and at the Powers Hotel and Coffee Shop, the best music venue in Fargo. That led to a booking with Sev Olson's band in Minneapolis, which led to her joining Will Osborne's band. After a series of bookings around the country, the band traveled to Palm Springs, California, where Peggy found work at the Doll House, a popular spot for movie actors.

At that point in her career, Peggy had not developed a distinctive style of her own. That occurred at the Doll House when she tried lowering her voice in an effort to silence what could sometimes be a boisterous crowd. The softer she sang, the more attention she received from the audience. Actually, Peggy was ahead of her time. Decades later, media researchers discovered that "cool" images offered the most powerful visual and auditory stimuli on television and radio. Peggy learned from experience that the "cooler" she was toward the audience, the more people seemed to appreciate her.

In 1941, at the age of twenty-one, she took her new vocal style to a booking at the Ambassador West Hotel in Chicago, where Benny Goodman, the most popular bandleader in America at that time, dropped by to hear her sing. Peggy did not know it, but Goodman's girl singer, Helen Forrest, had decided to join Artie Shaw's band in an apparent dispute with Goodman over money.

The next morning, Goodman called Peggy's apartment and spoke to her roommate, telling her that he wanted to offer Peggy a job. When Peggy received the message, she thought it was a joke at first, not believing it until she dialed the number left with her roommate and heard the band leader's voice on the other end of the line.

Goodman didn't waste any time gabbing: He told her that he wanted her to join his band. Shocked, Peggy said she would be delighted. All he said in response was, "Come to work and wear something pretty." Peggy got the most sought-after job in music, without ever going through the trauma of an audition. Goodman liked what he had heard at the Ambassador and didn't feel he needed to hear more.

Peggy showed up for work wearing a nice dress, as requested, and received yet another shock—there would be no rehearsal. She was simply handed a list of the songs she would sing that night. Luckily, she knew them all. Peggy went to extraordinary lengths to forge a career as a popular singer—and in the end all she needed was to be in the right place at the right time.

The first night went well enough, or so she thought. The next morning she was horrified to learn she had been savaged by the critics. Later,

Downbeat magazine ran a photograph of her with the caption: "Sweet Sixteen and Will Never Be Missed." Peggy was so discouraged that she told Goodman she wanted to quit. His only response was, "I won't let you."

Within days after joining Goodman's band, Peggy was sent to a recording studio with producer John Hammond to make a record with Goodman and his band. The night before, Hammond gave Peggy the sheet music to a song titled "Elmer's Tune," expecting her to know it from top to bottom when she arrived at the session. She did, but the session was a harrowing experience because in those pre-tape days, artists could not stop and back up to correct mistakes. It was a live performance, and everything had to be perfect.

At a subsequent session, Peggy brought her wind-up phonograph and a recording of Lil Green's "Why Don't You Do Right?" to play for the bandleader. Goodman paid Peggy ten dollars to record the song, with no royalties. At the time, she thought it was probably a good deal since her weekly salary was only seventy-five dollars. To everyone's surprise, the record was a smash hit and sold over one million copies. It made Peggy famous, but she never benefited financially beyond the ten-dollar recording fee she collected for the session.

For the next two years, Peggy toured with the Benny Goodman band, doing mostly one-nighters but occasionally settling into a hotel ballroom for an extended booking. Once, while she was performing at the New Yorker Hotel, Count Basie walked up to the bandstand and winked at her, intoning, "Are you sure you don't have a little spade in you, Peggy?" She took that as a high compliment.

Peggy soon began dating Dave Barbour, the guitarist in Goodman's band. When she learned that she was pregnant, she rushed to him to deliver the good news. To her surprise, he paused a long time, and then said, "Why, Peg, I hardly know you." That was not exactly what Peggy wanted to hear, and it devastated her; but he eventually recovered from the shock of parenthood and proposed to her after the birth of their daughter, Nicki. They married in 1943, the year Peggy left Goodman's band to move to California to focus on her recording career.

In 1944, Peggy signed with Capitol Records, beginning a long songwriting and recording career that produced a string of hits, including "Golden Earrings," which sold one million copies; "You Was Right, Baby"; "It's a Good Day"; "Manana," which sold over two million copies; "What More Can a Woman Do?" and "I Don't Know Enough About You." This time she made certain she received royalties.

Considering her stage presence and her good looks, it was perhaps inevitable that Peggy would gravitate to movies. Her first film was *The*

Jazz Singer, in which she played opposite Danny Thomas in a remake of the early Al Jolson movie. She followed that up with a role in *Pete Kelly's Blues,* in which she played an alcoholic blues singer. She was so convincing in the role that she was nominated for an Oscar.

Peggy's acting experience inspired her to write songs for films in which she was not cast as an actor. She wrote the theme music for *Johnny Guitar* and *About Mrs. Leslie,* and she contributed songs to two cartoon features, *Tom Thumb* and *The Time Machine.* Oddly enough, the motion picture that brought her the most fame was the Walt Disney animated cartoon *Lady and the Tramp,* for which she wrote the lyrics and created several voices. Her recording career did not suffer in the least because of her involvement with movies. Three years after the release of *Lady and the Tramp,* she recorded the song that made her a superstar: "Fever," the sultry, finger-snapping hit that earned her four Grammy nominations. She went on to record hits such as "I'm a Woman," "The Way You Look Tonight," and "Is That All There Is?" which earned her a Grammy for best contemporary vocal performance in 1969.

As Peggy's success continued, year after year, allowing her to have hits in the 1940s, 1950s, and 1960s, it brought inevitable comparisons to the troubled careers of predecessors such as Judy Garland and Billie Holiday. How had she stood up to the enormous pressures of the music industry without resorting to drugs and alcohol? How had she survived, when others had not? Peggy's answer surprised a lot of people. "My strength came from the training I got as a girl, working as a hired hand on a farm," she told an interviewer. "I shucked grain. I pitched hay. I drove the water wagon for a threshing ring." Whether that experience gave her strength or simply reminded her of her humble beginnings and kept her motivated to succeed, she felt she was a product of her history and therefore had something to live up to.

The first half-century of the women's revolution in music came full circle in July 1971, with the death of Louis Armstrong. Lucille Armstrong, Louis's widow, asked Peggy Lee to sing the "Lord's Prayer" at the funeral in New York. Sitting in the audience that day, anonymous to most of the mourners, was the woman who initiated the women's revolution in music, Lil Hardin Armstrong.

Besides being survivors, Peggy and Lil had a great deal in common. Both women had personal lives marked by failed relationships (Lil had two marriages; Peggy had four), but neither succumbed to the "bad girl" reputations that characterized many of their contemporaries. Also, at that time, Peggy and Lil were the only women performers who found success as songwriters, an aspect of the music industry that was almost exclusively male.

Peggy never spoke to Lil that day. Indeed, she probably did not even know Lil was in the audience: She was so nervous about singing that she stared at Louis's corpse for the duration of the song. Also staring at the corpse was Lil, who never stopped loving the man with whom she had written so much inspired music.

Peggy left the funeral that day destined to achieve even greater success as an entertainer, and to live another thirty-one years. But Lil returned to Chicago, heartbroken about the loss of her only true love in life and despondent over the diminishment of her career. Seven weeks after her return, she was asked to perform in a memorial concert for Louis at Chicago's Civic Center Plaza.

When Lil's turn came to take the stage, she sat down at the piano and played W. C. Handy's "St. Louis Blues," a tribute not only to Louis, who had recorded the song in the late 1920s, but to her Memphis roots. She played the song loudly, with her usual wrist-snapping vigor; then she ended with a ringing chord that resonated long after she had struck the keys. She held onto the chord, tightly, as if drawing sustenance from it, then, to the astonishment of everyone in attendance, she tumbled off the piano stool, dead of a broken heart at the age of seventy-three. An era had come to an end.

2 The Modern Era Begins: 1954-1959

Elvis Presley—the man Madonna once called God—stood in the same place each time he listened to playbacks in the early days at Memphis Recording Service. With his hand braced against the wall for support, he lowered his head and listened to the sound of his own voice as the reel-to-reel tape spun round and round, filling the room with music.

One day, while listening to playbacks, his hands were dirty, maybe from his job as a truck driver at Crown Electric, or maybe from poking around the dark corners of the studio, leaving a perfectly outlined handprint on the light-colored wall. It embarrassed him at the time and he tried to rub it off, but the defiant handprint refused to budge.

For years afterward, young girls came into the studio to gaze at the handprint. Sometimes they stood in awe, breathless, as if they were at a religious shrine. Other times they touched, caressed, and kissed the handprint. Sometimes they measured their own hand against it. Always, they talked to it as if it had human feelings and could hear and understand and care about what they had to say. Then, one day, the handprint disappeared, covered over by an unsentimental painter.

Those looking for a starting point for the second phase of the women's revolution in music—the precise moment when little girls' dreams began to grow into the reality of womanhood, and the precise place where the dreams began to take root—need look no further than Presley's handprint. That it no longer exists hardly matters. That it took more than forty years for the dream to be realized matters even less. All that matters today is what the handprint stood for to an entire generation of American women—and to the daughters and granddaughters who bought into the dream.

By the time Marion Keisker started working with Sam Phillips at Memphis Recording Service, she was in her mid-thirties, the divorced mother of a young son. Her job title was secretary, but she was much more than that to Phillips, who depended on her good judgment and people skills to keep him in business.

Marion first met Sam in 1946, four years before he opened the studio. They both worked at radio station WREC, a CBS affiliate at 60 on the dial. Sam was an engineer and Marion was an on-air personality, the host of a popular talk show, "Meet Kitty Kelly." She made her debut on the station in 1929 at the age of twelve, appearing on a weekly children's show, "Wynken, Blynken, and Nod," and remained a presence at the station until joining the staff in 1946 to become Kitty Kelly.

By post-World War II standards, Marion was light years ahead of her time in her professional aspirations. She was intelligent, ambitious, energetic, and perhaps most important of all, aggressive in her pursuit of a career. In addition to playing the role of Kitty Kelly, she was on the air five days a week pulling duty on various shows; after hours, she worked on a nightly show, "Treasury Bandstand," which was broadcast from the top floor of the Peabody Hotel, a landmark gathering place for mid-Southerners. In later years, she recalled—to her own amazement—that she had written, directed, or produced as many as fourteen shows at a time for the radio station.

By the time Sam rented a building in 1950, located down the street from the Peabody (WREC's offices were located in its basement), he and Marion had worked closely together at the radio station for four years. By all indications, Marion was very much in love with Sam, though the exact nature of her relationship with him was never discussed by either person, since he was married at the time. At first, Sam tried to operate the studio while holding down his job at WREC. He worked at the radio station in the mornings and early afternoons, left to open the studio for a few hours, then returned to his job at the radio station in the evenings, then back again to the studio later at night. That wasn't an unreasonable time schedule for a studio because musicians tend to be nocturnal creatures; besides, musicians in Memphis all had day jobs of one kind or another.

For the most part, Memphis Recording Service operated as a vanity studio. Sam recorded bar mitzvahs, weddings, and birthday greetings. He transferred tapes to records and made off-air checks for radio stations. A separate enterprise was a record label he named Sun Records. For that, he recorded musical groups and pressed the tapes into actual records. If he got lucky, a radio station somewhere would play the record. Sam didn't get lucky often. There was not a long line of musicians waiting to get into the studio to work with him. That first year, he learned that the most commercial recordings he could make were of black musicians performing the music native to the region, the blues. He took those recordings and sold them, for modest amounts, to record labels in Chicago and Los Angeles that specialized in African-American music.

Creatively, Sam was quite successful, discovering talented black musicians who later went on to great fame: Howlin' Wolf, Joe Hill Louis, and Walter Horton, to name a few. Financially, he always seemed to be on shaky ground. All he could do was release the records, sit back and wait to hear from a record label, and then sell the master tapes. Unfortunately, there wasn't much money in that type of operation.

After a year-and-a-half of burning the candle at both ends, the pressure of working eighteen- and twenty-hour days got to Sam. His boss at the radio station criticized him at every opportunity. The studio brought in very little money. He had a wife and two sons to support. Emotionally, Sam was spent. Twice he was admitted to Gartly-Ramsay Hospital to undergo electroshock treatments for depression.

Abruptly in June 1951, Sam handed in his resignation at WREC to devote his full efforts to Memphis Recording Service. He printed up business cards that read: "We record anything—anywhere—anytime." To Marion, Sam must have resembled a wounded bird. In the early 1950s there was quite a stigma attached to mental illness; anyone who had ever been admitted to a mental hospital, or subjected to elec- troshock treatments, was viewed with distrust and sometimes derision. The only rung lower on the social ladder was reserved for those who committed racial transgressions. By working with black musicians in his studio, Sam violated that social convention as well. As if that were not enough, his engineering job was the lowest in the radio station pecking order. At the top was the general manager, then the on-air personalities, then the sales staff—and, at the very bottom—the lowly engineers. Sam was hardly a big shot.

By contrast, Marion was a local celebrity. Newspaper articles called her "Miss Radio of Memphis." It was her voice people heard interviewing the celebrities that came to town for performances or special events. It was her voice that made Memphians feel good about themselves. And it was her vivacious personality that helped two generations of Memphis women define themselves in the post-World War II economy.

If Marion was in love with Sam, it would explain why she gave up her high-profile job at WREC to work with him at the studio. Although she was identified as the secretary, she was Sam's partner in every sense of the word: She was the public persona of the company and greeted the customers; she did the bookkeeping and the billing; she was the business manager and made the arrangements for the distribution of the records; and she wrote up all the contracts and sent out the letters.

One day, after concluding that the front door made a bad impression on the public, she bought a new one with her own money and had it installed. Years later, in an interview with Jerry Hopkins, Marion put the early days in perspective. "I threw over the whole thing [the radio career] for the record company," she said. "The only sleep I got in those days was at the desk."

For the first three years, Sam generated a lot of attention for his work with African-American recording artists, but that recognition did not translate into financial success. Whatever promises Sam made to Marion when she left her job at the radio station, it was becoming clear that they might not come true. Three years is a long time to watch a company flounder, especially under the leadership of a man whose greatest claim to fame was his association with African Americans at a time when it was against the law for people of color to eat in white-owned restaurants or enter public facilities such as libraries or swimming pools. Sam was a rebel—and rebels don't attract money.

Marion became more aggressive as a talent scout. After three years it had become clear to her that Sun Records was never going to be successful promoting black artists. What Sam needed was a white artist, someone who would be embraced by the community she had represented so well as "Miss Radio of Memphis."

If she could find a white singer who could sing like the black singers Sam worked with, well . . . then she would have something. As there were no white singers standing in line outside the studio, she paid particular attention to the people who came into the studio to make vanity recordings. When someone wanted to make a birthday or holiday greeting for someone special, they could come into the studio, pay four dollars, and speak or sing into a microphone, recording the message onto an acetate disk that resembled the records sold in the stores. If Marion felt the client had talent and would be a possibility for the record label, she would turn on a separate tape machine and recorded the brief session so that she would have a copy to play for Sam.

That was how Marion discovered Elvis Presley. "I first saw Elvis on a Saturday afternoon—it was a busy, busy afternoon and for some reason I happened to be alone at the time," she said. "The office was full of people wanting to make personal records. It was a stand-and-wait-your-turn sort of thing. [Elvis] came and said he wanted to make a record. He sat down [with his guitar] . . . and while he was waiting his turn, we had a conversation. . . . He said he was a singer. I said, 'What kind of singer are you?'

"'I sing all kinds,' he said.

"'Who do you sound like?'

"'I don't sound like nobody.'

"I thought, 'oh yeah—one of those.'"

Marion took Elvis into the back room to record the acetate. When he was about one third of the way through the first song, she turned on the tape player. She got part of the first song and the entire second song on tape. Later, she realized that Elvis had been unaware that a second machine had taped him.

When Sam returned to the studio, Marion played the tape for him. He was impressed, but felt that the singer needed a lot of work. He asked if she had his name. She did. She showed him a piece of paper that said: "Elvis Presley—good ballad singer—hold." Unimpressed, Sam told her to do just that—hold it until he asked for it again.

Marion kept pitching Elvis to Sam, and Sam kept putting her off. One day while they were having coffee at a restaurant next door to the studio, she brought up Elvis' name again, this time in front of guitarist Scotty Moore, who had been urging Sam to tell him what kind of talent he was looking for. Sam had released a record by Scotty's band, the Starlite Wranglers, that hadn't sold well, and Scotty wanted Sam to give him another chance.

Sam suggested that Scotty get in touch with Elvis and audition him at his house. If Elvis was any good, Scotty could bring him in for a taped audition. Marion didn't win the way she wanted to—on the merits of her good musical judgment—but she did win.

In later years, Marion told the story of Elvis' discovery with pride, then as the years wore on, with some bitterness. Her story was that she took Elvis to Sam because he was fond of saying, "If I could find a white man who had the Negro sound and the Negro feel, I could make a billion dollars."

Unfortunately, no one can recall Sam ever saying anything remotely like that. Scotty Moore swears he never heard Sam say that. One suspects it was Marion who made that comment—and for good reason. Sam was more comfortable working with black recording artists. He recorded very few white singers and musicians. Sam never dealt with the public. That was Marion's job. She knew Sam was not going over very well in the white community. That was a bitter pill for a woman in love. It was Marion, not Sam, who had the greatest motivation to make a Great White discovery.

Once Elvis' career took off, Marion tirelessly worked the media on his behalf. On the morning of July 27, 1954, Marion took Elvis into the newsroom of the Memphis *Press-Scimitar* to do his first interview. Edwin Howard, the reporter, agreed to do the interview on Marion's recommendation. Later, he wrote: "The boy's hair looked as if it had been cut by a lawn mower, but the trademarks were already there: Flat top, duck tail, and sideburns. He was shy and, except, for saying, 'yes sir' and 'no sir,' let Marion do all the talking."

Once she saw how people reacted to Elvis, Marion gave Sun Records everything she had; from that point on, even her family took a backseat. Long days became long nights. Early one morning, about three o'clock, she fell asleep at her desk while doing the bookkeeping. Suddenly, she was awakened by the sound of her name.

"Marion . . . Marion . . . Marion," the voice said.

She lifted her head up off the desk and standing before her was Elvis, looking white as a ghost. "I thought you were dead," he said, his voice shaky. He explained that he was driving by the studio on his motorcycle and had spotted her through the open blinds, slumped over her desk, looking every bit the crime victim.

That first year, Marion worked feverishly on Elvis' behalf. She phoned radio stations, worked the press, and attended the recording sessions, doing what she could to help. During one session, they were recording a cover of "I Don't Care if the Sun Don't Shine"—first recorded by Patti Page in 1950—when everything came to a sudden halt. Elvis only knew one verse. "Don't worry," Marion told the boys. "Take a break." While they sat around and drank Cokes and smoked cigarettes, Marion hastily wrote a second verse for the song. It began, "I don't care if it's rain or snow/drivin's cozy when the lights are low/and I'm with my baby . . ."

Elvis finished the recording with her lyrics, and a few days later Sam took their only copy to a record convention in Nashville. He played the song for several people at the convention, then called Marion and told her to go ahead and master the record. He said everyone liked it and he was taking orders like crazy.

Some time later Marion received a telephone call from the song publisher, who told her the original writer, Mack David, would have to approve any changes made to the song. Marion airmailed her only copy to New York and awaited the verdict. To her surprise, the publisher called back and said David loved the new lyrics. Sam could release the record, but there was a catch: Marion would have to sign a disclaimer relinquishing any rights she might have acquired in the song with the new lyrics. Eager to do anything she could to further Elvis's career, she gladly signed the papers; but, for years afterward, she felt a tinge of anger whenever she heard the song on the radio with her lyrics.

Shortly before Sam sold Elvis' contract to RCA Records in November 1955, he purchased a radio station with money that he received from Holiday Inn developer Kemmons Wilson. The station, which was located in a Holiday Inn on Third Street, was given the call letters WHER. It was the first all-female radio station in the nation.

For the station's general manager, Sam chose Dotty Abbott, well known locally as an actress and broadcaster. Also hired were Sam's wife, Becky, and a staff of female salespersons and announcers, including Marion, who was removed from her position at the recording studio and hired as an announcer/news reporter for the station.

With her transfer to the radio station, the Sun Records partnership forged by Marion and Sam was effectively over. On her last visit to the recording studio, she angrily took down the door she had purchased and installed. She was not happy about relocating to WHER—hadn't she helped build Sun Records into the giant that it became?—but she did not let anyone know how unhappy she was.

"As it happened, mine was the first voice to be heard on WHER," she later wrote in an article published by the Memphis Brooks Museum of Art. "When the time came to run the required pre-opening engineering tests, I went on the air after midnight with a prepared text giving the station's call letters, assigned frequency, and location and asking listeners to call the station to help establish range and transmission quality. One caller, sounding very puzzled, commented: 'You sound like a lady!' I replied, 'I thank you, and my mother thanks you.'"

Marion lasted less than two years at WHER. In the fall of 1955, she and Sam had a big fight—their last big fight—and Marion stormed out of the radio station and joined the Air Force. She made the mistake women have made throughout history: She gave her talents in the name of love, a trade that always ends poorly for the woman.

Marion never made a dime off of Elvis' career, and she received little credit for her contributions to Sun Records. As the years went by, she remained loyal to Sam, but she became less and less supportive of the role he played in Elvis' career. At times, she openly disputed Sam's version of events. The only recognition she ever received came from the person who most mattered—Elvis himself.

While she was in the Air Force and stationed in West Germany and Elvis was in the Army in the same country, she was allowed to attend an event at which he was scheduled to appear. He was shocked to see her there, especially showing the rank of captain. He gave her a big hug, but not before asking, "Do I kiss you or salute you?"

The Army captain in charge was outraged to see an Air Force captain there—and a female to boot. He ordered her to leave. She refused. At that point, Elvis stopped and addressed his superior officer. "Captain, you don't understand," he said. "You wouldn't be having this thing today if it wasn't for this lady!"

"You mean, this WAF captain?" he asked.

"Well, it's a long story," Elvis explained, "but she wasn't always a WAF captain." Elvis went on to tell the story of how she had discovered him, but while he spoke to the captain he surreptitiously extended his arm behind his back, out of sight of the captain, reaching out to touch Marion, a gesture that made her heart melt. That was thanks enough for Marion, which was a good thing, because that was all the thanks she ever received.

◆◇◆◇◆◇◆◇◆◇◆◇◆◇◆◇◆◇◆

For the first half of the twentieth century, women were visible in American music, but only as vocalists, a distinction that made them seem more powerful than they really were. For the most part, they were considered attractive, personality-gilded facades for the big-money operations going on behind the scenes.

Despite their place in the spotlight, women were financially subservient in the music industry. Their compensation was usually restricted by the convention that women not earn more than men, or by unscrupulous managers and handlers who took advantage of their lack of experience in business matters—an easy thing to do in the industry's very fluid cash-and-carry economy.

By the 1950s, most of the successful bands and orchestras were still fronted by women, and a healthy portion of the recordings issued each year featured women vocalists. Peggy Lee, who had scored huge hits in the 1940s, continued to dominate the charts, as did Patti Page, who had her biggest hit ever in 1950, "Tennessee Waltz."

That special position began to erode in the late 1940s, when male crooners such as Bing Crosby and Frank Sinatra—and "singing cowboys" such as Roy Rogers and Gene Autry—gave male-gender respectability to the profession by recording songs that appealed to the same female record buyers that had made stars of the female singers. By the early 1950s, male singers such as Nat King Cole, Perry Como, Tony Bennett, and Eddie Fisher had bumped industry-wide record sales up a notch.

Even so, female artists were still going strong, led by the Andrews Sisters, Teresa Brewer, Eileen Barton, Rosemary Clooney, Della Reese, Kay Starr, Vera Lynn, and Doris Day. In 1951, at the age of twenty-three, Rosemary Clooney had a million-selling hit with "Come on a My House," a song that featured lyrics by noted author William Saroyan and music by his cousin, Ross Bagdasarian, who was famous at the time for creating a novelty act named The Chipmunks. Della Reese scored her first major hit during this time with "And That Reminds Me (of you)," a song that led *Billboard* to declare her America's "most promising singer."

The balance of power changed drastically in 1954, with Elvis Presley's first recordings at Sun Studios in Memphis—and it would stay that way almost until the end of the century—but women remained strong contenders throughout the 1950s. In fact, that decade gave them their best showing until the 1980s.

From the beginning of 1954 through 1959, forty-five female solo artists made the Top Twenty, compared to 108 male solo artists, giving women 29% of the total. The biggest female hitmakers were Jo Stafford, Kay Starr, Gogi Grant, Patti Page, and Debbie Reynolds, who directed their efforts toward melodic pop songs. That percentage would drop during the 1960s and 1970s, exposing the myth that the 1950s was a stifling period for women.

Female songwriters also did relatively well during the 1950s, though most of their hits were as co-writers with male partners. There is no way to know how many of the male co-writer credits were authentic and how many were "add-ons" provided to give the women marketplace credibility. For example, "Heartbreak Hotel" was Elvis Presley's first release for RCA and his first number-one single. Songwriter credits list Presley, Tommy Durden, and Mae Axton. Actually, Presley had nothing to do with writing the song (his manager Colonel Tom Parker routinely added Presley's name as a songwriter to all of his songs as a means of increasing his income). Durden gave Axton the idea for the song when he showed her a newspaper story about a suicide victim who left a note saying, "I walk a lonely street." How much of the song Durden actually wrote we may never know, although the evidence is strong that Axton wrote the entire song herself.

Other hit songs co-written by women include Carole Joyner's "Young Love" (1957), recorded by Tab Hunter; Felice Bryant's "Wake Up Little Susie" (1957), recorded by the Everly Brothers; Rose Marie McCoy's "I Beg of You" (1958), recorded by Elvis Presley; Barbara Ellis and Gretchen Christopher's "Come Softly to Me" (1959), recorded by a trio, The Fleetwoods (Ellis and Christopher were two of the vocalists); and Ann Farina's "Sleepwalk" (1959), an instrumental recorded by her two brothers.

One of the first woman to be sole author of a number-one pop record was Sharon Sheeley, whose "Poor Little Fool" provided Ricky Nelson with his sixth hit in 1958. (Earlier in 1949, Cindi Walker wrote Eddy Arnold's Number One hit, "Take Me in Your Arms and Hold Me.") Sheeley was a prolific songwriter and a major influence on the music of the 1950s. Professionally, her life was gilded and she could do no wrong, but her private life was chaotic and marred by tragedy. In 1960, Sheeley went to Europe to tour with her boyfriend, singer Eddie Cochran

("Summertime Blues"). Midway through the tour, she and Cochran decided to return to America to get married. As they were riding in a taxi to the London airport, one of the tires blew out, sending the taxi crashing into a lamppost. Sheeley and Cochran were both seriously injured in the accident. Sheeley recovered, but Cochran later died of head injuries sustained in the accident. You might say she was unlucky in love.

Sheeley's success as a songwriter was the exception. Marion Keisker's experience at Sun Records was more typical of what women faced in the 1950s. Despite high profiles as vocalists, women were non-existent in positions other than secretary or receptionist.

In 1990, *Ladies' Home Journal* saluted Frances Preston as one of the fifty most powerful women in America. Nearly a decade earlier, *Esquire* magazine had called her one of the most powerful people in the music business. As former president of Broadcast Music, Inc. (BMI), Preston oversaw a worldwide empire that is one of the financial bedrocks of the music industry. BMI is one of three licensing organizations—the other two being American Society of Composers, Authors, and Publishers (ASCAP), and SESAC—that collect hundreds of millions of dollars in royalty payments annually for songwriters.

As chief executive officer of the largest of the three agencies, Preston had plush offices in New York and Nashville. It was possible to become successful in the music business without having your name cross her desk, but it is not very likely. As influential as she became, it was not always that way. In the 1950s, in the early stages of her career, Preston found the going rough and demoralizing. "I was young and fairly attractive and people thought, 'Oh, look what BMI sent to me,'" she says. "You really had to be the Ice Woman to let them know that you were there for business. When you started talking they knew you knew about the business, but you had to be a little bit smarter. Your homework had to be done. The least they knew to talk about was performing rights, so I spent quite a bit of time going to seminars to learn every aspect of the business so that I could converse about whatever they wanted to talk about. There were instances when people would remind you that you were a woman."

Preston began her career in 1950 at radio station WSM in Nashville. WSM was best known for its Saturday broadcasts of the Grand Ole Opry, which had premiered at the station twenty-five years before Preston started work there as the receptionist. WSM was an NBC affiliate, and despite its reputation as the home of the Opry, the bulk of its programming was popular and classical music. In addition to broadcasting the Opry, WSM fed several programs each week to NBC. One was a big orchestra show called "Sunday Down South" that featured vocalists Dinah Shore and Snooky Langston.

Frances' introduction to the music business at WSM was an eye-opener. "Those were days when song pluggers came down from New York to plug their songs, but none of them were women," she says. "The days of radio and no women executives ... at that time, if you were a woman, you could be a clerk in a department store, you could be a nurse, a telephone operator, a secretary—that's basically it. You were very limited because you were expected to get married and raise a family. When I got married and didn't stop work to rear my children, it was quite controversial."

In 1952, the station decided to celebrate the Opry's birthday by inviting other country music broadcasters to Nashville to participate in a week-long convention; that convention became what is today called Country Music Week. The following year, BMI decided to use the occasion to give awards to its songwriters. The New York executives were so impressed by Preston's intelligence and organizational abilities that they offered her a job in 1955 coordinating a BMI branch in Nashville.

For two years, she worked out of her home; then in 1958 BMI opened an office in Nashville and put her in charge. "BMI, I must say, was one of the few major music companies that really believed in women," she says. "The gentleman who hired me, Judge Robert Burton, was president of BMI for a while and he had more women executives than any company ever dreamed of having in the music industry. He just had a lot of faith in women executives."

As head of the BMI office in Nashville, Preston often was told that she had gone as far as she could go in an industry that considered women a decorative asset but a business liability. She never believed that was true and she made up her mind to prove everyone wrong. She was convinced that in the music business, women could do just as well as men. Unlike Marion Keisker, she wanted more out of life than a kind word: She wanted to be a player.

◆◇◆◇◆◇◆◇◆◇◆◇◆◇◆◇◆◇◆

Kay Starr was living with her family in Memphis when, at the age of fifteen, she was offered a job singing with jazz violinist Joe Venuti's dance band. Despite her young age, her family allowed her to accept the job. While fronting for Venuti, the teenager was asked to fill in for Marion Hutton, Glenn Miller's vocalist, who was hospitalized briefly for an illness. Starr, whose real name was Katherine Starks, recorded two songs with Miller, "Love With a Capital U" and "Baby Me."

Mesmerized by the glamour and excitement of the music business,

Starr left her family behind in Memphis—her father worked for a sprinkler company and her mother raised chickens—and relocated to California, where she moved in with Venuti and his wife. During World War II, while traveling extensively on unheated transport planes to entertain American troops, she contracted pneumonia and lost her voice. It was a year-and-a-half before Starr regained her voice, but, when it finally returned, it was more mature and seemed wrapped in a husky resonance, which she put to good use. In 1948 she signed a recording contract with Capitol Records, turning out a string of hits, including "Side by Side" and a number-one single, "Wheel of Fortune."

In 1956, after signing a contract with RCA Records, Starr prepared for her first session with her new label. From the beginning, nothing went right for her. The RCA studio had a large floor area and a high ceiling; she felt intimidated by the vastness of the studio and simply did not feel comfortable singing in that setting. By the time she adjusted to the room itself, she was given another surprise: A string section. She had never recorded with strings, and the thought terrified her. But if she thought RCA was through with its surprises, she was wrong: The label had one more card up its sleeve.

A little over two months before the session began, RCA had signed Elvis Presley to a recording contract. A&R executives at RCA felt they had stumbled upon something with this new music called rock 'n' roll. For her first session, they gave Starr a tune titled "Rock and Roll Waltz." Who better to usher in the new music from Memphis than a girl from Memphis who had connections to the big-band era?

Starr may have heard of Elvis Presley by then, but it is doubtful since his success at that time was confined to a handful of Southern states. Starr was offended by the song. In fact, she suspected it was a joke they were playing on her. She had built a reputation for singing serious songs that expressed serious emotions. "Rock and Roll Waltz" sounded like a nursery rhyme. When she found out they were serious about the song, she did her best with it, though she later confided her heart really was not in it.

By February 1956, "Rock and Roll Waltz" was the number-one single on the pop charts with sales of over one million. Starr was stunned. The song she felt was a joke became the first number-one single ever charted by RCA. But there was more: It was the first song to ever have the words "rock 'n' roll" in the title—and, most importantly, it secured Starr a place in history as the first woman in the modern era to score a number-one hit. The bewildered Kay Starr had become the reluctant queen of rock 'n' roll.

Two months later, Starr found out what all the fuss was about when Elvis Presley bumped her out of the Top Twenty with the Number One hit "Heartbreak Hotel." For the next several months—and into the start of the new decade—American music underwent a spirited gender-based tug-of-war as rock 'n' roll struggled to define itself as a male medium. The women refused to go quietly.

About six weeks after "Heartbreak Hotel" made Elvis Presley a household name, Gogi Grant, a striking, thirty-two-year-old brunette from Philadelphia, knocked him out of the number one spot with "The Wayward Wind." In retrospect, it is obvious that American music was undergoing radical change—with the battle lines drawn along traditional gender-related themes of aggressive exploration versus nurturing self-assessment—but at the time it seemed more like a cultural change than one related to gender.

Rock 'n' roll was an invention of the South. Many critics considered it crude, sexual, and devoid of redeeming social value. The South had already given the world the blues, jazz, bluegrass, and country music. Would the South once again dictate American musical tastes? Now we know it had more to do with gender differences than cultural differences, but at the time no one understood that.

Unlike Kay Starr, Gogi Grant did not have a string of hits to pave the way for her. RCA Records initially signed her, but when none of her releases—all recorded under her real name of Audrey Brown—made the charts, she was dumped by the label. Grant's career looked bleak until Dave Knapp, a former RCA executive, started up an independent label named Era Records.

Knapp signed Brown to his new label and changed her name to Gogi Grant. A song was selected for her first session, but when she met with the writers and they played her some of their other material, she expressed an interest in another song, "Suddenly There's a Valley." The songwriters, both males, looked at each a little strangely, and when Grant asked why, they confessed that they thought the song should be sung by a man. Challenged by their comment, Grant recorded "Suddenly There's a Valley" instead of the song the men had chosen for her. The record went to Number Nine on the charts and made her an overnight sensation.

After completing a twenty-eight city promotional tour, Grant returned to the studio to record a follow-up song, "Who Are We?" It took less than three hours to record, so with the time remaining, they decided to record a second song. Herb Newman, the executive in charge of Era Records, asked Grant to come into his office. He showed her the dog-eared manuscript of a song he had written with Stan Lebouysky while they were students at UCLA. The song was titled "The Wayward Wind."

Like her previous hit, the lyrics were written for a man. Grant said she liked the song and wanted to record it if he would allow her to rewrite the lyrics. That was fine with Newman, so Grant changed the lyrics to reflect a woman's point of view. In the remaining fifteen minutes of the session, they recorded the song and prepared for the release of "Who Are We." When "Who Are We" peaked at Number Sixty-two, Newman decided to release "The Wayward Wind." It took the song only five weeks to move into the Number One slot.

Unaffected by the raging gender and cultural battles taking place on the pop charts were African-American female artists recording for R&B labels. Almost from the beginning, women R&B singers were given equal status with men—creatively, if not financially—and over the years, they seemed immune to the ups and downs experienced by women striving for positions on the pop and country charts.

One of the most successful R&B singers of this era was Etta James, who had a Number One hit in 1955 with "The Wallflower," which she followed up with a Number Six hit, "Good Rockin' Daddy." A few years later, she scored as a back-up singer on Chuck Berry's "Back in the U.S.A." and "Almost Grown." Sadly, she never made the Top Twenty on the pop charts and did not achieve her due until the 1990s when she was awarded a Grammy for *Mystery Lady,* an album that saluted Billie Holiday.

From June 1956, when Gogi Grant went to Number One with "The Wayward Wind," until August 1957, males dominated the top of the charts, with hits from Elvis Presley, Pat Boone, Guy Mitchell, Perry Como, Buddy Knox, and Tab Hunter. It was in August that actress Debbie Reynolds knocked Presley out of Number One with "Tammy," a syrupy ballad that rode the soundtrack of the movie *Tammy and the Bachelor.*

At the time, Reynolds was married to singer Eddie Fisher, who until Presley's arrival, was RCA Records' top artist. The more success Elvis had, the less Eddie had. Reynolds had not put much thought into her recording of "Tammy." She sang it accompanied only by a piano. Later, when movie executives decided to release the song as a single to promote the movie, strings were added to the track to give it a fuller sound.

Reynolds was surprised at the success of the record, as was everyone else, but her biggest surprise came from her husband. "From Eddie, there wasn't a word of congratulations or joy; not a momentary kick that his wife was on the charts," Reynolds wrote in her autobiography. "I was surprised by the record's success. I could be happy but I couldn't be glad. I had offended my husband without even trying."

It is strange that an actress—not a committed singer—was able to topple Elvis from the charts. But the success that accompanied "Tammy" created tensions in Reynolds's marriage, and was indicative of the professional and gender-based tensions that would develop in the years ahead. Reynolds' 1957 success was the last Number-One hit scored by a solo female artist until the dawn of the new decade.

◆◇◆◇◆◇◆◇◆◇◆◇◆◇◆◇◆◇◆

Brenda Mae Tarpley started singing in public in 1949 at the age of five, when she sang her version of "Take Me Out to the Ball Game" at a county fair in Conyers, Georgia—and won first prize in the competition. Musically, she was a child prodigy with an amazing memory. Her mother was proud to tell people that even as a very young child Brenda could hear a song twice and then sing it back without missing a word.

In the beginning, Brenda's musical talents were a novelty for her family. Her father was a construction worker and her mother worked in a cotton mill; together they eked out a hardscrabble living in rural Georgia for their family of three daughters and a son. The Tarpley family didn't own a record player; the only music Brenda was exposed to either came into their home over the radio or from street-corner and front-porch musicians. Most of what Brenda heard was R&B and gospel—Ray Charles, Fats Domino, and Mahalia Jackson—because that was the music that her neighbors enjoyed.

Brenda might have remained a neighborhood novelty but for a freak accident that turned her world upside down. In May 1953, just five months after of her seventh birthday, her father was killed at a construction site when a hammer fell on his head. The accident left the Tarpley family destitute. It was then that Mama Grace Tarpley, seeing all the attention that Brenda was getting with her singing, investigated the possibilities of a music career for her daughter. Soon Brenda Tarpley became Brenda Lee.

On weekdays, Brenda attended school, doing her best to be a good student; but on weekends she boarded a bus to travel to the bookings around the state that her mother arranged for her. Soon she was the principal breadwinner of the family. When she returned to school on Mondays, she often was so tired that she put her head down on her desk and slept until past noon. Aware of how desperate Brenda's family was for money, the teacher allowed her to sleep in class.

That routine continued for three years. Then in 1956 Brenda got the big break that she and her family had dreamed about: She was invited to appear on an Augusta, Georgia, television show with country star Red Foley. He was so impressed with Brenda that he invited her to perform on his popular television program, "Ozark Jubilee."

Equally impressed was Foley's manager, Dub Allbritten, who took her on as a client. Instead of focusing on getting Brenda a recording contract (females of any age were a hard sell with record executives then, but a little girl—forget it!), Allbritten targeted television. Savvy managers were quickly learning that it was the best way to go over the heads of record executives and take their case directly to the public.

Television was still in its infancy, but it was a very effective vehicle for reaching a female audience. In short order, Allbritten got bookings for Brenda on the "Perry Como Show," then followed that up with appearances with Ed Sullivan and Steve Allen.

Brenda became a national star, almost overnight, without ever making a record. Decca corrected that oversight before the year was out and signed the twelve-year-old to a recording contract. Decca's most immediate problem was how to package her. Since she was not a country singer per se, record executives, with Allbritten's approval, decided to fit her into the rockabilly mold exploited so well by Elvis Presley.

Legendary producer Owen Bradley supervised her first session. "Jambalaya," her first single, did not chart, but it did garner a favorable review in *Billboard,* which predicted that she had the talent to skyrocket "to great heights, not only in the country field but in the pop field as well." The flip side, "Bigelow 6-200," was successful, but not a big hit.

Not until the following year did she make the charts. It was with a song entitled, "One Step at a Time." The song is probably most notable for a line that offers an indirect reference to Elvis Presley: "Every old hound dog once was a pup."

By the fall of 1957, Allbritten and Decca were concerned about sagging public interest in their thirteen-year-old child prodigy. When Allbritten, a close friend of Colonel Tom Parker, learned that Presley was going to visit the Grand Ole Opry, he sensed an opportunity for his client. The visit was a spur-of-the-moment decision by Presley (he had driven to Nashville to give Parker an early Christmas present), and before going to the Opry he stopped by a Nashville clothing store to buy something to wear.

To Allbritten's delight, Brenda, looking much younger than thirteen, was photographed backstage at the Opry with Presley, who put his arm around her and clasped her hand, leaving her positively beaming as she looked up at him with admiration and something akin to lust. It was a great photograph and Allbritten used it for all it was worth to promote Brenda's career in the months ahead. Brenda performed that day at the Opry for first time, but to Albritten's surprise, neither the performance nor the publicity shot with Presley boosted her career.

Brenda recorded a string of bop songs in 1958 and 1959, including "Rock the Bop," "One Teenager to Another," and "Dynamite" (the song that earned her the nickname, "Little Miss Dynamite"), but nothing really clicked. Allbritten decided to book her in Europe, with the hope that overseas publicity would generate greater interest in the States.

Everything went smoothly, until the promoter of a show at the Olympia Music Hall in Paris learned Brenda was a child—not an adult as he had been told. The offended promoter canceled her appearance. Allbritten, taking a cue from his friend Colonel Parker, planted a story that Brenda was actually a thirty-two-year-old midget. The press ran with the story. Once it was published, Allbritten denied that she was a midget, and then he denied that he had ever planted the story.

The resulting controversy forced the promoter to reinstate Brenda as the opening act. She was so popular in Paris that the show was held over for five weeks. She was then asked to tour Italy, Germany, and England. When she returned to the States, she was an international star—and poised to zoom to the top of the pop charts with her first Number-One single, "I'm Sorry."

Brenda's experiences as a female in the music industry are unique for several reasons. Her young age—and the fact that she always looked even younger than she was—coupled with her status as a fatherless child, elicited protective feelings from most of the male authority figures she encountered in the business.

"My experience is probably different than most [women], in that I started out so young," she says. "I was looked over so closely by my mother, and then when I acquired my first manager, he was like more of a father figure than a manager and he cared about me as a person, not just as a product. All the people around me really cared about me and didn't take advantage of me. I didn't encounter any of the things [other women have faced], but then I didn't live in California or New York. I lived in Tennessee, where I had a legal guardian who saw to it that no one could spend my money without me knowing where it was going."

By the time "I'm Sorry" went to Number One in July 1960, money—or the lack of it—was no longer a problem in the Tarpley household. Brenda was a genuine pop star, the first female pop star of the modern era. Although still a teenager, there was nothing girlish about her powerful voice and there was nothing childish about the sensual overtones of her music. That was one reason that her Nashville record label was hesitant to allow her to release "I'm Sorry." Male executives thought she was too young to be singing about unrequited love. They were so concerned that they held the record up several months out of fear of a backlash in the Bible Belt.

People were amazed by Brenda's ability to be something she was not. Was she a grown woman in disguise? Or was she a child in disguise? Or was she something else entirely, something so exotic that it didn't yet have a name? They flocked to auditoriums and concert halls by the thousands to see the little girl who sounded liked a sex kitten. They thought that if they could only see her, they would know the truth.

Technically, Brenda was a pop star by virtue of the fact that her songs were topping the pop charts; but her music was closer to rock 'n' roll and she was viewed as more of a rock artist by the teenagers who bought the records. For five consecutive years, both *Billboard* and *Cashbox* named her the most programmed female vocalist on radio.

At a 1962 tour in England with Gene Vincent, they were billed as the "King and Queen of Rock." Brenda was embraced as a female rock 'n' roller not just by the fans, but by the performers—most of them males— who were defining the new genre. Jerry Lee Lewis wanted Brenda to tour with him, but Mama Tarpley, perhaps mindful of the negative publicity Lewis got for marrying his 13-year-old cousin, put her foot down and refused to allow her daughter to tour with a man she called a barbarian.

Later that year, Brenda followed up "I'm Sorry" with her second Number-One hit, "I Want to Be Wanted," knocking off the charts the dominant males of the decade: Elvis Presley, Chubby Checker, and the Drifters. More Top Ten hits followed: "Dum Dum," "Emotions," "Break It to Me Gently," "All Alone Am I," and "Losing You." When she opened at New York City's most popular nightclub, the Copacabana, a *Billboard* reviewer wrote that she had the fire to be a "teenage Sophie Tucker."

◆◇◆◇◆◇◆◇◆◇◆◇◆◇◆◇◆

Matching the success women were having on pop charts in the 1950s were the women of country music. While the general perception among record executives on Nashville's Music Row was that "girls don't sell," there was a string of female recording artists whose success defied conventional wisdom.

Patsy Cline, Minnie Pearl, Kitty Wells, the Carter Family—all were breaking new ground for women. Of all the women who emerged during that time, it was probably Kitty Wells, whose real name was Muriel Deason, who made the greatest impact. By the time her single, "It Wasn't God Who Made Honky Tonk Angels," was issued by Decca Records in 1952, she was discouraged that any woman could have a career in music. To her surprise, the record went to the top of the country charts and stayed there for weeks, selling more than 800,000 copies, a huge number at that time. It was the first time a woman had ever topped the country charts.

Wells never thought the song would be a hit because it went against the flow. It was a gutsy, pro-feminist ballad that tore into lying, cheating husbands. Women loved the song and they bought it and played it for their husbands. Male record executives—and in those days all record executives were male—thought it was just a fluke.

Wells quickly took the title "Queen of Country Music" (a title she wore until the end of the century), and while she was no feminist—and the women who adored her would never have considered themselves feminists—she became an underground hero among the women of her generation. Wells followed up her early success with a string of hits, including "I Can't Stop Loving You" and "Love Makes the World Go 'Round," but none of them had the strong pro-female perspective of "It Wasn't God Who Made Honky Tonk Angels," and she eventually lost the momentum initially gained from the hit.

Minnie Pearl, whose real name was Sarah Cannon, made an impact on the music industry, not with her musical talents but with her humor. As a member of the Grand Ole Opry, she was a familiar figure to country music fans for over five decades. From the moment she stepped out on stage wearing an old-fashioned dress and a flowered straw hat with a price tag dangling in full view—and yelled out, "How-Dee! I'm just so proud to be here!"—she connected with music fans in ways that transcended the simplicity of her homespun comic routines.

One of her favorite routines went like this: "I was coming out of the back of the auditorium—and it was dark—and this fellah comes up and he has a gun in his hand. He says, 'Give me your money.' And I say, 'I don't have any money.' And then he looks me up and down and says, 'You really don't have any money, do you?' And I say, 'No, but if you'll do that again, I'll write you a check.'"

Technically, Minnie Pearl's talents lay beyond the realm of music, but she was so much a part of everything that was—and still is—the music business, that most observers would be hard-pressed to exclude her on a technicality. "I think the star among all was Minnie Pearl," says BMI's Frances Preston. "She was a genuine person who cared for other people and gave back to her industry."

No discussion of the women of country music in the 1950s would be complete without a mention of Patsy Cline. She did not enter the picture until late in the decade, but her influence was so great that she seemed to overshadow everyone else. Cline, whose real name was Virginia Hensley, was a product of the new medium, television.

She had tried to break into country music since the age of sixteen, but no one was interested and she ended up making a living as a dancer. Then in 1957, at the age of twenty-five, she was given an opportunity to appear on "Arthur Godfrey's Talent Scouts," one of the most popular nationally televised shows of its time. She sang "Walkin' After Midnight" and won first prize and a recording contract with Decca Records.

For ten years, jaded male record executives in Nashville had failed to spot Cline's simmering talent. It was the television audience that made her a star. Women viewers identified with her immediately. They could see themselves in her woman-next-door face and they could hear the long-suffering hurt in her emotion-drenched voice. They responded by making "Walkin' After Midnight" an instant hit.

Record executives followed up with a series of songs that they thought women wanted to hear. They were wrong, and Cline's career stalled because of their bad judgment. Not until 1961, did she rebound with an irrepressible song titled "Crazy." She followed that hit up with "I Fall to Pieces."

By 1963, she was one of the most popular female singers in the country. Her career ended abruptly on March 6, 1963, when the single-engine Comanche in which she was riding crashed during a thunderstorm, killing all aboard.

Even in death, her powerful voice and haunting face tugged at heartstrings. That is as much a result of the influence of television as it was her music. She was the first woman to go over the heads of male record executives to appeal directly to a female television audience. The music industry was slow to grasp the importance of that strategy, but, once it did, it embraced it with a passion and never looked back. Once again, it was a woman, both brilliant and stubborn, who had led the way.

3 Freedom Is Just Another Word: The 1960s

For a decade that began with the chart domination of Brenda Lee and Connie Francis and ended as the second-worst decade of the modern era for female recording artists, the 1960s has an undeserved mystique for unbridled political liberalism and newfound sexual freedom for women. Free love? Most people thought so at the time.

As the decade began, Connie Francis, whose birth name was Concetta Rosa Maria Franconero, knocked Elvis Presley and the Everly Brothers off the top of the charts with her 1960 hit "Everybody's Somebody's Fool." Two years earlier, the twenty-two-year-old Italian American thought her career was over. She had recorded ten songs for MGM Records, and none of them had made the charts. She was preparing for her final session with MGM by playing the song list for her father, a roofing contractor who had taken an interest in his daughter's career. When he heard the songs, he grimaced and told her they were no good. He gave her a 1923 song, "Who's Sorry Now?" with the admonition, "Now there's a song."

Connie went to the session with the songs that had been chosen for her by her producer, but during the final fifteen minutes, she asked to record "Who's Sorry Now?" out of respect for her father. Actually, she thought the song was much too old-fashioned to be a hit. Her thoughts were probably not even on music that day. MGM had made it clear it had lost interest in her; she had applied for a scholarship at New York University and had every intention of getting out of the music business.

"Who's Sorry Now?" lingered for months after its release and showed no indication it would chart. Connie wasn't surprised. None of her records had ever charted. Late one afternoon, as she was sitting down to a big Italian dinner with her family, she turned on the television; she had grown accustomed to watching Dick Clark's "American Bandstand." She heard Clark say something about a new girl singer who was going straight to the top. "Well, good luck to her," said Connie, thinking her own career was finished. Suddenly, she heard the song—her song—and started screaming: "Dad! Dad!" After being mentioned by Dick Clark, "Who's Sorry Now?" peaked in the Top Ten and opened the door for a second hit, "My Happiness," which peaked at Number Two.

For her first Number One hit, "Everybody's Somebody's Fool," Connie bumped Elvis off the top of the charts. For her second Number One, "My Heart Has a Mind of Its Own," she displaced Chubby Checker, who had become a national sensation with "The Twist." Connie was the first woman to have two consecutive singles at the top of the charts. In between Connie's two hits, Brenda Lee scored with her Number One, "I'm Sorry." With Presley's movies doing so well at the box office, Connie was asked to do a film of her own. She asked two New York songwriters, Howard Greenfield and Neil Sedaka, to write the title song for the movie, *Where the Boys Are*. The result made Connie a multimedia celebrity and opened the door for Sedaka to have a solo career of his own.

Connie starred in three more MGM films: *Follow the Boys, Looking for Love,* and *When the Boys Meet the Girls*. A year-and-a-half later she scored with "Don't Break the Heart That Loves You," another song that had been recommended by her father. The intervening months had allowed Brenda Lee to have another Number One, "I Want to Be Wanted," and two black girl groups—the Shirelles with "Will You Love Me Tomorrow," and the Marvelettes with "Please Mr. Postman"—to make history by becoming the first black girl groups to top the charts.

Knocking Connie out of Number One was eighteen-year-old actress Shelley Fabares, a co-star on the popular television sitcom, "The Donna Reed Show." Tony Owen, the show's producer, asked Shelley to record a song for the show, but she was not a singer and she was reluctant to do the song. She didn't relent until Owens convinced her that it was necessary for an upcoming episode. To everyone's surprise, "Johnny Angel" was an instant hit, peaking at Number One in 1962. Two years later, Shelley left the "Donna Reed Show" to pursue a recording and movie career. None of her subsequent recordings made it into the Top Twenty. She was right the first time: She was not really a singer. But she co-starred in three movies with Elvis and in one movie with Fabian, who emerged as a major recording star later in the decade.

"Don't Break the Heart That Loves You" was prophetic for Connie Francis. Later that year she recorded two songs—"Second Hand Love" and "Vacation"—that made it into the Top Twenty, but by 1963 she was history as a hit-maker. She continued to perform in nightclubs until 1974, when she was brutally raped in a Howard Johnson's motel in New York. Emotionally devastated by the rape, she was unable to perform for six years. No sooner did she recover from that trauma than she learned that her brother had been murdered, gangland style, at his New Jersey home.

For the first two or three years of the decade, women stood toe-to-toe with their male competitors. Besides Connie Francis, Brenda Lee, and the emerging girl groups, solo performers such as Nancy Wilson made a significant impact. Reviewing Wilson's 1964 album, *How Glad I Am,* the critic for *Playboy* magazine wrote that the singer was "ultrafancy throughout." In the same issue, the magazine gave a good review to a new album by Peggy Lee and a bad review to Barbra Streisand for her album, *People*: "Color us disenchanted...the latest LP from the hottest female property in show business goes over with a whimper, not a bang." That review aside, *Playboy* was one of the few magazines that consistently gave good reviews to female recording artists.

Female recording artists were in deep trouble by mid-decade, and by the end of the decade they had been displaced almost entirely by male artists. Figures for the decade show that of 292 solo recording artists to make the Top Twenty during the decade, only seventy-one (24%) were women. Since the 1950s, women had lost five percentage points, and the numbers were destined to get even worse. Women were experiencing a backlash. A 1962 article in *Time* magazine about the newly emerging folk movement is indicative of the tone used toward women by the media: "It is not absolutely essential to have hair hanging to the waist—but it helps. Other aids: No lipstick, flat shoes, a guitar. So equipped, almost any enterprising girl can begin a career as a folk singer."

By the mid-1960s, rock 'n' roll had been around for a decade. The role of women in the industry was changing, not so much because rock 'n' roll displaced women on the pop charts (it had ten years to do that), but because music was evolving into a genre that didn't really have a place for women. The reasons for that turnaround could be argued until doomsday: The changing role of women in society, the emergence of the feminist movement. Arguments could be made that women themselves were changing music simply by changing the rules of the game. That is a valid argument, but a more convincing one is the influence of the growing rage that men of the 1960s were feeling toward society in general.

Eighteen-year-old men were being asked to fight in Vietnam in a war that made no sense to growing numbers of people, including scores of male recording artists who were treated with disdain by their conservative elders. The result was a vaporous rage that billowed and spewed forth music characterized by angry lyrics and driving, hard-edged rhythms that went out as a clarion call to a new generation of record buyers. Male recording artists expressed anger not just at society, but at those who had been excluded from the unreasonable demands of the war: Women.

The response from women is surprising in retrospect. They provided "free love" to the men expressing the rage, and proclaimed to the world that they were now free from the shackles of society. At the time, such expressions seemed revolutionary, a vehicle for dramatic social change. Today we can look back to that revolution and see that it was not so much a release from bondage as an invitation for abuse. Women went from being the stars of the recording industry to being backup singers and groupies. While proclaiming their freedom, they had unknowingly sold themselves into even deeper bondage. They could damn well have sex with any man they wanted, but they could damn well forget about competing with men on the charts.

If men were exerting such domination over women, why would female record buyers—still the majority—purchase records that reflected that attitude? Why would they buy records such as Leslie Gore's "You Don't Own Me" one minute, then turn around and buy Dion's "Runaround Sue" or Elvis Presley's "You're the Devil in Disguise"? The answer would seem to be that when they wanted meaningful lyrics, they turned to female artists, but when they wanted to dance, when they wanted to tap into that inner male rage that skewed their hormonal balance, they flocked to the male artists who were not ashamed to give it to them. For those women who exchanged sex for the right to dance, it was the dancing that apparently had the most meaning in their lives, for it was the dancing that gave them the freedom they had been promised in sex.

◆◇◆◇◆◇◆◇◆◇◆◇◆◇◆◇◆◇◆

Nothing about Estelle Axton smacked of the music business. She was a former schoolteacher, forty years of age, married with two children, working as a bookkeeper at Union Planters Bank in Memphis. She stood out in a crowd because of her red hair, which in the South of the 1950s was a rarity. Redheads were uncommon enough that whenever someone encountered one, it was always good for a comment or two. Axton fit the redhead stereotype: Shy but surprisingly outspoken when challenged, temperamental over small details, ambitious, and eager to prove herself.

When her younger brother, Jim Stewart, came to her in 1958 with a business proposal to start up a record label, it came as a surprise. Jim worked in the bonds department of a rival bank. After serving for two years in the army, earning a degree in business from what is now the University of Memphis, he had settled into a button-down career as a banker. Everyone in his family knew he had an interest in music. He played fiddle in several swing bands and occasionally performed on country music segments aired on radio station WDIA, which normally adhered to a black music format. But his musical excursions were viewed more as a hobby, something akin to a grown man playing with a Lionel train set.

Jim's proposal was simple. He wanted to start up a record label, but didn't have the money to buy a recording machine. If Estelle would provide $2,500 for the machine, she could be his partner. Estelle said she didn't have $2,500. "But you have a house, and you have several years paid into it," Jim said.

When Estelle talked to her husband about loaning the money to Jim, his response was, "No way!" But the more Estelle thought about it, the more she liked the idea. Finally, she talked her husband into mortgaging their house and investing the money in Jim's proposed record label. They bought a one-track Ampex recorder and set up shop in a vacant grocery in a small community a few miles from Memphis. The building was owned by Jim's barber, who told them they could have it rent-free if they would work with his sixteen-year-old daughter, who had stars in her eyes. The biggest thing in the news then was Sputnik, the Russian satellite that had become the first man-made object in space, so they named their company Satellite Productions.

After more than a year of experimenting in the former grocery with the barber's daughter—without the slightest hint of success—Estelle and Jim decided they would have to move their studio to Memphis if they were to ever have any hope of recovering Estelle's investment. With the help of Chips Moman, a guitarist who had been working with Jim, they located a vacant movie theater. "The guy that owned it rented it to us for $100 a month," says Estelle. "Can you imagine a whole theater for $100? We ripped out all the seats and put a partition down the middle to compact the sound. The screen was up on the stage and that was where we put the recording machine that I had paid $2,500 for."

Once they had the studio set up, they opened a record shop next door in space that had been occupied by a barbershop. Estelle and Jim kept their day jobs, but after work they put in time at the site of their new venture, with Jim working in the studio and Estelle operating the record shop. Like the recording studio, the record shop was put together piece-meal. Estelle took orders for records from the people she worked with at the bank, then she went to Poplar Tunes, the largest record store in town, and bought the records for sixty-five cents and then re-sold them for one dollar at the bank. With the profit, she bought records for her own store.

For the longest time, it was the record shop that kept the studio afloat. None of the early records issued by Satellite Productions were successful. One day, Rufus Thomas, a popular black disk jockey on WDIA, came by the studio to pitch some ideas. He brought his 16-year-old daughter, Carla, and they sang together on a song he had written called "Cause I Love You." Jim and Estelle thought it was good enough to release as a record. It sold well enough locally—about 15,000 copies—that Atlantic Records head Jerry Wexler offered them $1,000 for the right to distribute it nationally. It ended up selling about 35,000 copies, which was not a huge number, but impressive enough to give Jim and Estelle exposure as record executives.

They were sitting around the studio with Rufus and Carla, trying to come up with another idea, when Carla said she had a song. "As soon as Jim and I heard that song, we knew it was a hit," says Estelle. "It's funny—when you hear a song you know if it's got something in it that will sell." With the $1,000 they had received from Wexler, they took Carla to Nashville to record her song, "Gee Whiz," in a state-of-the-art studio. They played the recording for Wexler, who promptly signed Carla to a five-year contract and released the song on Atlantic. "Gee Whiz" peaked at Number Thirteen on the pop charts in March 1961, making Carla a teenage singing sensation.

All of which came as quite a shock to the teenager. Those were the days of segregation in Memphis. Blacks were prohibited by law from using public libraries and swimming pools. It was illegal for them to request service in white-operated restaurants and hotels. One can only imagine Carla's feelings when she traveled, as she was ushered into a brave new world where she was treated even better than the white people back home. No other black teenager in Memphis had ever had such an experience.

At the time, Carla really didn't grasp the significance of what was happening. "I'm going to be honest—no, I didn't," she says. "I was young. Being young and black in the Sixties—it was a thrill just to record. The kids are so sophisticated now. It took me awhile to see the significance of what I was getting into. What I thought was fun, was a business. There were so many things on the business end that I didn't know."

Over the next few years, Carla outgrew her label as a "teen queen," and went on to record a series of solid rhythm & blues records, one of them a duet with Otis Redding ("Tramp"). When she went to Europe as part of the Stax/Volt Revue (Satellite Productions had become Stax Records after a California company named Satellite threatened a lawsuit), she was enthusiastically received by everyone, including Beatle Paul McCartney, who went to the Bag of Nails to hear her perform in a club setting. "There's an old saying, that what comes from the soul, reaches the soul," she says. "From the blues came soul music and it reached out and grabbed people, and I don't think people have been the same since." When interest in soul music tapered off in the 1970s, so did interest in Carla's career. She eventually found a new career in the public school system, but she continued performing into the late 1990s at special events and soul music revivals.

Carla opened doors not just for other black entertainers, but for women in general, especially white women who felt rebellious over the race issue. One of those was Rita Coolidge, who had become addicted to Memphis soul while attending college at Florida State University. A native of Nashville, where her father was a minister, she had performed in church from an early age. While she was in college, her parents moved to Memphis; upon graduation, she went to Memphis to spend the summer with her parents before returning to college to pursue a master's degree in art. To earn extra money that summer, she sang radio jingles for a local company. That led to some studio work, and before she knew what had happened, she was hooked on the record business, especially the soul music recorded by female singers such as Carla Thomas.

By 1968, Estelle and Jim had built Stax Records up into the premier soul music independent in the country. Otis Redding. Booker T. and the MG's. Sam and Dave. The Mar-Keys. There seemed no end to the hits turned out of that old movie theater. In addition to Stax, hits were flowing like crazy from American Recording Studio, which had been opened by Chips Moman, and from Hi Records, which was operated by black producer Willie Mitchell. Rita was never able to gain entry into Stax, but she was a frequent visitor at American and Hi. To Mitchell, she was a novelty. He recalls that she used to come to his studio, which was located in a black neighborhood, and sit there until all hours of the night, quietly watching, listening, soaking up the music like a sponge. That amused Mitchell because it simply was not done by white girls in Memphis at that time. "I knew she was a singer, but we never did anything she wanted to sing on," he says. "Anytime we had a gig in Memphis, she came and observed what we were doing. She liked the rhythm section. She liked the feel of Memphis music."

After spending a year—instead of the summer, as originally planned—in Memphis, Rita returned to Florida State to pursue her education. Then it hit her: Music was what she wanted, not an academic education. "If I hadn't spent that year in Memphis, I don't think I would have ended up in the music business," she says. "I went back and realized that I was hooked on the music business and didn't want to further my education. I wanted to further my musical career." Rita returned to Memphis and began singing in nightclubs with her sister, Priscilla, and continued doing radio jingles, sometimes with her friend Donna Weiss, who was perfecting her talents as a songwriter.

Rita recorded one of Weiss's songs, "Turn Around and Love You," at American, but before the record was released, she got an offer to tour as a backup singer with the Los Angeles-based Delaney and Bonnie. She moved to the West Coast and discovered shortly after getting there that "Turn Around and Love You" was a Top Ten hit on Los Angeles radio stations. Rita went on to establish herself as a recording artist with A&M Records and to work with some of the leading male vocalists of her generation: Eric Clapton, Joe Cocker, and Graham Nash. While out promoting her first album, she met Kris Kristofferson in an airport; they became traveling companions and then got married and had a daughter. Rita's friend, Donna Weiss, also moved to Los Angeles, where she co-authored "Bette Davis Eyes," one of the biggest hits of the 1980s. Rita's sister Priscilla shocked polite Memphis society, first by dating Booker T. Jones, the leader of Booker T. and the MG's, then by marrying him. Such things simply were not done in Memphis—at least not in those racially charged days.

By the time Rita Coolidge was finding a new life in California, Estelle Axton was being squeezed out of Stax Records by business interests in California. Over the years, Stax had grown too large for a brother-and-sister operation. When Estelle and Jim got word that Atlantic Records was being acquired by Warner Brothers, they learned Stax would have to renegotiate its distribution agreement with Atlantic. By then tensions between Atlantic head Jerry Wexler and Jim and Estelle were well established.

Estelle's relationship with Wexler had deteriorated early on, with the 1961 success of the Mar-Keys' instrumental, "Last Night." When Estelle first heard the song, she just knew it was a hit and she pressured Jim to release it as a single. Jim didn't like the song. Neither did the song's producer, Chips Moman. Neither thought it would sell. Estelle continued to argue for the song's release. Jim and Chips thought she wanted the song released because her son, Packy, played saxophone on it, but that wasn't the case. She had been studying the records in her shop, and she just knew "Last Night" was a hit.

Finally, Jim agreed to release the record. It was an instant hit in Memphis, but when Atlantic released it to national buyers, sales stalled. Estelle blamed it on Atlantic and told Wexler he wasn't doing a very good job. "He wasn't promoting it," says Estelle. "He didn't believe in it. He didn't believe it was a hit, but I knew from experience that it was. I was arguing with Jim about it, and he said for me to get on the phone and talk to Wexler about it. I did. I told him that it had been a hit in Memphis and a record that could be a hit in Memphis could be a hit anywhere. Well, he didn't like my attitude at all. He called Jim back. He said, 'Don't let your sister get on the phone anymore to me. I don't want to talk to her.'" Estelle laughed when she told the story years later, but that is because she got the last word in that argument when "Last Night" zoomed to Number Two on the pop charts, making it the most successful record in Memphis recording history. "Well, I proved [Wexler] wrong," she says. "I didn't want to lose that record. I knew it was a hit."

When Stax Records was sold to Gulf & Western, Estelle was offered 4,000 shares of Gulf & Western stock, along with a yearly salary of $25,000 for five years. There was one added condition: She had to agree not to re-enter the music business for five years. Estelle agreed to those terms—and laughed all the way to the bank. About the time her five-year term was up, Stax went into bankruptcy, with Jim and the others losing everything they had invested in the company.

Estelle had 4,000 shares of valuable stock, and she still had an ear for music. With her son-in-law as a partner, she started up a new label named Fretone. One of the songs she recorded for her new label was "Disco Duck," a tune recorded by Memphis disk jockey Rick Dees. As the doors to Stax Records were being permanently shut in 1976, "Disco Duck" went to the top of the charts. Again, Estelle had proved that she was more than just another "girl" executive. "Disco Duck" was the first Number One record ever ushered onto the charts by a female record executive and—as of 2005—still stands as the last Number One pop record to come out of Memphis.

Estelle Axton never received the recognition she deserved for her efforts at Stax. She received even fewer accolades for her success with "Disco Duck," which initially sold over two million copies. Yet, by any yardstick, she is the most successful and influential female executive in recording history. "Estelle never got credit for it," says BMI's Frances Preston. "She ran the place [Stax]. She was the glue that kept it together. That's what so many women have been—the glue that holds things together. Behind so many of the big names are women who have held things together."

◆◇◆◇◆◇◆◇◆◇◆◇◆◇◆◇◆◇◆

Carla Thomas was one of the first black women solo artists of the modern era to make the Top Twenty, but she was not the first black woman to do so. Two girl groups, the Chantels and the Chordettes, already had cracked the Top Twenty. Three months before "Gee Whiz" peaked, the

Shirelles, a black girl group from New Jersey, became the first to have a Number-One single when "Will You Love Me Tomorrow" knocked Elvis Presley off the top in 1961. "Will You Love Me Tomorrow" was released by Sceptor Records, a tiny New Jersey label owned by Florence Greenberg, whose daughter, Mary Jane, was a classmate of the four students who sang under the name the Poquellos. Mary Jane urged her mother to listen to the group; she did and signed them to a contract. Not surprisingly, she suggested they change their name. They chose the Shirelles, although afterward no one could remember the reason why.

Greenberg released their first single "I Met Him on a Sunday," on her own label, Tiara Records. When the record charted at Number Forty-nine, Greenberg thought they would be better off if she leased the next two records to Decca Records. Neither record charted. Not ready to give up on the Shirelles, Greenberg decided to release their next single, "Dedicated to the One I Love," on her own label, which she renamed Sceptor. The record barely made it into the Top One Hundred. The next song, "Tonight's the Night," made it just inside the Top Fifty. By that time, Greenberg had hired Luther Dixon, a former member of the Four Buddies, to produce the group. When time came to choose a follow-up song to "Tonight's the Night," Dixon told Greenberg and the Shirelles that he wanted to use a tune by two new songwriters, Gerry Goffin and Carole King.

When the Shirelles listened to the demo of "Will You Love Me Tomorrow," they hated it. They thought it sounded too white for a black girl group. Not until they got into the studio and started recording the song did they change their minds. During production Dixon added his own special rhythm & blues touch, and Carole King came into the studio to help out, playing kettle drums when needed.

"Will You Love Me Tomorrow" scored a number of firsts: It was the first record by a girl group to go to Number One, the first to be released by a label owned by a woman, and the first chart-topper for Carole King, who went on to become one of the most influential songwriters of the 1960s and 1970s. (A decade later, King would score a Number One hit as an artist with "It's Too Late/I Feel the Earth Move.")

Female label owner, female songwriter, female singers—it was a new experience for women in the music business. The gate had been opened, but there was more at stake than new opportunities for women. Coupled with that were new opportunities for African Americans. Florence Greenberg in New Jersey—and Estelle Axton in Memphis—did more than simply flex their newly discovered clout, they pricked the conscience of white America and paved the way for black entertainers to enter the mainstream. The African-American/white female coalition would prove to be unbeatable.

In between "Will You Love Me Tomorrow" and the Shirelles's second Number One hit, "Soldier Boy," emerged yet another Number One hit from a black girl group, "Please Mr. Postman." The Marvelettes, a Detroit high-school quartet that auditioned for Berry Gordy, Jr.'s record label, Tamla Records, recorded the song. Gordy was a former boxer and Ford Motors mechanic who had a knack for music. He had launched Tamla Records in 1959 (he wanted to name the label Tammy, after the Debbie Reynolds' hit of the same name, but trademark restrictions forced him to use Tamla) and had found some success with a girl group named the Miracles, but a Number-One record eluded him.

When "Please Mr. Postman" was first offered to the Marvelettes, group member Georgia Dobbins liked the melody but hated the lyrics. She asked the three male songwriters if she could change the lyrics. She completely rewrote the song, keeping only the title. Meanwhile, she learned that her mother was seriously ill. Georgia taught the other group members how to sing the song, then dropped out of the group to take care of her ailing mother. "Please Mr. Postman," with twenty-two-year-old unknown Marvin Gaye on drums, went to Number One in 1961, providing Gordy with his first hit.

Encouraged by that success, Gordy formed a new label, Motown (short for motor town) and sought new talent. He was immensely successful with several of his male acts—the Temptations, Marvin Gaye, Eddie Holland, the Miracles, and Little Stevie Wonder—but Motown's biggest claim to fame would come from its female acts. More than any other male record executive in America, Gordy had become a believer in the musical power of the female. He was unable to get another Number One with the Marvelettes, but he was able to find success with three female acts that became legendary in the 1960s and 1970s: The Supremes, Martha and the Vandellas, and Mary Wells.

Detroit-born Mary Wells proved that Gordy's faith in women was well placed when her song "My Guy" went to Number One in 1964. Before that, she had recorded a number of singles that made the charts: "The One Who Really Loves You," "You Beat Me to the Punch," and "You Lost the Sweetest Boy." Mary was the first person signed to the Motown label and the first to have a Number-One hit. "My Guy" went on to become a classic, but, unfortunately, it was her last single to make the Top Twenty. Mary was the first major artist to leave the Motown fold and in 1990 she was diagnosed with throat cancer and died shortly thereafter.

Martha Reeves was working for Gordy as a secretary when he pulled her out of the office and into the studio to sing background with two other women on a Marvin Gaye session. Two of the songs, "Stubborn Kind of Fellow" and "Hitch Hike," were two big hits for Gaye and convinced Gordy that the women had a future as a solo recording act. As Martha & the Vandellas, they scored with four Top Ten hits: "Heat Wave," "Nowhere to Run," "Jimmy Mack," and "Dancing in the Streets," which peaked at Number Two. After the group ran out of steam in the 1960s, Martha Reeves continued to record as a solo artist, although without ever achieving the commercial success of the group.

Motown's biggest selling and most enduring group was the Supremes, a trio made up of Diana Ross, Mary Wilson, and Florence Ballard. The group provided Motown with its third Number One hit when "Where Did Our Love Go" topped the charts in 1964. The Supremes were not an instant success, however. They had released eight singles, all of which had failed to make the Top Twenty. Gordy continued to release the group's records because he believed in them, particularly in Diana Ross. The Supremes followed up the success of "Where Did Our Love Go" two months later with their second Number One, "Baby Love." For the next five years, they would give Motown some of the most memorable hits of the decade: "Come See About Me," "Stop! In the Name of Love," "My World Is Empty Without You," and "You Can't Hurry Love." In 1969, Diana Ross broke away from the group to pursue a solo career, but not before contributing to "Someday We'll Be Together," the group's twelfth Number-One hit. Other girl groups, such as the Dixie Cups with their Number-One hit, "Chapel of Love," the Shangri-Las with their hit, "Leader of the Pack," and the Angels with "My Boyfriend's Back," were competitive, but only the Supremes survived as chart-toppers until the end of the decade.

◆◇◆◇◆◇◆◇◆◇◆◇◆◇◆◇◆◇◆

The 1960s was an interesting decade for female country singers. The explosion of rock music and the British invasion cut deeply into country music sales; especially affected were sales by female artists. In spite of those limitations, the decade produced two of the strongest female voices in country music history: Loretta Lynn and Tammy Wynette.

Loretta's rise to fame is legendary by now. Most people have heard the story of the "Coal Miner's Daughter," as told in the movie and autobiography of the same name. From humble origins in Butcher Holler, Kentucky, she became—almost by grit alone—a household name at a time when American society was undergoing its most convulsive upheaval since the Civil War. Her success didn't come overnight, but it almost did. From 1961 to 1962, she went from being a wannabe with a record out on a small label no one had ever heard of, to a regular on the Grand Ole Opry with a Top Ten hit, appropriately entitled "Success." That year *Cashbox* identified her as the most programmed woman in country music.

If Loretta's contributions began and ended with her output of passionate, heartfelt songs, that in itself would be enough to justify her fame, but there is more to her story than great music. Just as important were her efforts to obtain equality for women. Minnie Pearl once credited Loretta with battering down the barriers for other women in the music business, and there is truth to that.

Loretta knew about breaking down barriers because she had to do it just to survive; it had nothing to do with gender. After her first record, "I'm a Honky-Tonk Girl," was financed by a Vancouver lumberman and released on a label named Zero Records, she and her husband, Mooney, struck out in their old Mercury on a promotional tour, with a goal of visiting as many radio stations as they could in three months. Radio DJs were so shocked to see her breeze into the studio, they played her record. No one told Loretta that recording artists—especially female recording artists—did not dare call on radio stations, for fear of offending someone. So she followed her instincts. How was she going to get her record played, she reasoned, if she didn't get out and ask people to give it a listen? Loretta's common sense forever changed the way records were promoted and it lifted the hearts of other women who dreamed of being brave and creative and free at heart.

The first years of Loretta's career coincided with the birth of the women's liberation movement. Betty Friedan's *The Feminine Mystique* found a growing readership during that time, and the National Organization of Women was formed. Loretta was never what most women would call a feminist, but if her actions and public statements had been uttered by an educated woman without a rural Southern accent, she would probably have been branded a flaming feminist. Loretta was never shy about expressing her opinions to interviewers or to anyone in the audience who had questions about the role of women in American society, but her strongest statements were issued in her music, where she was an eloquent voice on the issue of women's rights.

Loretta's most recurring theme was that women should have control over their lives. Her belief that the birth-control pill was an important advancement for women was expressed in her 1975 song, "The Pill." She caught hell for that song. Some radio programmers refused to play it, and arch-conservative preachers held her up as an example of how women were going straight to hell, but she never apologized for it. Some of her best songs in the 1960s and 1970s were reflective of women's issues.

Sometimes the titles are enough to explain the content: "We've Come a Long Way Baby," "I Wanna Be Free," "You Wanna Give Me a Lift (But This Gal Ain't A-Goin' That Far)," and "When the Tingle Becomes a Chill." In her 1973 hit, "Hey Loretta," she sings about a runaway housewife who calls for women's liberation to begin in her life "right now." Says Loretta in her autobiography: "Sure, I've heard people say men are bound to run around a little bit. It's their nature. Well, shoot, I don't believe in double standards, where men can get away with things that women can't. In God's eyes, there's no double standard. That's one of the things I've been trying to say in my songs. . . . There's plenty of songs about how women should stand by their men and give them plenty of loving when they walk through the door, and that's fine. But what about the man's responsibility? . . . No woman likes to be told, 'Here's the deal.'"

Of course, it was Tammy Wynette who wrote the book on "Stand by Your Man," the title of her 1969 Number One county hit and her autobiography. "Stand by Your Man" resurfaced in the early 1990s as a topic of national debate when Hillary Clinton told a television interviewer that she would not be a "Stand by Your Man" type of First Lady. Tammy was offended by the remarks, as were many of the singer's fans. If Hillary had done a little more research or perhaps had been a fan of country music, she would have had a greater appreciation of the contributions Tammy had made to women's rights. Even before Hillary's comments, Tammy had received criticism from the women's movement. "I don't see anything in that song that implies a woman is supposed to sit home and raise babies while a man goes out and raises hell," she wrote in her autobiography. "But that's what women's lib members thought it said."

In a *Newsweek* magazine article, under the headline "Songs of Non-Liberation," Tammy was described as a "platinum-haired divorcee" by a reporter who then went on to explain that "the way she sings, almost manfully, about how tough it is to be a woman, accounts for her edge over her rivals." The article, written by Eleanor Clift, is interesting because although the reporter berated Tammy for her country ways, observing the required political correctness of the times, it was obvious that she was impressed by the singer's accomplishments. Unless Clift's article was rewritten by a male editor, it serves as a reminder that sexism was not reserved solely for males. Despite the fact that *Newsweek* poked fun at Tammy for not being attuned to women's liberation, the masthead of that issue indicates that only one of the magazine's forty-five top editors was female.

Tammy's beginnings were not unlike Loretta's. Born in a tar-paper shack near Tupelo, Mississippi, she had to overcome a series of obstacles, including a very bad marriage and health problems, to find success as a recording artist. Her first experience with music occurred at her mother's place of employment, a Memphis dry-cleaning establishment owned by Scotty Moore's brother, Carney. It was where Scotty and his bandmates, Bill Black and Elvis Presley, gathered to rehearse in an upstairs room.

"I would go down there after school, and they just shoved me back and forth in those old [laundry] carts," Tammy later recalled. "The day I remember the most was the one when they were coming down the stairs and Auzella [Carney's wife] looked up and said, 'My, my, my—look at the stars! Elvis was nothing then, but he looked at her with that little smile, and he said, 'Auzella, one of these days I'll wrap you up in hundred dollar bills.'"

Later, after Elvis had earned enough money to buy a house for himself and his parents, Auzella asked thirteen-year-old Tammy if she wanted to go with her to drop off some Christmas presents at his house. "I got to see the inside of Elvis' house," Tammy said of his white-carpeted home. "When I got back home, I said, Mother, that rug that you walk on—it comes up around my ankles!"

Despite that tempting glimpse into the music business, Tammy didn't sign her first recording contract until 1966, by which time Loretta was already the reigning queen of country music. But her success came quickly enough, first with "Apartment #9" in 1967, and then later that year with "Your Girl's Gonna Go Bad." She became even more popular than Loretta on the concert circuit, and by the late 1960s she had entered the "legend" category with classics such as "D-I-V-O-R-C-E" and "Take Me to Your World."

Tammy followed in Loretta's footsteps by recording songs that presented a strong female perspective. "Unwed Fathers" offered a criticism of men who abandoned women when they got pregnant. "Another Chance" tells the story of a victim who survives. By the time she found success on the charts, male vocalists still accounted for the great majority of sales. "Because of this the producers would always sign a man before a woman," Tammy wrote in her autobiography. "The labels were convinced that women, who buy most of the records anyway, would spend money to hear a male singer quicker than they would to hear another woman."

A series of failed marriages, including one to country star George Jones, kept Tammy in the news throughout the 1960s and 1970s.

Through it all she displayed the same survivor's instincts possessed by Loretta, and she was able to move past her personal problems and focus on her career, turning out one hit after another well into the 1980s. She was still a popular concert draw in the late 1990s and continued with her recording career right up until her death in 1998.

About the same time that Loretta and Tammy were making inroads for women in country music, West-Coast, blues mama Tracy Nelson moved to Nashville. In 1965, when she released her debut album, *Deep Are the Roots,* Tracy was a student at the University of Wisconsin, where folk-blues albums were popular. Reaction to the album was good enough for her to pack up and move to San Francisco, where she thought she would find an even greater acceptance of her music. It was during the height of the hippie free-love and cheap beads era, and Tracy was appalled at what she saw. She formed a rock band named Mother Earth, recorded an album in 1968 that brought comparisons to Janis Joplin, then hit the road with the band to promote the album.

The last date on the tour was Nashville. While there, Tracy got word from her record label that they wanted a new album, so she decided to stay in Nashville and record it there. She and the band rented a farm west of the city and settled into a recording routine at a studio named Bradley's Barn. One day, after the album was finished and the band had returned to California, Tracy's producer, Pete Drake, took her by Music City Recorders, a studio owned and operated by Scotty Moore. That meeting with Moore resulted in a decision to record a second album, a collection of country songs with Nashville session musicians and Moore as engineer.

Tracy had been every bit as offended by the San Francisco hippie scene as most country session players would have been had they witnessed it for themselves, but she was like nothing any of them had ever seen. In their eyes, she was the epitome of the west-coast hippiedom they had read about and seen on television. She cussed a blue streak. She flashed an occasional marijuana stash in the studio. She dressed like a man, wearing jeans and pullover shirts. She was absolutely fearless.

Rose Drake, Pete's widow, laughed when she talked about it years later. "We had never heard women say four letter words before," she says, "and Tracy threw them out like there was no tomorrow. If Tracy saw that her language was embarrassing the men, she would escalate the tempo of her profanity. It was unbelievable what she came out with. They were afraid to bring people into the studio because they didn't know what Tracy was going to do next."

When the Nashville album, *Make a Joyous Noise,* was released, it was issued as a two-disc set—one disc country, the other a rock collection they called "city" music. Tracy ended up liking Nashville so much that she bought a farm and stayed. She mellowed considerably in the 1980s, but she continued recording her special blend of blues-rock, releasing a critically acclaimed album in 1996, *Move On,* and a 1998 album recorded with Marcia Ball and Irma Thomas, *Sing It!*

◆◇◆◇◆◇◆◇◆◇◆◇◆◇◆◇◆◇◆

Janis Joplin escaped the San Francisco music scene by a different route: Heroin. She had grown up in Port Arthur, Texas, a conservative oil refinery town where men were men and women were women, and the twain never met except on Saturday night. She had a very hurtful and confused childhood, primarily because she felt different from the other girls and didn't seem to fit their concept of what a little girl was supposed to act like. She was so despised that other students sometimes threw things at her. Adolescence amplified her childhood hurt a hundredfold.

Janis' solution to her adolescent pain was to run away from home at the age of seventeen. She enrolled in a school to learn to become a keypunch operator, but that didn't last for long. The only thing she could do really well was sing, so in 1966 she gravitated to the Haight-Ashbury district in San Francisco, where she hoped to connect with a band. Her reaction to the hippie scene was every bit as negative as Tracy Nelson's, and she quickly returned to Texas. The following year a San Francisco band, Big Brother and the Holding Company, contacted her and asked if she would be interested in returning to the West Coast. Janis jumped at the offer. Big Brother and the Holding Company was the house band at the well-known Avalon Ballroom, and singing for them would mean steady work.

Janis and the band recorded an album for a small label; a single from the album, "Down on Me," attracted a lot of attention but did not make the Top Twenty. Not until the following year, when she gave an electrifying performance at the Monterey Pop Festival, did she attract the attention of a major label. Columbia Records signed her to a recording contract and released an album, *Cheap Thrills,* followed by a single, "Piece of My Heart," that made it onto the charts in 1968. Buoyed by the success of the album, Janis left the band and recorded a solo album, *I Got Dem Ol' Kozmic Blues Again.* When that album failed to sell as expected, she stopped performing for a while, then reemerged with the Full Tilt Boogie Band to work on what would be her final album. Songwriter Kris Kristofferson stayed with her for a short time during this period; when he

53

moved on, he left a song with her titled "Me and Bobby McGee."

Janis had been an alcoholic for years, but by 1970 she had become a full-blown heroin addict. She died of an overdose on October 4 in a hotel room littered with empty whisky bottles, before work on her album was completed. When it was released posthumously in 1971, "Me and Bobby McGee" went to Number One on the pop charts. Like soul singer Otis Redding, Janis died without knowing her work would ever receive widespread acceptance. It probably would not have mattered to Janis. Her voice was powerful—filled with gut-wrenching angst—but not especially melodic. She was a sexual creature, on and off stage, but not what you would call physically attractive, except when she sang, and then everyone agreed she was absolutely beautiful.

Music to Janis was a lifestyle, not an art form: It was who she was, not what she did for a living. With her untimely death evolved a mystique that has continued to the present day. With the passing of time, it has become apparent that her popularity was due as much to the intensity of her performances as to her recordings. It was her pain that made her different, the fact that she seemed to be dying, spiritually and emotionally, each time she stepped out on stage. People seemed mesmerized by the sight of her. Their faces showed the same awe and titillation reflected in the faces of people watching a public execution. Or a train wreck. Janis was giving her life for her fans—right there on stage—and it was riveting to those who witnessed it. "Have you ever been loved?" she once asked a friend. "I haven't. I only feel it on stage."

Janis stood alone in the 1960s in her efforts to adopt the male persona. Most women wanted success, but as women. The first woman to turn the tables on men by using the same technique perfected by Elvis was Frank Sinatra's daughter, Nancy. In 1961 Frank started up his own record label, Reprise, and Nancy was one of the first artists signed. Her first single, "Cufflinks and a Tie Clip," died a quick death, but no one at the label was about to give up on Frank's daughter.

For five years, Nancy released single after single, with none of them making the Top Twenty. Finally, after fifteen successive failures, Reprise turned to successful writer/producer Lee Hazlewood and asked him to help. "You're not the virgin next door," Hazelwood told Nancy, according to *Time*. "You've been married and divorced. You're a grown woman. I know there's garbage in there somewhere."

Hazelwood wrote a song he thought would do the trick. "These Boots Are Made for Walkin'" was a brassy, no-nonsense anthem to female liberation. It went to Number One in 1966, giving Nancy the first chart-topper by a woman since Connie Francis' 1958 hit "Stupid Cupid." Hazelwood, who also produced the record, was savvy enough to take the Presley formula and use it for Nancy. The lyrics were designed to appeal to women, and Nancy's appearance—short skirts and hot pants that showed off her toned thighs, coupled with a striking girl-next-door face and Playmate of the Month body—was designed to appeal to male record buyers.

That same formula had worked for Leslie Gore two years earlier, though the sex appeal aspect was not consciously stressed because of the singer's young age. In June 1963, her first release, "It's My Party," went to the top of the charts. Leslie was only seventeen at the time and attending a New Jersey high school. The record, which was produced by newcomer Quincy Jones, was devoured by female record buyers, who identified with the song's stand-up lyrics. It caught the attention of males, who thought she was cute but sexy.

If it appears unseemly to equate sex appeal to an underage teen, it must be remembered that in the early years of the rock era, the vast majority of records were purchased by teenagers. Over the years, the median age increased, stretching into the fifties and sixties as many of the early rock stars, such as the Rolling Stones, approached their sixties. But in the beginning, it was a teenage thing—and it is a fact that teenage boys are attracted to teenage girls. Leslie followed her first hit with a string of Top Ten hits that advocated the radical concept that men had no right to tell women what to do or what to say. It was strong stuff for its time, and it ultimately cost Leslie her male audience and her supremacy on the charts.

Balancing that more daring approach were a number of singers who preferred to remain in territory defined by female artists in the 1950s. Nancy Wilson was able to crack the Top Twenty with only one song, "(You Don't Know) How Glad I Am," but she maintained a strong nightclub base and received positive reviews from pop-oriented magazines such as *Playboy*, which described her as "the girl with the golden voice." Falling into that same category was Barbra Streisand, who was recognized by *Playboy* as the "hottest female property in show business." Although that assessment was based primarily on her theatrical work—she appeared on Broadway in *I Can Get It for You Wholesale* and *Funny Girl*—she had a Top Twenty hit in 1964 with "People," a song taken from *Funny Girl*. Streisand was a chart contender throughout the decade, but her best work was yet to come.

Female singers were in abundance in the 1960s, though not in as great a supply as male singers (there were three males for every woman who made the Top Twenty). Petula Clark, Dusty Springfield, Gladys Knight and the Pips, and Dionne Warwick were all major players on the charts in the 1960s, but of that group only Petula made it to the top—first with

"Downtown," then with "My Love." Petula also made history by becoming the first British female artist of the modern era to top the charts.

One of the strongest voices of the 1960s belonged to Aretha Franklin, a Memphis-born soul singer who zoomed to the top of the charts in 1967 with "Respect." The song had been written by Otis Redding, who had released it earlier, only to watch it founder on the charts. Redding was perplexed by the success of Aretha's version. How could a woman have a hit with a song he had tried—and failed—to score with? It was the same melody. Same lyrics. But way opposite results. He was stumped.

❖◇❖◇❖◇❖◇❖◇❖◇❖◇❖◇❖◇❖◇❖

Throughout the socially turbulent 1960s, BMI's Frances Preston was responsible for the entire southern region of the country. Her job required her to travel throughout the South to meet with BMI-affiliated songwriters and to sign up new songwriters. Musically, it was an exciting time. Southern rock and rhythm & blues were exploding all over the charts. It was a troublesome time in that racial integration was still a source of strife. Her job was to meet with songwriters, no matter the color of their skin, which made her an easy target for racists who didn't approve of racially mixed conversations.

Once she went to Memphis to meet with a new composer signed to BMI, Phineas Newborn, an enormously talented jazz pianist. He was a good catch for BMI. The only problem was that he was an African American. Meeting with him presented a dilemma for Preston. BMI did not have an office in Memphis, nor did Newborn, who lived in a black neighborhood that offered no potential for a business conference. Where would they meet? They couldn't meet in a restaurant or coffee shop because blacks were prohibited from entering public facilities used by whites. Recalls Frances: "I was staying at the Peabody Hotel, so I thought, what's wrong with meeting him in the lobby of the hotel? So, we were sitting there, papers were spread out and we were signing contracts and the manager came over.

"He said, 'Get that nigger out of the hotel.'

"I said, 'Excuse me. We're just sitting here signing some papers.'

"He said, 'I said get that nigger out of this hotel.' Then he looks at Phineas and said, 'Nigger you know better than to be in this hotel lobby. Get out of here.'

"Phineas was embarrassed to death and I just wanted to die."

The hotel manager turned his attention back to Frances, his face reflecting the disdain he felt for what he obviously perceived to be a fallen white woman, a disgrace to his race. "Are you staying in this hotel?" he demanded.

"Yes."

"Okay, get your bags and get out. We don't want your kind in this hotel."

As she was going out the door, Frances had the last word: "You'll regret this," she said over her shoulder. When she returned to Nashville, she telephoned that city's most powerful resident, Governor Bob Clement, who happened to be a close friend. Then she called her father, who was a proud Rotarian; he, in turn, called the higher ups in that organization; overnight an ugly racial incident was transformed into a cause for the governor's office and, of all people, the Rotarians. "We got that guy fired," she says proudly. "Not only did I have to go through the 'woman' bit, I had to go through the racial bit. Between the two combined, I was always on a crusade."

The Memphis incident is revealing because it provides insight into why Frances was able to become a top-ranked executive. When she encountered the problem at the hotel, she did not go to the NAACP, or to individuals in the state who had reputations for backing liberal causes; she went to a conservative, white governor and an organization that had a history of racial and sex-based exclusion.

Frances knew that if she wanted a problem fixed, she had to appeal to individuals who had the power to bring about change. In that instance, her problem-solving instincts were right on target. The payback to the Rotarians was that she became their first female member, once they opened their doors to women. Later, she became the first professional woman to be accepted into the Friar's Club; the only other women, at that time, were entertainers Liza Minnelli and Nancy Sinatra.

◆◇◆◇◆◇◆◇◆◇◆◇◆◇◆◇◆

Roberta Lee Streeter was inquisitive from an early age. In the early 1950s, when her family lived in a multi-unit house in a pleasant neighborhood in Greenwood, Mississippi, she played in the fenced-in backyard with a six-year-old boy who occasionally dropped by to visit his cousins who lived in the house. Sometimes they squirted the water hose. Other times they poked around, peering into storage sheds and behind vine-covered trees.

One hot summer day, Roberta said, "Wanta' see something?"

The little boy said, "Sure."

Roberta, who was a year older, led the little boy inside, moving quietly through the dark shadows of the house. Without either of them saying a word, they made their way past a gauntlet of oscillating electric fans that purred with quiet efficiency, sending loose currents of cool air scooting through the house. When they entered the back bedroom, where her mother was lying on the bed, she looked up at Roberta. "Hi, honey," she said; then she looked at the little boy, surprised to see him in the room.

Roberta swept her arm out toward her mother, saying proudly, "See!"

The little boy looked at the mother, who was cradling an infant to her breast. The little boy had seen infants before, but he had never seen a female breast. He stared at the woman's breast, seemingly paralyzed; then he heard Roberta say, "Let's go back outside," then slowly backed out of the room, as Roberta broke into one of those skipping gaits of which little girls are so fond.

Eventually, both the little boy and Roberta moved away from Greenwood. Roberta left a few years later, moving with her mother first to Houston, Mississippi, then to Palm Springs, California, where she attended high school. After studying music at the Los Angeles Conservatory of Music and philosophy at UCLA, she did secretarial work for a while, then put together a song and dance team in 1966 and struck out for Las Vegas.

By then, she had changed her name to Bobbie Gentry. Within a year she had built up a successful nightclub act. She wrote all of the group's material and performed with them as a singer and hoofer. Clearly she was not intimidated by the display of bare breasts that permeated the Vegas nightclub scene. Most Vegas acts were thrown together by men; Bobbie's success was unique for the times. She was aggressive, but she had a charming, sultry way about her—part of that Southern upbringing, no doubt—that allowed her to deal effectively with men and get what she wanted. Vegas is a tough town, but Bobbie was not in the least intimidated by the city's reputation.

One day Bobbie made a demo of a song she had written, "Mississippi Delta." She gave it to a song publisher, who played it for Kelly Gordon at Capitol Records. Gordon took one look at Bobbie—she was darkly exotic, with a striking face and long, waist-length black hair—and he signed her as an artist. Capitol agreed to release "Mississippi Delta" as a single, but since they needed something for the flip side, they sent Bobbie into the Capitol Records studio on Vine Street in Hollywood to record another song she had written, "Ode to Billie Joe." It took less than an hour to record the song, with Bobbie accompanying herself on guitar. Later, Gordon added strings to the track and listed himself as producer.

Capitol wasn't all that excited about "Ode to Billie Joe." It was too long. It couldn't be categorized and it couldn't be aimed at a specific audience. They reminded Bobbie that she was entering the market as a solo female singer, a category that wasn't doing very well on the charts. In July 1967, "Mississippi Delta" was released. It was a good song, but not one that was likely to break out of the pack. To everyone's surprise, disc jockeys all over the country flipped the record over and started playing "Ode to Billie Joe."

On August 5, 1967, "Ode to Billie Joe" debuted on the Hot 100; three weeks later it bumped the Beatles's "All You Need Is Love" out of Number One and prevented Diana Ross and the Supremes' "Reflections" from moving up. Bobbie was stunned by the record's success. So was Capitol Records.

In September, accompanied by Gordon, Bobbie returned to Houston, Mississippi, for a homecoming celebration sponsored by the town. By that time, everyone in the country wanted to know about Bobbie Gentry. "Ode to Billie Joe," with its mysterious reference to something being flung from a river bridge, had intrigued the nation. A media contingent befitting a presidential candidate descended upon tiny Houston. Gordon was inundated with requests for interviews. *Newsweek* was there. So was *Time*. The wire services. Who is this Bobbie Gentry, they demanded— and what's the deal with that song?

Gordon turned down all the media requests, saying that Bobbie just wanted to enjoy the homecoming celebration. Among those requesting an interview was the author of this book, a student reporter from the University of Mississippi, who had been sent to cover the homecoming for *Mississippi* magazine. He was among those turned down by Gordon, and if memory serves, he was not too happy about that.

Later in the day, when everyone, included Bobbie, was seated in a banquet hall, the reporter approached the singer and asked for an interview. Neither Bobbie nor the reporter knew it at the time, but the reporter was the little boy she had escorted into her mother's bedroom that hot summer day nearly twenty years earlier. Bobbie looked over the reporter for the longest time. She had heard the question, clearly, but something was preventing her from giving the answer Gordon had instructed her to give. The reporter could not take his eyes off of the singer. There was a connection there that neither understood. Finally, Bobbie nodded, the words following at a slower pace. "Okay," she said. "Meet me after the reception and we'll talk then."

"Bobbie!" Gordon said, shaking his head. "You don't have time."

Bobbie did the interview—it was the only one she granted—but the reporter did not understand why until years later when he learned that Bobbie Gentry and Roberta Streeter were one and the same. Bobbie herself didn't know why. During the interview, the reporter asked her if "Ode to Billie Joe" was meant as a veiled protest of some kind. Opposition to the war in Vietnam was at its zenith, and the national media analyzed every book, record, and movie created by the under-thirty generation with suspicion. There was talk among the reporters at the banquet that Bobbie might be a subversive of some kind, so asking her if she was a protest singer seemed appropriate. Bobbie laughed at the question. "No, I am not a protest writer," she said. "My theme is indifference. I am not protesting. I am trying to call attention to the indifference that individuals possess even while discussing a boy who has jumped from a bridge."

After the interview, the reporter offered to give Bobbie a ride back to the Memphis airport in his Mustang convertible. As they were walking toward the car, Gordon came running up, clearly agitated. "What are you doing?" he demanded.

Bobbie told him.

"No, no," he said, taking her by the hand.

"Sorry," Bobbie said, looking like a woman who did not enjoy taking orders from a man, even if he was her producer and a big-shot record executive. Years later, she would complain about her treatment as a woman. Said Bobbie, "I originally produced 'Ode to Billie Joe,' and most of the others, but a woman doesn't stand much chance in a recording studio." No matter what a woman did in the studio, the record always contained a man's name as producer when it was released.

"Ode to Billie Joe" sold over three million copies and won three Grammys. Bobbie continued writing and recording songs that focused on women—"Fancy" was about a prostitute, "Belinda" was a stripper, and "The Girl from Cincinnati" was about a movie star who had been forced to earn stardom in the backseat of a thousand different cars—but none of her subsequent efforts ever achieved the level of success of "Ode to Billie Joe." In 1969, she married Bill Harrah, president of the Desert Inn Hotel in Las Vegas. They divorced soon thereafter and she married singer Jim Stafford. That marriage lasted less than a year, and she divorced him shortly after giving birth to their baby.

When "Ode to Billie Joe" was made into a major movie in 1976, she returned to Mississippi for a visit. Interviewed by a reporter for the *Delta Democrat-Times*, she said she thought the song had been successful because people were tired of male-dominated psychedelic rock groups. Said Bobbie, "There were no songs on the charts by female recording artists then. But all the drawbacks turned into advantages."

Bobbie wrote and recorded more than seventy songs in the 1970s—and she starred in her own television series on BBC-TV in London—but she was unable to recreate her earlier success and eventually dropped out of sight.

◆◇◆◇◆◇◆◇◆◇◆◇◆◇◆◇◆◇◆

Following in Bobbie's footsteps was Jeanne C. Riley, a Kentucky-born singer who moved to Nashville from Texas in 1966 in hopes of landing a recording contract. She recorded demo after demo, but none of them caught anyone's attention. She was working as a secretary when she was asked by Shelby Singleton, Jr. if she would come into Sun Records to sing on a record titled "Harper Valley P.T.A." Singleton had purchased Sun Records from Sam Phillips and had relocated the label to Nashville. The song had come his way from songwriter Tom T. Hall, who had recorded the demo with a female singer whose voice Singleton felt was too soft to sell the song.

"Harper Valley P.T.A." tells the story of a widowed mother who is attacked by the P.T.A. for what it considers loose morals. It is an angry song, one that lashes out at hypocrisy and promotes the right of women to follow their destiny. Singleton sensed that the song was right for the times. Everyone, it seemed, was on edge in 1968. The Vietnam War was raging. Martin Luther King and Robert Kennedy had both been shot to death. Anger was palpable in the air.

Jeanne was no different. She was angry about the anger. When she stepped up to the microphone, all those pent-up feelings—anger at the way society was falling apart, anger at the way her music career was going nowhere—came bellowing out in "Harper Valley P.T.A." Singleton had records pressed within twenty-four hours of the session and sold nearly two million copies within two weeks.

On September 21, 1968, "Harper Valley P.T.A." was the Number One record in America, outselling the Rascals' "People Got to Be Free" and the Beatles' "Hey Jude." If Jeanne had once lain awake at night, dreaming of a hit record, that dream turned into a nightmare as she struggled to adopt the "fallen woman" image depicted in the song. That fall she attended the Country Music Association Awards to accept the honor for the Single of the Year. She showed up at the nationally televised event wearing a floor-length gown. When Singleton learned of that, he ordered the gown cut off into a mini dress, and he provided Jeanne with silver boots to wear with the dress. Jeanne was humiliated by the incident, but it was just one of many in which she was forced to be someone she was not.

The success of "Harper Valley P.T.A." came close to destroying Jeanne. It ruined her marriage and led her to experiment with marijuana. She pulled herself out of that morass in 1972 by becoming a born-again Christian, but she never again had a major hit. It had become a common theme in pop music: When male artists had hit records, they seemed to thrive on the success, using it as a stepping stone to even bigger things, but, invariably, when female artists had hits, it unleashed a barrage of professional and personal hurdles that few women were able to overcome.

In July 1969, six months before the end of the decade, *Newsweek* recognized what was happening to women in the music business and expressed hope that the situation would improve. "For all its individuality, the rock-music scene has lacked the personal touch," wrote Hubert Saal. "Largely, it has been a world of male groups, of pounding, thunderous music that drowns out the words, which are rarely of moment. It needed the feminine touch and now it has got it." As proof, the magazine offered profiles of five women—Joni Mitchell, Elyse Weinberg, Lotti Golden, Laura Nyro, and Melanie—that Saal predicted would turn things around with their "feminine touch." Saal showed impeccable taste in his selection, but a soothsayer he was not.

4 | Stayin' Alive: The 1970s

"Hey, I want the big 'un!"

The anonymous voice shot out of the audience like a lightning bolt, up onto the stage, where four women and a man stood frozen in their tracks. One of the women—the terrified object of the catcall—was an attractive, rather buxom musician. From the demeanor of the all-male audience, it would be reasonable to conclude that the musicians were part of an adult entertainment revue of strippers, drag queens, and bawdy comedians. In reality, the group was a folk and bluegrass band named the Good Ole Persons.

They were performing at a trade show in a small town in northern California when the incident occurred. The 1970s had brought hope to small towns in that part of the state. The economy was showing signs of expanding, and real-estate sales were booming. To accentuate the positive, the movers and shakers in the town held a huge trade show, inviting representatives from all the major businesses of the region.

In between serious-minded presentations from real-estate firms and chambers of commerce from surrounding communities, the 400-plus men in the audience were treated to slide presentations of nude women. Bare breasts and protruding buttocks were projected onto the huge screen amid thunderous applause and screams of approval. Taking all that in were the Good Ole Persons, who stood backstage patiently awaiting their cue to perform. They couldn't believe their eyes and ears. They were folkies, for God's sake—the Good Ole Persons!

Once they took the stage, it quickly became apparent the audience was not there to hear music. "We were all very young—sweet things," says Laurie Lewis, a vocalist and fiddle player with the group. "We were terrified. They were screaming and yelling, and we were doing our sweet little songs. We lasted for about three songs, then got off stage."

Lewis went on to become one of the top female bluegrass fiddle players in the country and she can laugh about it today, but at the time it was difficult to see any humor in the situation. The tradeshow audience was indicative of how attitudes toward women had changed in the 1970s. By the time the decade ended, it would prove to be the worst in history for female recording artists.

From 1970 through 1979, 270 solo artists charted hits in the Top Twenty. Of those, only sixty-two (23%) were women. Individual recording artists, such as Cher, Diana Ross, and Carly Simon, scored sizable hits, but for women as a whole the decade was an unmitigated disaster. The situation on the business end was even worse. When the decade began there was one female top executive in place—BMI's Frances Preston—and when the decade ended, there was still only one female executive in place.

If you chose one word to describe the war between the sexes in the 1970s, it would be "strident." Feminist Kate Millett's scorched-earth policy toward men in *Sexual Politics* drew an equally bellicose response from Norman Mailer, who wrote an article for *Harper's* magazine, "The Prisoner of Sex," that offered the male perspective. In 1972, *Time* magazine wrote a cover story about the raging gender war, noting that, "The most lordly male chauvinist and all but the staunchest advocate of Women's Liberation agree that women's place is different from man's. But for the increasingly uncomfortable American woman, it is easier to say what that place is not than what it is." The magazine focused on the disparity in music, noting that an all-female rock group in Chicago belted out verbal attacks against male musicians. "Rock is Mick Jagger singing 'Under My Thumb,' it's all right," sang the women. "No, Mick Jagger, it's not all right!"

Music itself reflected the conflict, with lyrics from male songwriters and artists that alternated between indifference and outright hostility toward women. Reflecting the axiom that Number One records required a healthy mix of male and female buyers, many of the chart-topping hits recorded by males in the 1970s fell in the "sensitive guy" category. Al Green's "Let's Stay Together." Stevie Wonder's "You Are the Sunshine of My Life." Charlie Rich's "The Most Beautiful Girl." The biggest exception was Chuck Berry's "My Ding-a-Ling," a song that went to Number One despite being about the singer's penis (female record buyers must have had their reasons for helping it become a hit).

The sexual liberation of women, begun in the 1960s with optimism, reached a crescendo in the 1970s with the addition of a new word to the lexicon—groupie. Male rock stars accumulated large gatherings of women in their teens and early twenties who followed their heroes from city to city, offering sexual favors to the entertainers and to their roadies. They would do anything to get backstage to meet their heroes.

Typical was the young teen that begged and pleaded with the stage crew of one male artist to get backstage to meet him.

At the high end of the groupie spectrum were those women, invariably glamorous-model types, who pursued rock musicians as potential mates. One of the most famous is Bebe Buell, whose union with Aerosmith's Steven Tyler produced a daughter, Liv Tyler, who achieved fame of her own as an actress. Buell, a former *Playboy* playmate, who in addition to dating Tyler was linked to Todd Rundgren, Elvis Costello, and Rod Stewart, told the magazine in 1997 that she hated to be called a groupie. "I think it's sexist," she said. "Nobody calls males groupies."

In addition to the gender war, the other variable in the 1970s was the introduction of payola. Scores of grand jury and FBI investigations rocked the industry, resulting in executive shakeups at several major record labels. The investigations began after federal officials linked a CBS Records official to a heroin ring operating between New Jersey and Canada. The trail led investigators from illegal drug operations to industry payoffs, all channeled through company promotions departments. Payola affected women because it involved record companies paying off radio programmers to play certain records. Invariably, those chosen records were by male artists, unless on rare occasion the record companies decided they wanted their "bitch" to do battle with a competitor's "bitch."

Once the payola was exposed, it brought attention to another inequity in the system: All of the radio program directors of that era were males. They chose the records that received air time, and they, as a group, decided which records would make the charts that reflected airplay. For that reason, the charts that listed hits based on airplay and the charts that listed hits based on sales were not always in sync. Sales charts reflected female buying habits. Airplay charts reflected the opinions of male program directors. Guess which charts showed women in the most favorable light.

◆◇◆◇◆◇◆◇◆◇◆◇◆◇◆◇◆◇◆

Early in the decade, sex was the key to success for many women. Melanie Safka, who performed and recorded simply as "Melanie," had a Number One hit in 1971 with "Brand New Key." Ostensibly, the song—delivered with the playful resonance of a child's voice—was about a little girl who needed a key that would fit her skates. Almost from the instant it was played on radio, it created a firestorm of protest from people who interpreted the song in terms of sexual imagery. Some radio stations banned it.

Melanie was stunned. She had composed the song in about fifteen minutes to use as an uptempo change-of-pace tune during her concerts.

Two years earlier, in an interview with *Newsweek,* she had confessed discontent as an entertainer: "There's no one to share my experiences with and I get very low sometimes. . . . I feel like a product, a machine. It's as if I'm wearing a nun's habit. I feel there are things I can't say and that people coming up to me don't know how to talk to me."

The success of "Brand New Key" only amplified her alienation. She had spent three years building a reputation as a serious artist who had important things to say, but after the success of "Brand New Key," everyone wanted her to continue with that cutesy, little girl image. That kind of success was not what Melanie had in mind when she started out, so she quit performing and returned to her South Jersey home, where she devoted the next four years to the more traditional female role of raising a family. In 1975, she attempted a comeback—falsely concluding that America had gotten over its obsession with sex—but by then it was too late to recapture her audience.

The same sort of thing happened to country singer Tanya Tucker with her hit, "Delta Dawn," but with a major difference: Tanya really was a little girl. Once, she was roundly booed by a Grand Ole Opry audience during a performance in which she flaunted her blossoming sexuality and sang several rock-oriented songs that ran counter to her image as country music's "darlin' little girl."

Tanya was twelve when she and her father left their home in Las Vegas to travel to Nashville for her first recording session. She had been discovered by a female songwriter, Dolores Fuller, who had pitched her to Billy Sherrill, artists and repertoire director at Columbia/Epic Records. Sherrill liked what he heard and wasted no time setting up a session. The first single out of that session was "Delta Dawn," a gutsy song written with a much older woman in mind. Before the year was out, "Delta Dawn" was a Top Ten hit and Tanya was a country-music star.

"I thank the lucky stars and the Good Lord for that song," says Tanya. "If I cut it now for the first time, I think it would be a hit. I was fortunate to have latched onto that one, and that was all Sherrill's doing. If it hadn't been for Sherrill, I probably would have been a rodeo queen or something. Any other producer would have stuck me with some puppy dog song. I wasn't used to singing those songs. I had sung mature songs all my life. I was singing, 'You Ain't Woman Enough to Take My Man' when I was eight years old."

Looking back, it is difficult to understand how people could have missed Tanya's woman-child message, but they did. She sang adult songs that dealt with adult themes, and she did so in an adult voice, and she wore mini-skirts and Nancy Sinatra-style boots. In a 1973 feature about country music, *Newsweek* published a photograph of Tanya with the caption: "Teenage mythmaker." Did the magazine know she was only thirteen? Probably not, because she looked much older in the photograph.

"I wasn't allowed to date until I was sixteen, and I really didn't worry about that too much," she said in 1988; then hearing her own words, she broke out into self-effacing laughter, "I still don't worry about it [dating]. It's just as bad now as it was then."

In 1978, fed up with all the criticism, Tanya went to Los Angeles to record a rock-influenced album titled *TNT.* It was one of the top-selling country albums of 1979 and proved, once and for all, that Tanya was at her best when she was being herself. By then, being Tanya meant traveling in the fast lane. Drugs. Alcohol. A failed engagement to Glen Campbell. By the 1980s, Tanya had become fodder for the tabloids, as she seemed to drift from one misfortune to another. In an interview with *Newsweek,* she blamed some of her troubles on the fact that she is a woman. Bemoaning the fact that women were not allowed to vote until the 1920s, she said: "I can't imagine that. Probably 100 years from now they're going to be saying that about us. 'Wow! You mean they couldn't get drunk and screw anybody they wanted? God! Poor girls!'"

Tanya Tucker has received more criticism for the excesses in her personal life than praise for her leadership on women's issues, but surely the latter is more appropriate. Over the years she has been a tireless, if not always politically correct, advocate for women's rights. Following in Tanya's footsteps, both musically and in the arena of gender politics, was Helen Reddy, an Australian who recorded a remake of "Delta Dawn" that became a Number One pop hit in 1973.

"Delta Dawn," which was written by two men—Alex Harvey and L. Collins—was embraced by women long before it ever became a hit. Harvey recorded it first on an album he did for Capitol. One of the backup singers at the session was Tracy Nelson, who sang the song at the Bottom Line in New York. In the audience that night was Bette Midler, who decided to use the song in her nightclub act. Response was so good that she included the song in her album, *The Divine Miss M.* While out promoting the album, she did the song on "The Tonight Show" with Johnny Carson, thus giving it its first national exposure. Watching television that night was Billy Sherrill, who thought the song would be perfect for Tanya Tucker. The lesson was obvious: If women like it, it's probably a hit.

"Delta Dawn" was Helen Reddy's second Number One hit in less than twelve months. In 1972, she had topped the charts with "I Am Woman," a song that unabashedly celebrated the female gender. Her record label hated the song and didn't really want to include it on her album. Her producer thought it made her sound like a lesbian. Her friends told her it would ruin her career, but the song struck a chord with Helen, who had experienced difficult times after moving to America from Australia. When time came to choose songs for her first album, she deliberately looked for material that would project a positive image for women.

Helen was vindicated when the song went to Number One, but it was not until the following year, when she was awarded a Grammy for top female vocalist, that she expressed her sentiments about the women's movement to a national television audience. After accepting the award, she said, "I want to thank everyone concerned at Capitol Records; my husband and manager, Jeff Wald, because he makes my success possible; and God because *She* makes everything possible."

Helen was subjected to an outpouring of approval from feminists and hostility from right-wing zealots and religious fundamentalists who considered the song and her remarks about a female God as blasphemous. "I Am Woman" quickly became the theme song for the women's liberation movement, and Helen encouraged those associations at every opportunity. She had another Number One hit with "Angie Baby," but by mid-decade her career as a hit-maker was over. She continued to perform, even starred in her own television variety show, but by 1982 her professional problems had spilled over into her personal life as her divorce from Wald elicited headlines about his cocaine use and their unfriendly battle over custody of their son. The following year she married a drummer, Milton Ruth, but when that marriage ended in divorce, she told *People* she had no interest in ever again getting married: "What can any man give me that I can't give myself?"

By the mid-1990s, Helen had focused on a career as an actress. She appeared on Broadway in the musical *Blood Brothers*, and she went out on the road to tour with Willy Russell's comedy, *Shirley Valentine*. After one performance, she told a reporter for the *Arizona Republic* that she sometimes thought people were disappointed not to hear her sing. "For some people, it's a nice break to come to see me and not have me sing 'Delta Dawn' and the rest of it," she said. "But there's the inevitable person who walks out upset because I didn't do 'I Am Woman.'"

David Letterman did a "Late Night" spoof on the women's liberation movement by asking Helen to repeatedly pop out onstage to sing lines from "I Am Woman." The comedy bit called for Letterman to shoo her off stage each time she appeared. It was all in good fun, and Helen was not averse to poking fun at herself, but it was also a commentary on the fragile link that always exists between music and politics, no matter how noble the intent: A song is a song is a song.

✦◇✦◇✦◇✦◇✦◇✦◇✦◇✦◇✦◇✦

Linda Ronstadt began her career in the 1960s with the folk-rock trio, The Stone Poneys, but success did not come her way until 1975, when her recording of "You're No Good" went to Number One. The ten years prior to that she jumped around quite a bit musically in an effort to find herself. Her greatest liability was also her greatest asset: She could sing just about anything and do it justice. For that reason, no one quite knew what to do with her. If you do everything well, nothing you do stands out. What did stand out was Linda Ronstadt herself. She was petite and attractive, and she had a shy way about her that endeared her to everyone who met her or watched her perform. She was small-townish and worldly at the same time. Every small town in America has a girl singer that everyone just *knows* is good enough for the big time. Linda was *America's* singer that everyone just knew was good enough for the big time.

When "You're No Good" struck Gold, *Rolling Stone* magazine did a cover story on her titled "Linda Ronstadt: Heartbreak on Wheels." It was an acknowledgment that she had made it into the inner sanctum of rock 'n' roll. The article pointed out that, at age twenty-eight, she still looked and talked like a little girl. If the magazine writer was struggling to define his subject, so was Linda struggling to find herself. "I'm very dissatisfied with everything," she said. "I'm hard to please and very restless, so it's always a battle between that and my real deep desire to have a home and roots."

Success brought Linda new problems, but it was always the old problems—true love and the stress of putting together and keeping a band—that kept her on the ropes. Relationships were always a hassle for her. Like many women, she tried to please. She had a hard time standing up for herself. "I was so unsure of myself," she told Mark Bego. "I have a tendency to let other people shape me. If I'm going with someone and he gets at all critical of my music, the bottom falls out for me."

Linda traveled to Nashville in 1970 to appear on the Grand Ole Opry and to record an album titled *Silk Purse*. She hated the album, primarily because she was never able to get into a comfortable groove with the Nashville musicians, but the experience convinced her that her future as a recording artist lay in country-rock. When she returned to Los Angles, she put together a first-rate group of musicians who would eventually rename themselves the Eagles and have a few hits of their own. She found them easy to work with, but she knew that they were too talented to remain her backup band.

Finding and keeping a band would always be a problem for her. Male musicians didn't want to work for a woman—at least never for long. Frankly, she didn't know how to talk to them, how to give orders to men. She knew they felt working for a woman was not cool, and a secret part of her agreed with them. In the 1970s rock 'n' roll was a guy thing; it was one of the reasons she kept flirting with country music. It was the only place she could find comfort with kindred spirits such as Emmylou Harris.

Linda first went to hear Emmylou perform after friends told her she was doing the same type of music. She became an instant fan and friend. Emmylou was indeed doing her style of music—only better, Linda confessed to friends. Linda asked her to sing on her album, and she sang harmony on "I Can't Help It," which won a Grammy. It was during this same period that Linda was drawn to the music—and uncritical persona—of Dolly Parton, who then was a successful country artist but not yet a pop star. The three of them—Linda, Emmylou, and Dolly— began recording together as a trio during this time, but it would take a decade for them to complete enough material for an album.

For Linda, her friendships with other female performers were what kept her sane. "In the old days we couldn't afford psychiatrists," she told Bego. "Maria Muldaur, Bonnie Raitt, Wendy Waldman, and I kept each other from having nervous breakdowns for years. And my attitude towards anyone who is new on the horizon is that if they're good, and it's honest, then it has to be helped; those people have to be brought in. My feeling about girls that are better than I am is that we need 'em, because they'll make the music better, and I can learn from them. There's always somebody who's better than you."

Linda's success from mid-decade on caught her off guard. She really was not prepared for all the attention she received from the media and from the increasing numbers of people in the industry who wanted something from her. She charted eight Top Twenty singles in the 1970s, including "Blue Bayou," "That'll Be the Day," and "It's So Easy." But her success made it even more impossible, or so it seemed to her, to have a decent relationship with a man. For a time, she swore off being anyone's "girlfriend." She told a reporter from *People* that what she wanted was a relationship with someone who was an equal. "I'm so disorganized," she joked, "what I really need is a good wife."

❖◇❖◇❖◇❖◇❖◇❖◇❖◇❖◇❖◇❖

Bonnie Raitt's first love was the blues. By the age of twelve she had taught herself to play guitar so that she could experience the music firsthand, but growing up in Los Angeles, where her father, John Raitt, worked as an actor, did not put her in personal contact with many blues musicians. She compensated by listening to all the blues records she could find. Memphis Minnie was her favorite. To hear her play blues guitar was more than a musical experience, it was a religious epiphany. The very idea that a *woman* could play guitar like that inspired Bonnie.

Those aspirations take on added significance when you consider that Bonnie's parents were Quakers, not thought of as a religion that stresses female self-reliance, and she spent her summers attending Quaker camps. By the time Bonnie was eighteen, her father had moved to the East Coast, where he found steady work as a Broadway singer, so she packed up and went East to attend college.

Bonnie enrolled at Radcliffe College in Cambridge, Massachusetts, where she spent several years as a student, working in local coffee houses during her off-hours. Her audience, for the most part, was an eclectic mix of educated white kids her own age that grooved on the straightforward blues rhythms and soulful intonations she had mastered. There was something alluring about the diminutive redhead using her delicate, ivory-toned fingers to connect with her guitar, exploring the dark and mysterious recesses of the bottomland blues that had originated in the Mississippi Delta.

There came a time when Bonnie had to choose between getting a formal education at Radcliffe and a more worldly education in music. She chose the latter, trading the certainties of college for the chaos of one-nighters in nightclubs in New York, Boston, and Philadelphia. She also headed South, taking a plane to Memphis, then renting a car to drive down into Mississippi, where she sought out bluesman Fred McDowell in his hometown of Como. Fred taught her to play slide guitar, and Sippie Wallace gave her lessons on how to phrase the songs so they would sound authentic.

Bonnie wanted her music to be real. She wanted to carry on a tradition, not adapt old music to something new. In the early years, she surprised more than one down-and-out bluesman with words of praise and questions about his guitar technique. Lamented Bonnie: "I'm always sad because I was lucky enough to know a lot of the great blues people, the traditional blues artists as well as the ones from Chicago—and a lot of them have passed on, and unfortunately that music heritage has been relegated to some kind of cult."

With a college following that was almost cult-like, Bonnie moved to Los Angeles in 1971 and signed a recording contract with Warner

Brothers. Her self-titled debut album, recorded at an abandoned lakefront summer camp in rural Minnesota, contained many traditional blues songs, and while it did not make a dent on the charts, it did solidify her fan base. There was a politics to music in those days. The Vietnam War was in its final throes, and Bonnie's generation viewed music as an expression of solidarity. There was no protest in Bonnie's music, but she performed a type of music that was more or less forbidden in polite, white society. Her considerable musical talents aside, Bonnie belonged to the hip crowd of her generation. Everyone liked her, especially other female performers. She was accessible, both to her fans and to the music media.

Even conservative, mainstream publications such as *Newsweek* found themselves infatuated with Bonnie. In 1972, less than a year after the release of her first album, the magazine's music writer, Hubert Saal, stopped by a New York rock club to sample her music. He was more accustomed to writing about the ballet and symphonies, but he left the club that night with the feeling that he had witnessed something special. "[Some might feel] it's kind of freaky for a girl who looks like Bonnie to be singing and playing the country blues of the black man," he wrote, describing her as a beautiful redhead. "But she draws gasps from the crowd when she lets herself go on the guitar." Bonnie told Saal that she didn't want to be a star. She just wanted people to enjoy her music, the way they would a visit with their friends. She needed the feedback, she said—and the love.

Between 1971 and 1987, Bonnie recorded nine albums for Warner Brothers, none of which were commercial successes. At a time when Donny Osmond, the Bee Gees, and America were sugaring up the charts in a decade that was disco bound, Bonnie stayed true to her musical roots, tipping her hat whenever possible to the traditional blues. Sometimes she would do more than tip her hat, as when she recorded a live duet with her hero Sippie Wallace on "Woman Be Wise." It is impossible to listen to the song without hearing Sippie's pleasure and pride at exchanging gut-wrenching vocals with the redheaded white girl who provided her with a new definition of sisterhood.

As Bonnie entered the 1980s—and her thirties—she found that her audience was changing. Her fan base was no longer young and no longer spending Saturday afternoons in the record store. Mortgage payments displaced rebellion as a topic of conversation. Middle age loomed on the horizon. The music business itself was changing. Radio was solidifying and specializing in specific formats. It was a rough decade for Bonnie. She wondered if her recording career was over.

In a 1986 interview, she expressed frustration at the way radio was segregating musical styles: "I, for one, am happy to see black music played more on the radio in the crossover sense, but I wish there was a way to obliterate those categories. When I was growing up there was no black or white radio, everyone just played good music. You could hear the Temptations, the Supremes, Sam and Dave, and the Beatles on the same radio station. I would like to see that situation come back because I think there are a lot of black musicians who have always been ignored, especially in the financial sense, considering the number of white artists who are making a lot of money having been influenced by what they do."

Despite her misgivings and her pessimism about the future, Bonnie ended the decade with a bang. After leaving Warner Brothers and signing with Capitol Records, she released her most successful album, *Luck of the Draw*. The first single, "Something to Talk About," gave Bonnie the first Top Twenty hit of her career, and a new audience, as women in their late teens and early twenties discovered Bonnie for the first time. The song was a defiant declaration of independence and became a favorite among liberation-minded strippers who danced to the song at gentlemen's clubs across the country.

By then, Bonnie's relationship with her audience was changing. Approaching fifty, she was no longer described as a young, beautiful redhead; instead she was hailed as one of the founding mothers of blues-rock, an elder in the church of get-down boogie. Bonnie responded by making herself less accessible to her fans and to the media. She no longer mingled with her fans after concerts, and she no longer returned calls to reporters. With success, she became the person she said she never wanted to become.

◆◇◆◇◆◇◆◇◆◇◆◇◆◇◆◇◆◇◆

Bette Midler was an anachronism, even by 1970s standards. With a big, polished voice and a saucy stage presence—once, at the height of President Richard Nixon's difficulties, she dedicated "Daytime Hustler" to the "divine Dick"—the five-foot veteran of *Fiddler on the Roof* played out the role of the unrepentant feminist. Critics were brutal—not in their criticism of her voice, which everyone seemed to agree was spectacular, but in their descriptions of the singer herself. Her body was described as "absurdly inadequate," and her mouth "toothy" and her nose compared to a "ski jump."

Such comments must have hurt Bette, but if they did, she never let on. Her first ambition, she told reporters, was to be a comedienne. Not until she heard an Aretha Franklin record did she decide she wanted a career in music. It was a good choice, though comedy would always be a part of her nightclub act. After signing with Atlantic Records in 1972, she released an album, *The Divine Miss M.*, that in addition to winning her a Grammy gave her a new identity as the "Divine Miss M."

Bette's approach to music was always theatrical. She competed with rock divas for space on the pop charts, but she had an entirely different outlook from contemporaries such as Bonnie Raitt and Linda Ronstadt. She was more at home on television, wearing a glitzy gown, than she was in jeans and T-shirt traveling across country in the back of a psychedelic rock 'n' roll van. It was her eighteen-month stint as a regular on the *Tonight Show* with Johnny Carson that launched her recording career.

Movies and television exerted a strong pull on female recording artists in the 1970s. Not all women wanted to travel the club circuit and perform for sometimes drunken audiences. Some women found the allure and glamour of movies and television irresistible. For those women, it was stardom that mattered—not some romantic notion of traveling the back roads to "live" their art.

Like Bette, Olivia Newton-John was dazzled by the bright lights. One of the few white female artists to have a Number One hit in the 1970s, she scored with "I Honestly Love You," a heartfelt ballad that resembled a solitary flower on a football field in the midst of a rough and tumble game. It initially attracted attention because it was so out of place.

The following year, Olivia followed up with "Have You Ever Been Mellow," her second Number One hit. It was considered a country song by the industry and by the awards committee of the Country Music Association, which honored her as the 1994 Female Vocalist of the Year and created a strange situation for Olivia, who really didn't consider her music to be country. She said as much to reporters. Her comments angered the country music establishment and led to a number of association members resigning in order to establish a competing organization, the Association of Country Entertainers.

Olivia was both hurt and confused by the protest. She tried to mend fences by opening for Charlie Rich and playing rodeos and livestock fairs; but not until she decided to record an album in Nashville—*Don't Stop Believin'*—was she able to feel accepted. Once that was done, she focused her attention on a television and film career. Her next Number One hit was "You're the One That I Want," a song from the movie *Grease*, which she co-starred in with John Travolta. Two years later, she starred opposite Gene Kelly in the musical *Xanadu*. The movie bombed, but a song from the soundtrack, "Magic," gave Olivia yet another Number One hit.

Olivia's biggest hit was "Physical," an upbeat song that was controversial because of lyrics that suggested a physical relationship. Some radio stations banned the record. Olivia was amused by the controversy, but she protested that people were taking it entirely too seriously. She continued to place songs in the Top Twenty—"Make a Move on Me" and "Heart Attack"—and she undertook a cinematic reunion with John Travolta in *Two of a Kind* and did a number of television specials, but another chart-topper eluded her, and by the 1990s her recording career had practically disappeared.

Throughout her career, Olivia seemed to struggle with her identity. She didn't think she was a country singer, yet that is where she found her initial success. She didn't think she was an actress, yet the public said she was. It was because of the movies, and not her heartfelt recordings, that she became a pop-music star. She was one of the most successful female solo artists of the decade, but she never seemed to connect with other female performers. If she showed leadership—and she did by becoming a role model for a generation of little girls who, taking a cue from "Physical," learned to speak in double *entendre*—it was accomplished by her actions and not her statements, for she never became a spokesperson for women's issues.

Another singer who seemed more at home in movies and television than in live concerts was Barbra Streisand, who sometimes suffered panic attacks before going on stage to sing. She found the controlled environments associated with television and movies much more to her liking, though she was not beyond succumbing to occasional flirtations with exhibitionism.

When the October 1977 issue of *Playboy* hit the newsstands, it featured Barbra on the cover, reclining blissfully in a gigantic, Freudian-inspired circle. She wore white shorts and a white T-shirt with the *Playboy* emblem. During the photo session, she took off her shoes and socks and stretched out in a pose calculated to show off her toned legs.

"Hey, guys," she said. "Now you can say I took it off for *Playboy*."

The magazine's editors were ecstatic. It was the first time a female celebrity had ever posed for the cover. The headline writer posed the question: "What's a nice Jewish girl like me doing on the cover of *Playboy?*" The editors addressed the headline to themselves as much as to the readers. Actually, it was a very good question. The answer could be found in the fact that Barbra had completed *A Star Is Born*, a controversial film she had co-starred in with Kris Kristofferson. Making the movie had been a nightmare. No one seemed to get along—and the principals spent more time arguing and doing midnight rewrites on the script than they did before the cameras.

Professionally, it was a very insecure time for Barbra: It had been three years since she had a Number One record and she had gone out on a limb and co-written a song for *A Star Is Born*. The movie took a roasting from the critics and was snubbed by the Academy of Motion Pictures Arts and Sciences, with the exception of the soundtrack song, "Evergreen," which she co-wrote for the movie. About the time she did the *Playboy* interview, she learned that "Evergreen" had become her second Number One hit. In an interview with record executive Joe Smith for his book, *Off the Record*, Barbra offered some advice to new artists: "Don't be afraid of the establishment. There are always those who are going to say, 'No you can't, no you shouldn't.' . . . You've got to do your own thing."

By 1977, Barbra felt fenced in creatively. She wanted to make hit records. She wanted to star in hit motion pictures. She wanted to do everything and she wanted to do nothing. For more than a decade, *Playboy* had been among Barbra's staunchest supporters, reviewing each and every record she released, often in glowing terms, such as the 1966 review of *My Name Is Barbra, Two,* in which the critic referred to the "epic success of the miraculous Miss Streisand." It was not popular at the time to say so—and among feminists it is still not a popular notion to suggest—but the magazine did as much to promote the careers of female performers as any major-circulation publication of its day. The Big Bunny adored female singers, and was not ashamed to admit it. Barbra knew that and found it hard to say no to being on the cover.

The interview itself was one of the best she had given. There were questions about her career and about her nose, but the best questions and answers revolved around issues specific to her gender. She was asked about the women's movement and about her own experiences in the business as a woman. She was asked if she considered herself a feminist. Says Barbra: "It's funny, I never thought about the women's movement while I was moving as a woman. I didn't even realize that I was fighting this battle all the time. I just took it very personally; I didn't even separate it from the fact that I was a woman having a hard time in a male society. Then they started to burn the bras, and I thought it was ridiculous, although I now understand it in the whole picture of revolution—one has to go to these crazy extremes to come back to the middle. Actually, I believe women are superior to men, I don't even think we're equal."

Barbra never said publicly that she thought Carly Simon was her biggest competitor, but she did admit to reporters that she co-wrote "Evergreen" because other female recording stars were writing their own songs. Carly Simon and Carole King were the two most successful singer-songwriters of the decade, and of the two, it was Carly who was dazzling the world with her toothy smile and sexy album covers. Her 1972 *No Secrets* album, which contained the Number One single, "You're So Vain," had a cover photograph of Carly that showed her nipples outlined against a thin blue pullover shirt. On the flip side was a close-up of her face, her sensual mouth, with lips parted, measuring an enormous five inches across, giving rise to any number of male fantasies.

Sex was a big part of the record business, but it was Carly who elevated it to an art form. She swore up and down that the sexy images were all unintentional. She explained to reporters that as a child she had mugged for her father (publisher Richard Simon, co-founder of Simon & Schuster) whenever he took her photo; it was a means of getting his attention, and if it was a habit she had been unable to outgrow . . . well, she wasn't going to apologize for it. Girls will be girls.

Carly was arguably the best lyricist of her generation. The songs not only expressed complicated emotions, they revolved around mysteries, such as the identity of the person she was writing about in "You're So Vain." If her success had been confined solely to music, more specifically to her songwriting, her place in American music history would be secure; but to her generation, Carly was more than a singer or songwriter. Not only was she married to singer James Taylor (the prototype of the sensitive male of the 1980s), she had friendships with male rockers such as Mick Jagger, who sang backup for her on "You're So Vain," she traveled in social circles only dreamed about by her fans. It was the extra-musical associations that made her an icon to other women. In the eyes of many women, Carly was the epitome of what a woman should be.

In songs such as "Anticipation," "The Right Thing to Do," or "Haven't Got Time for the Pain," Carly reached out to other women on a consistent basis with sympathy, attitude, and a sense of optimism. In some ways, Carly was very much a creation of the 1970s; the rock and pop era had progressed to a point where the public felt it needed royalty. It was at that point that Carly realized that her success had come with obligations attached.

Carly's problem was that she didn't want to be a rock- or pop-music princess. Music was not a lifestyle to her, not the way it was to Janis Joplin or Linda Ronstadt, and the harder the public pushed her in that direction, the more she dug in her heels. To Carly, it was the song that was important. Music was a vehicle though which she could express herself with the spoken word. As the 1970s wore on, Carly focused less on public appearances and more on her songwriting. She decided to try her hand at writing songs for the movies. Her first was "Nobody Does It Better," which she wrote and sang for the 1977 James Bond film, *The Spy Who Loved Me.* Years later, she would follow up with "Let the River Run," which she did for the movie *Working Girl.* Other movies followed, including the soundtrack for Nora Ephron's *This Is My Life,* which contained the song, "You're the Love of My Life." From movies, Carly moved on to books, writing a series of books for children, including *Amy the Dancing Bear.*

When Carly's marriage to James Taylor ended, she became a recluse, at least as far as the public was concerned. She went into her private self and closed the door. No public appearances. No sexy album covers. Carly said repeatedly during the 1970s that she didn't understand why people had labeled her with a "sexy" image. She was so convincing when she said it, it was difficult not to believe that she really meant it.

When she reappeared in 1995, at the age of fifty, to promote a new album titled *Letters Never Sent,* entertainment writers first focused more on her accomplishments and the fact that she had recovered from her stage fright than on her former "sexy" image, but then as she undertook more and more public appearances, there evolved a sense of amazement among the twenty-and thirty-something entertainment writers that Carly still had a sensual air about her—and at fifty!

The fourth television and motion picture diva to surface in the 1970s was Cherilyn Sakisian LaPierre, who thought from an early age that she would be an actress. And why not? She lived in Hollywood. Her mother was an actress. And she took acting lessons while attending high school. Everything pointed toward the movies as a career. Of course, something would have to be done about that name. It would have to be shortened to Cher.

When Cher first met Sonny Bono in a Hollywood coffee shop, he was twenty-seven and she was sixteen, though she told him she was eighteen. He worked as a promotions man for record mogul Phil Spector, who sometimes allowed him to sing background on the records he produced. Sonny thought it would impress Cher if he took her to one of the sessions on which he was asked to do background vocals.

Spector was impressed enough with Cher to allow her to sing background vocals, which led to him producing a single, "Ringo, I Love You," with Cher using the name Bonnie Jo Mason. The record bombed. Sonny encouraged Spector to give her another shot, but he declined. Sonny then persuaded Atlantic Records to sign them as a duet. As Sonny and Cher, they recorded a song written by Sonny titled "I Got You Babe" and paired it with "It's Gonna Rain." When they sent the tape to Atlantic Records head Ahmet Ertegun, he thought "It's Gonna Rain" was the better side. Sonny pleaded with him to release "I Got You Babe," but Ertegun was adamant. Before the record was released, Sonny took "I Got You Babe" to a Hollywood radio station and told them they could have it exclusively if they would agree to play it once an hour. They did, and the song became an immediate hit, establishing Sonny and Cher as one of the top acts of the 1960s.

Married by then, they followed up with "The Beat Goes On" and "All I Ever Need Is You." Not until Cher broke away as a solo act in 1971—and CBS Television was persuaded to air the "Sonny and Cher Comedy Hour"—did adult record buyers begin to take her seriously. The same year the television show began, Cher racked up her first Number One hit with "Gypsys, Tramps, and Thieves." She followed up with another Number One, "Half-Breed," then with "Dark Lady," which proved to be her last Number One single.

One of the highlights of the "Sonny and Cher Comedy Hour" were the verbal barbs they tossed at each other during the opening of the show. Viewers thought Cher's caustic digs at Sonny were humorous, but what they didn't know was that the couple had separated and were pretending to be happily married for the sake of their careers. After their divorce, they attempted a comeback show on CBS, but the show failed, with the audience apparently deciding that watching a divorced couple argue in public was not nearly as funny as it had been when they were married.

With her singing career on the rocks, Cher focused all her energies on her first love—acting. She was every bit as successful in the 1980s as an actress as she was as a singer in the 1970s. She appeared in films such as *Good Times* and *Chastity,* but it was not until *Silkwood* that she blossomed as an actress, earning an Oscar nomination as best supporting actress. With the release of her 1985 film, *Mask,* Harvard University's Hasting Pudding Club named her "Woman of the Year," an honor that previously had gone to the likes of Jane Fonda and Katharine Hepburn.

Cher's public persona cast her as a strong female who, despite always getting into trouble for things she did or said, was able to somehow come out on top; but if she was perceived as a role model for other women, it was more along the lines of what *not* to do. By the mid 1990s, good acting roles proved hard to come by and comebacks on the recording front seemed even more elusive. Enormously talented as a singer and as an actress, she was never able to bond emotionally with her female public; she gave love, or so she felt, but it was never returned. Into the New Millennium, she bore a reputation—richly undeserved—as a woman people loved to hate.

❖◇❖◇❖◇❖◇❖◇❖◇❖◇❖◇❖

There was more to the downturn women experienced in the 1970s than would appear from an analysis of numbers alone. It was in many ways the most unusual, perplexing, and disheartening decade of the modern era. By the mid-1970s, America had come to terms with the "race problem" by enacting laws that protected the rights of African Americans to vote, assemble, and travel with equal protection of the law, but what America had not done was change its way of thinking.

Despite all the gains won by the civil rights movement during the 1960s and early 1970s, black entertainers still found themselves segregated. We may never know how much of that was by choice, and how much was forced upon them by society; but we can know that whatever the cause, black women in the music business lived an isolated existence, one marked by anger, frustration, and hopelessness. It is one of the reasons black female artists felt resentment toward their white sisters whenever they appeared together at concert venues and found themselves dressed so radically differently.

They felt they were at the bottom of the pecking order. At the top were white male stars, followed by white females, then black males, and, at the bottom, black females. In spite of all the hardships—the cheating managers and agents, the sexually demanding club and venue managers, a fickle public, and perhaps worst of all, black boyfriends and husbands who demonstrated a preference for newly liberated white females—black female artists, projecting an indomitable spirit, produced a dazzling array of music during the decade. Diana Ross, Natalie Cole, Thelma Houston, Roberta Flack, and Gladys Knight & the Pips, all kept black women "staying alive" at the top of the charts.

With four Number One hits during the decade, most people would consider Diana Ross one of the dominant female voices of that era, and certainly she was the dominant black female vocalist. As the lead singer of the Supremes, she had participated in twelve Number One singles, so when she broke away to record her first solo project in 1970, she was under a lot of pressure to deliver. Thinking she needed a new direction, Motown's Berry Gordy asked an outside producer, Bones Howe, to supervise the project.

Howe was a proven hitmaker, with Number One singles by the Association and the Fifth Dimension to his credit. Midway through the project, Gordy realized that Howe saw Diana as a black Barbra Streisand. That was not a vision that appealed to Gordy and he dropped Howe from the project. Two Motown staffers, Nickolas Ashford and Valerie Simpson, were asked to take over production. They had written two hits for Marvin Gaye and Tammi Terrell—"You're All I Need to Get By" and "Ain't No

Mountain High Enough." They decided to rework the latter song, changing it from a duet to a solo effort.

Ashford and Simpson produced the record, and Ashford, who had started out singing gospel in a Baptist Church in Harlem, sang the soaring backing vocals at the end of the song. Gordy hated it, saying that at six minutes, it was much too long to release as a single. He wanted to change the song around, but they stuck to their guns and it was released as they had recorded it. Six weeks after "Ain't No Mountain High Enough" was released, it went to Number One, knocking another Motown record, "War" by Edwin Starr, out of the top slot. Fifteen years later, Ashford & Simpson would record a Top Twenty hit of their own as vocalists on 1985's "Solid," but it was their twin talents as songwriters and producers that made them unique during the 1970s. Some of their songs became giant hits—"Ain't Nothing Like the Real Thing" and "Let's Go Get Stoned."

With the success of "Ain't No Mountain High Enough," Valerie attracted attention for her contributions as a producer. She was the first woman to get production credits on a major hit. Unfortunately, it was not a facet of the music industry she wanted to pursue. What she really wanted was to become a solo artist. She attempted several solo projects and several duets with Simpson, but until the 1985 hit, none of the projects lived up to expectations. With her incredible talents in the studio, it is tempting to ponder what she might have accomplished if she had developed those talents and stayed the course as a producer.

Diana Ross followed "Ain't No Mountain High Enough" with "Touch Me in the Morning," which went to Number One in 1973. Between the release of the two songs, Diana made her acting debut in *Lady Sings the Blues*. Prior to the session for "Touch Me in the Morning," there was concern at Motown about the sexual implications expressed in the song's lyrics and concern about whether Diana's newfound career as an actress would divert her focus and energies from the work that would be required of her in the studio. Perhaps because of those fears, Diana was asked to record the song twelve times. Afterward, according to songwriter Ron Miller, engineers spent three hundred hours splicing the song together; the finished product did not contain "three syllables" in sequence from the same recording. By then, everyone was experiencing frustration with Diana. It even carried over into the media. In a 1974 review of her album, *The Last Time I Saw Him*, the *Rolling Stone* critic was brutal, calling the album "utterly facile" and "pretentious," then observing that Diana was "capable of simply making a fool of herself."

Diana had two more Number One singles that decade—"Do You

Know Where You're Going To," the theme from the movie *Mahogany,* and "Love Hangover"—but it was clear to everyone that Diana was more interested in her emerging movie career than her singing career. The glamour, the glitter associated with Hollywood, was all more than she could resist. Then there were the complications of the personal relationship that developed between Diana and Gordy. Diana's last solo single to go to Number One—and her last to be released by Motown—was "Upside Down," which peaked in September 1980.

Berry Gordy has been criticized for his infatuation with—and sometimes blind devotion to—Diana Ross, sometimes at the expense of his other female recording artists, but he was one of the decade's most outspoken proponents of female talent. He openly sought female talent for Motown and he hired women on a consistent basis. One of his executive assistants, Suzanne de Passe, played a major role in the direction the label took. Later, she left the music business to focus her efforts on film and television production with equally impressive results, proving that she was more than a stand-in for Gordy.

Biographer J. Randy Taraborrelli maintains that Gordy had a plan right from the get-go. He was a big admirer of Debbie Reynolds and Doris Day and wanted to build his company around black women of similar talents. "Gordy wanted a female artist to be the focus of his company, but it would have to be someone whose style could appeal to both black and white audiences," wrote Taraborrelli. "She would be a black woman who would make her race proud because they respected her worldly sophistication. She would also make whites comfortable because they understood her image and finesse. He certainly had nothing against black music, but [he] realized that it was limited mostly to blacks."

◆◇◆◇◆◇◆◇◆◇◆◇◆◇◆◇◆

In 1972, Clint Eastwood was filming *Play Misty for Me,* a suspense thriller about a disc jockey, played by himself, who was targeted for revenge by a female stalker. When time came to choose a song to play beneath the love scene between himself and Donna Mills, he remembered a song recorded by Roberta Flack in 1969.

The song, "The First Time Ever I Saw Your Face," had stuck with him. He called Roberta and asked for permission to use it in the movie. After the movie's release, it took just six weeks for the song to go to Number One. For Roberta, who at thirty-three had never had a commercial success, it seemed like a miracle. Encouraged, she returned to the studio. The following year she scored her second Number One hit with

"Killing Me Softly With His Song." A third Number One followed in 1974 with "Feel Like Makin' Love."

Also making an impact in the 1970s was Natalie Cole, daughter of Nat King Cole. She had only three Top Twenty hits that decade—"I've Got Love on My Mind," "This Will Be," and "Our Love"—but she received a great deal of media attention due to her paternal lineage. Sometimes it went to absurd lengths, such as the time she sang at a restaurant in Greenfield, Massachusetts, near the college she was attending. The sign on the door read: "Nat King Cole's Daughter Appearing Here." Her name was never even mentioned. She scored several Top Twenty hits in the 1980s, including "Miss You Like Crazy" and "Pink Cadillac," but her biggest—and most memorable—hit was probably 1991's "Unforgettable," which she sang with her father, courtesy of new technology that allowed their voices to be combined on the same recording.

If you are thinking at this point that the 1970s was an excellent decade for female solo artists—in view of all the incredible hits turned out by women—then you would be right from a creative standpoint. Women made some incredible music throughout the decade, despite the many restrictions placed upon them. Unfortunately, for every success enjoyed by female artists, males chalked up three successes. Since the business of music is one of numbers, it is to the numbers that we must go to evaluate the progress of the sexes. On that basis, it is clear that women made the worst showing of the modern era during the 1970s.

Seemingly unconcerned about the business of music was Grace Slick, the first female artist to breast-feed her baby on the pages of a national news magazine. Somehow it seemed appropriate in the 1970s for the acid queen of the 1960s to display a sense of radicalism on the subject of motherhood. During the heyday of Jefferson Airplane, she was a hard-driving rocker who dared to go where other women had never ventured. Usually, she was stone-cold drunk on Dom Perignon champagne by the time she walked out on stage, but her audience, which was itself usually stoned on LSD, seldom seemed to notice Grace's condition.

By the mid-1970s, when the group transformed into Jefferson Starship—and motherhood had put new demands on her—Grace was preaching the evils of drugs, although she did confess to reporters that she still had a deep appreciation for a good bottle of wine. Jefferson Airplane had two Top Twenty hits in the 1960s, but it was more successful in the 1970s, scoring five hits, including "Runaway," "Count on Me," and "Miracles." The group didn't survive the 1970s, though technically it had a Top Twenty hit in 1980 with "Jane."

Grace Slick was not a solo artist, but she had a strong influence on other women who respected her independence and rebelliousness. She was living out the rock 'n' roll lifestyle, because she chose to and not because she didn't have other options. In the minds of many, she was the rich girl gone bad. Her parents were well-to-do and had sent her to Finch College, the same exclusive girls' school attended by President Richard Nixon's daughter Tricia. She was a former model who performed at gritty outdoor festivals, not afraid of the mud and slime and boisterous overtures of her admirers.

Once, when invited to a tea at the White House, she arrived with 600 micromilligrams of LSD with the intention of lacing the tea, only something came up and she got distracted from her mission. In a 1976 interview, Grace told a reporter that she had no intention of ever growing up. Her goal was to still be hanging out at bars when she was seventy-five, though she jokingly conceded that she didn't expect to be picked up nearly as much by men at that age.

**There's Something Happening
Out There: The 1980s**

"Janis Joplin was dead—there were a lot of singers around, but they were doing different things than what I wanted," says Pat Benatar, referring to her musical mindset going into the 1980s. "I wanted to do a certain kind of thing—and the people I was emulating were men."

Pat was among the first of the women rockers to adopt the hard-driving, guitar-propelled rock 'n' roll that had come to represent pop music's new direction for male artists. Mick Jagger and Keith Richards of the Rolling Stones. Robert Plant and Jimmy Page of Led Zeppelin. Those were Pat's heroes as she was learning the guitar during the 1970s. By the time her first album, *In the Heat of the Night,* was released, her male competitors—bands such as Queen and Pink Floyd—were hogging the singles charts with Number One hits like "Crazy Little Thing Called Love" and "Another Brick in the Wall."

Pat responded with a second album, *Crimes of Passion,* which generated a million-selling single, "Hit Me With Your Best Shot." The song created an image for Pat. The sexy one. Not satin-dress sexy like Diana Ross. Not sweet-voiced sexy like Olivia Newton-John. Pat's sexy image had a rough, cutting edge to it.

Pat was the strongest, most aggressive, female rocker to emerge from the 1970s, but she was not alone. Other women rockers were hitting the charts. Deborah Harry of Blondie. Joan Jett and the Blackhearts. What they discovered was that the system was rigged so that they had to compete with each other, not with their male competitors. Radio programmers would not air records from female artists back to back. Often they would not even air two female records in the same thirty-minute segment. It was a situation that made Pat—and the other female artists—livid. Says Pat: "There were many times when clearly you had the record that was being requested the most, but they would say, 'We already have a girl on the playlist.' And if it was me on the playlist, then my other peer group would not get on. They would say things like, 'We can't play the Pretenders record because we just played you.' It was a constant problem—and it still happens."

Pat's talents were recognized at the 1981 Grammy Awards when she was given the first Grammy ever awarded in a brand new category: Best Rock Vocal Performance, Female. It was an award she would take home every year for the next three years. In the early 1980s, Pat was the epitome of what the industry thought a female rock star should be: Bold, sexual, energetic (all five feet two inches of her), an advocate of in-your-face, guitar-driven music.

Ironically, by the time the industry decided that it was acceptable for women to project aggressive images, Pat decided that was no longer what she wanted. She was approaching thirty, had met the man of her dreams—she had married guitarist/producer Neil Giraldo in 1982—and was looking for new challenges. "If you want to be sexual on stage, that's fine, but if you decide you don't want to do it anymore, people will refuse to let go of it," says Pat. "That was a big problem once I decided I had enough. I was twenty-six when I started—a young, single person. Very quickly I met my husband and it changed the way I wanted to look as a performer. The problem was, I was already locked in peoples' minds."

Besides the public's reluctance to let go of her old image, there was something else that bothered Pat during that time. Despite all the Grammys, the hits, and the million-selling records, Pat was not immune to old-fashioned sexual harassment. "I had all kinds of radio program-mers saying, 'Come over here and sit on my lap.' That sort of thing. 'Let's see if we can get that record played.' It was truly amazing. I felt like I was in a movie. You can't possibly allow that kind of thing to happen, but they have the power to make your life hell. You couldn't come right out and say, 'Kiss my butt.' You had to say, 'Oh, no thank you,' because they were in positions of power. It was very demoralizing. People say, 'What's the big deal?' But it was a big deal. I'm a little person, but I am always ready for a fight, and when I was young, I was a maniac, constantly doing battles with people over those things."

That problem was compounded by the shortage of other women to talk to about it. Most of the people she worked with were males. Usually, the only women she came into contact with were publicists, not a group she felt comfortable confiding in about problems concerning the media. She talked to her husband about the problems she was experiencing, but it didn't make her feel better. Nothing can savage a relationship quite so much as a female complaining to a male that she is always fending off sexual overtures from other males. "This was a whole new thing for everyone involved and there was very little support at the female end," says Pat. "It would have been nice to have someone to commiserate with. It was always a struggle because I spent most of my time arguing. I think it would have been easier to explain what I wanted to another woman."

Pat felt like she was part of a movement, but it was not always easy to define what kind of movement. "My age group was probably the first true product of the women's movement," she says. "It had a great influence on women my age. We were thirteen and fourteen when it came full blown. But we had a lot of dissent, even within our own ranks, because we were afraid of being lumped together as feminists in negative ways. Even though we had camaraderie among us, we tried to downplay the fact that we were female. Our attitude was, 'Let's just play the music and get on with it.' It was about war, not refinement. There was a gauntlet. You were out there trying to get through the day."

There were few places for young women to turn for help in those days, says Pat: "It was my intention to have younger females relate to me because I hated it so much when I was young, with guys singing, 'Let me take you back to my room little girl.' What do they think? That we have no feelings? I would like to take *you* back to *my* room, how about that? I don't think we could see clearly what it was we were trying to accomplish because we were being battered every single day."

Not until she gave birth to two daughters, Haley and Hana, did Pat undergo an attitude change. "Motherhood was the first step to dropping all the guards I had up from being so defensive," she says. "Because you can't do that with children. It opens up everything. Your writing. Your perspective. Every aspect of your life. Raising daughters is not the same as raising sons. I teach my daughters about strength. There's not a question in their minds that they can't do things. Their gender never enters into it." The change in Pat's life became apparent when she went onstage, decked out in rock 'n' roll black, only to look down to see the remnants of baby vomit clinging to her shoulder.

"I believe that men and women are separate in the way we view things, not that we are not equal—just different," says Pat. "With the group of women that I belonged to in the beginning, it was said we had a mostly male audience screaming, 'Take your clothes off!' But it was from the beginning a predominately female audience who related to what we were doing. It was unique for them to see someone like themselves up there. My husband is my collaborator, my producer, but we view things differently, even when we write songs. When his influence is heavy into the lyrics, the song is another thing entirely. You can separate our songs by who wrote what."

✦◇✦◇✦◇✦◇✦◇✦◇✦◇✦◇✦◇✦

During the 1980s, music was more about gender war than artistic refinement. As women rockers like Pat Benatar gained acceptance, two exclusively male alternatives—rap and heavy metal—increased in popularity. The lyrics of both musical forms sometimes expressed hostility toward women, while recruiting them as fans and groupies.

Denna Winstein, writing in *Heavy Metal: A Cultural Sociology*, concluded that the "anti-female posturing of heavy-metal stars relates less to misogyny than to a rejection of the cultural values associated with femininity. Men act, women are acted upon—through sight, touch, or merely imaginative transformations. Power, the essential inherent and delineated meaning of heavy metal, is culturally coded as a masculine trait."

Toward the end of the 1970s, a feminist organization named Women Against Violence Against Women threatened to boycott Warner Records because of album covers the organization considered degrading to women. The dispute was resolved, but came to a head again in 1984 over videos aired by another Warner-affiliated company, MTV.

Elayne Rapping, writing in *The Guardian,* complained that women were being depicted in the videos as "bitches, teases, castigators, and all-around sex-things." She was right, but there was more to it than that. The war of the sexes, as it spilled over into the 1980s, was complicated by the acceptance of large numbers of women of what was admittedly anti-female music. Those women did not gravitate to the music because they hated themselves, but rather because they were reacting to mothers and grandmothers who appeared weak and inadequate to them. They felt that if they attacked women they perceived to be weak, it somehow made them stronger, more like men.

The gender tug-of-war that was beginning to take hold resulted in the best decade yet for women solo artists. In the years from 1980 to 1989, seventy-three female solo artists made the Top Twenty charts. That translated to 31% of the total chart placements. Male solo artists received 69% of the total; a strong, dominant showing, but their worst numbers yet—and a harbinger of things to come.

Ironically, it was a woman, a former *Playboy* bunny, who introduced white America to rap music. By 1981, Deborah Harry—the lead singer for Blondie—had already had two Number One hits. The first, "Call Me," was the title song for the movie *American Gigolo;* the second was "The Tide Is High." Blondie was already soaring when Deborah and band member Chris Stein decided to write a song based on the new music they had been hearing in the Bronx and in Brooklyn.

For a southern-born girl—Deborah was born in Miami, Florida, but raised by adoptive parents in Hawthorne, New Jersey—the rap parties she and the other band members attended in New York struck a surprising cultural chord. One day, Chris suggested they write and record a rap song of their own. The result was "Rapture," the first rap song to ever make the pop charts.

Blondie did a follow-up album, *The Hunter,* but none of the singles released charted in the United States ("Island of Lost Souls" peaked at Number Fifteen in Great Britian). After the band broke up and her writing partner, Chris Stein, became ill, Deborah attempted a solo career. Between 1982 and 1989 she charted two singles in the Top Twenty, but the magic was gone. A review of her 1987 album, *Rockbird,* was typical of the times: "The only drawback evident on *Rockbird* is the lack of commercially viable songs," wrote Becky Russell in *Nine-O-One Network.* "With the exception of hard-core Blondie fans I doubt a very large percentage of the general public will hear her album."

Everyone still loved Deborah, or so they said, but without hit songs that love would not translate into a long career. Taking up the slack in the rocker category was Joan Jett. With her coal-black hair brushed up to Sex Pistol-punk standards, her heavy black eyeliner, and her big, pouty, Mick Jagger look-alike lips she added a sense of drama and sex appeal. She played her Gibson guitar slung low, massaging its neck with nimble fingers that induced unavoidable phallic associations. For the males in the audience, it engendered a hormonal surge. For women, it elicited knowing smiles, for they knew what she was doing and why—and they approved.

Joan wasn't born with the knowledge to do that; she picked it up out on the road. From 1975 to 1979, she sang and played guitar with an all-girl group named the Runaways, eventually discovering that she could not have picked a worse decade to be a female guitar player. When the Runaways called it quits, Joan went to England as a soloist. While there, she started working with ex-Sex Pistols Steve Jones and Paul Cook, who had decided to try their hand as producers. For their first effort with Joan, they chose a song that had been recorded several years earlier by the Arrows. "I Love Rock 'n' Roll" was written by Arrow band members Jake Hooker and Alan Merrill as a response to a song the Rolling Stones had recorded entitled "It's Only Rock 'n' Roll (But I like It)." Hooker and Merrill were offended by the Stones' song because rock 'n' roll was everything they lived for; they wanted to write a song in response.

Joan's version of "I Love Rock 'n' Roll" was released only in Holland on the flip side of a remake of Leslie Gore's "You Don't Own Me." Meanwhile, Joan returned to California long enough to put together a new band. This time she chose only male musicians and named the group Joan Jett and the Blackhearts. She took the band straight to Europe because she felt no one would take them seriously in the United States. Europeans, she felt, were more accepting of women rock musicians.

Eventually, Joan returned to the States to perform at a concert in New York. Unknown to her, "I Love Rock 'n' Roll" co-writer Jake Hooker was in the audience, along with producer Roy Thomas Baker. After the show, they talked about recording an album, but Baker only wanted to produce that one song, so they were unable to reach an agreement. Instead, Joan teamed with producer Kenny Laguna to do an entire album that included a re-make of "I Love Rock 'n' Roll." When the record was released, it went nowhere. Undaunted, she undertook a dizzying schedule of one-nighters. She performed the song everywhere she went. "I ain't no punk rocker," she screamed to the audience, a reference to criticism she had received from radio program directors that she only played punk rock. "I play rock 'n' roll."

Responding to Joan acting as cheerleader for her own record, women by the thousands started calling in to radio stations to request the song. Program directors had no choice: They had to play the record. By March 1982, it was the Number One record in the country. Joan was astonished by public reaction to the record. Nothing associated with her many years on the road had prepared her for the success that followed. In an interview with *Bam* magazine, she said, "People might expect me to be sick of it by now, the title and all, but when you sit there and look at that Gold record and you think of your accomplishments—I mean, to come back and do what we did is so incredible in itself that I can't believe it sometimes."

Joan followed up the success of "I Love Rock 'n' Roll" with "Crimson and Clover," which peaked at Number Seven in 1982. It would be six years before she had another Top Twenty hit. Her last hit was 1988's "I Hate Myself for Loving You," which barely made it into the Top Twenty. It was Joan's last Top Twenty hit, proving that she—like Pat Benatar and Deborah Harry—was about a decade ahead of her time.

◆◇◆◇◆◇◆◇◆◇◆◇◆◇◆◇◆

When teenager Annie Mae Bullock was picking cotton on a plantation east of Memphis in the 1950s, Ike Turner was one of the most successful and powerful black men in the Mid-South. As a talent scout for West Coast record labels that specialized in rhythm & blues, he was allowed access to Sam Phillips's studio at Memphis Recording Service. At a 1951 session with his band, the Kings of Rhythm, Ike recorded "Rocket 88," which was subsequently released by Chess Records. The record went to

Number One on the rhythm & blues charts, giving both Chess and Ike their first chart toppers. "Rocket 88" was the precursor to the first rock 'n' roll songs recorded in Phillips' studio by Elvis Presley and some historians consider it the first rock 'n' roll song ever recorded.

Annie Mae did not meet Ike until she and her mother moved to St. Louis in the late 1950s. Annie Mae was at a nightclub with her sister one night to hear Ike's band, when the drummer, who was dating her sister, came over to their table to instigate a little jive talk. To the drummer's surprise, Annie Mae took the microphone away from him and started singing. Ike was so impressed with her spunk that he asked her to travel with the band.

Two years later, after she got pregnant, they married and Annie Mae changed her name to Tina Turner because she and Ike thought it sounded better. Tina became the star of the Ike & Tina Turner Revue, a high-voltage rhythm & blues show that featured Ike on guitar, Tina on vocals, and a group of high-stepping female background singers. Their first hit record, "A Fool in Love," made them stars on the black nightclub circuit.

In the early 1970s, they extended their popularity to young, white rock 'n' roll audiences with a remake of Creedence Clearwater Revival's "Proud Mary." They did well as a touring band and their records sold reasonably well, but none topped the charts. Finally, in 1976, after years of what she has described as an abusive relationship, Tina and Ike divorced. Tina pursued a solo career, but for years it looked as if her career was stalled. Then, in 1982, she signed with Capitol Records. Her first single, a re-make of Al Green's 1971 hit, "Let's Stay Together," charted, but failed to make the Top Twenty. Not until the time came to do an entire album did she record "What's Love Got to Do With It." When the song hit Number One in 1984, Tina was forty-five; not only did the song rejuvenate her career, it made her America's first middle-aged sex symbol.

Tina was successful because she overcame every barrier put before her: Age, sex, and race. She was embraced by the women's movement, which saw her as a modern day Joan of Arc, all of which mystified Tina. "The first I heard of women's lib was when *Time,* magazine ran this picture of some women waving their bras in the air," she said in her autobiography. "Great picture, but I didn't really get it. Was it supposed to mean that just because you took off your bra you were now using your mind? I couldn't really relate to that 'movement' kind of thing. They were talking about 'liberation'—but liberation from, like, housework. That was the least of my problems. My problem was simply survival."

As a result of the single's success, attention was focused on the entire album, *Private Dancer.* Over the next two years, the album spawned two additional Top Twenty singles—"Private Dancer" and "Better Be Good to Me"—and it sold over ten million copies. At the 1984 Grammy Awards she was given awards for Best Female Rock Performance, Best Female Pop Performance, and Record of the Year.

With her success, Tina proved that age had nothing to do with it. In the process, she became every woman's hero. "After I left Ike, I began to wonder about equality—socially, racially, spiritually, and between men and women," she wrote in her autobiography. "Even knowing that men are physically stronger, I cannot believe that we women are not equal. . . . This is why I have not given up on men."

Sharing the spotlight with Tina Turner in 1984 was Cyndi Lauper, whose "Girls Just Want to Have Fun" peaked at Number Three on the Top Twenty. Male reviewers wrote Cyndi off, poking fun at her light-hearted approach. *Newsweek* derisively called her a "new-wave Gracie Allen." Not writing Cyndi off was her target audience—young women who felt that equality included the right to have as much fun as men.

Cyndi followed up with "Time After Time," which went to Number One. She was thirty-one at the time, still young enough to be an effective salesperson for her eccentric, little-girl persona. She dressed like a new-wave diva, but sang in a sing-song voice that always seemed only a step or two away from breaking out into laughter. Whatever the critics said about her—and it was usually male writers who gave her the hardest time—it soon became evident that she was not posing as an eccentric. She truly was what she appeared to be: A free spirit, a little girl trapped in a woman's body.

Cyndi made history in 1984 when two additional singles—"She Bop" and "All Through the Night"—made the Top Ten, making her the first artist of the modern era to have a debut album that generated four Top Ten hits. Unfortunately, Cyndi's quirky light had a short wick and by 1989 her brief, flickering flame had extinguished. She made several comeback attempts, most notably in 1997 with a new album, *Sisters of Avalon*. Before the release of the album, nervous record executives tried to put Cyndi—and her early success—in perspective. "There are certainly some precon-ceived notions that we have to overcome," Epic vice president David Massey told *Billboard*. "We believe that with perseverance and the right exposure, we can gradually knock down any barriers ahead."

When Cyndi hit the interview circuit to promote the album, both she and her interviewers honed in on the women's movement. *Interview* maga-zine asked her if she felt the music industry was sexist. "It is, but I don't dwell on it, because my world isn't like that," she said. "I decided a long time ago the only way to change things was for me to change my environment."

Cyndi may have been successful in changing her immediate environment, but as she made more and more personal appearances it became apparent that she was not going to blend into the environment at large. The market for her music was still the same—young girls and women in their early twenties—but was she still the same? At thirty-one with her delightful persimmon hair, she was able to reach that market. At forty-four, she seemed less like a playful free spirit and more like the scary old woman who lived in the attic. Seeing her attempt to fit into the little-girl persona she had worn so well in the 1980s was painful, almost as unsettling as seeing Mick Jagger do the turkey-strut at age fifty-four. Cyndi's 1997 album proved that girls can't always have fun.

Benefiting from Tina Turner's unrepentant sexuality and Cyndi Lauper's gender-bending experimentation was Detroit-born Madonna Louise Veronica Ciccone, a former doughnut shop clerk and ballet dancer who had a knack for the dramatic. As Tina and Cyndi were topping the charts in 1984 and raking in handfuls of Grammy awards, Madonna was testing the waters with a series of singles, none of which hit.

Not until the release of *Like a Virgin* did it become apparent that she had a future in the music business, when the single went to Number One on the singles chart, establishing Madonna as a major player. She was shocked by the record's success because she disliked the song and had complained while recording it that the lyric "like a virgin" did not offer a good musical hook. The following year, she released "Material Girl," which went to Number Three, and "Crazy for You," which peaked at Number Two. At the same time the records were charting, she tried her hand at acting with a role in the movie *Desperately Seeking Susan,* for which she received rave reviews.

Madonna blended her flair for the dramatic with a level of sexuality never before displayed in popular music. For the most part, the media was stunned by her sudden ascent into stardom. *Time* called her the "sultriest of the video vamps." She told the magazine that she identified with Susan in the movie because she was "a free spirit and does what she wants." With the release of her third album, *True Blue, Newsweek* alluded to her "Marilyn Monroe look," with begrudging admiration in an article written by Cathleen McGuigan: "Way back about sixteen or seventeen months ago, there were certain oracles of pop who predicted that Madonna was just a flash in the pan—a very hot flash, but no more authentic than the gaudy baubles she wore, draped by the yard across an expanse of bare flesh."

Madonna garnered her share of male record buyers with her willingness to exploit her sexuality, but she won the hearts of an even larger audience of women who admired her boldness. She had become the female Elvis. Critics could call her tawdry all they wanted (they had called Elvis worse), but her message was getting through, and the more criticism she received, the more determined her audience became to adopt her viewpoint, style of dress, and attitude toward men. By 1987, *Rolling Stone* magazine was describing her as "something a bit better than another hot or controversial celebrity: She is an icon of Western fixations."

Throughout the 1980s, Madonna ruled the charts with a string of Top Twenty hits, including "Papa Don't Preach," "Express Yourself," and "Who's That Girl." She stayed in the tabloids with a marriage and a divorce to actor Sean Penn. Then she co-starred in another movie, *Dick Tracy*, with Warren Beatty, with whom she was linked romantically. By that time, she had fallen into a pattern of bad relationships and bad movie roles, but none of that mattered, because the more negative publicity she received, the more acceptance she received from her fans.

Madonna ended the decade and began a new one in controversy as MTV refused to air the video for her single, "Justify My Love." Under criticism from feminists over videos from male artists that critics said degraded women and advocated violence, MTV banned Madonna's video on grounds it was too sexually explicit. It was a bitchy way for the network to strike back at the feminists.

Madonna responded by hitting the interview circuit, milking the controversy for what turned out to be millions. *Time* called her efforts a "program of self-defense and self-promotion." In a masterful stroke, she appeared on "Nightline" with Forrest Sawyer, who aired the video on the pretense of examining the issue of censorship. Thus, the video that was too lurid for MTV saw the light of day on a network news program. Sawyer knew that Madonna's appearance would only boost sales of both the video and the record, and he found the irony irresistible. "In the end, you're going to wind up making even more money than you would have," he said during the interview.

"Yeah," Madonna replied. "So, lucky me!"

Madonna was not the only strong female voice of the 1980s, but she was the dominant one; it was her iron-willed reluctance to accept neither her own defeats, nor dominance from a male-dominated industry, that inspired a new generation of younger female artists to look for the flickering light at the end of the tunnel—no matter how dim it appeared in the distance.

❖◇❖◇❖◇❖◇❖◇❖◇❖◇❖◇❖◇❖

Ask people in the business who they think was the most successful woman in country music in the 1980s and invariably they will answer, Dolly Parton. Narrow that group down to a female-only audience—and ask them who they most admire in country music—and, once again, the answer will be Dolly Parton.

"You can't deny what Dolly has done," says BMI's Frances Preston. "Brains, drive, know-how—you can talk about managers all you want to, and Sandy Gallin [Dolly's manager] is one of the best managers in the business, but when it comes to Dolly Parton, she has handled her own career. Dolly knows what Dolly wants to do and what Dolly wants to be. I have always loved her line, 'I paid a lot to look this tacky.'"

Dolly was no overnight sensation. By the time her first Number One pop single, "9 to 5," topped the charts in 1981, she had spent fourteen long years in the trenches of country music, first as a struggling new artist with Monument Records, then as a singer with Porter Wagoner. It was Wagoner who succeeded in getting her signed to his label, RCA Records. She had a series of country hits during the 1970s—"Coat of Many Colors," "Jolene," and "Love Is Like a Butterfly"—but the audience for country music was limited and Dolly wanted more out of life. She set her sights on the bright lights of Hollywood.

With the release of the movie *9 to 5,* in which she co-starred with Jane Fonda and Lily Tomlin, Dolly became an international star. Her acting won universal praise from magazines and newspapers that had a long history of ridiculing the women of country music. There was something about Dolly with which the public could identify. That mystified Dolly since she was admittedly a self-made woman—a big-breasted caricature of a Barbie doll dressed in a form-fitting dress and a fuzzy, big-haired wig. Other women had tried that approach, but Dolly succeeded where the others did not because she never took it seriously. She gave men what they said they wanted, and she laughed about it all the way to the bank. It was an attitude that made her especially endearing to other women. If men didn't get the joke . . . well, that was their problem.

"Many an old boy has found out too late that I look like a woman but think like a man" Dolly wrote in her autobiography. "It is a great mistake to assume that because I look soft, I do business that way. Just like the first prostitute who realized she was 'sittin' on a gold mine,' I know what I have to sell, and nobody goes prospecting in my gold mine without first buying the mineral rights."

Dolly pursued a movie career throughout the 1980s, playing opposite Burt Reynolds in *The Best Little Whorehouse in Texas,* and opposite Sylvester Stallone in *Rhinestone,* but she stayed in touch with her music fans, scoring her second Number One in 1983 with "Islands in the Stream," a duet with Kenny Rogers. Dolly and Kenny followed up with a Christmas album and a joint American tour the following spring.

The 1980s was an incredible decade for Dolly, but by her own admission, the crowning achievement, not just of the decade but of her entire career, was the release of the album she recorded with Linda Ronstadt and Emmylou Harris, *Trio*, which was released in 1987 to rave reviews. Dolly told interviewers that she sounded better on that album with the other women than she ever had sounded alone. Linda and Emmylou were equally flattering in their comments about Dolly.

The three women were unable to arrange their schedules to promote the album the way each wanted to, but it took off without much help and eventually went Platinum. Of the three women, only Emmylou had never had a Top Twenty hit on the pop charts. At times, Linda and Dolly seemed embarrassed that they had achieved a level of financial success that Emmylou had not, and their public comments, awkward at times, reflected that sense of unease. Emmylou's career received a jolt from the album, but for some reason the public never took to her the way it did to Dolly and Linda.

By the mid-1980s, the major beneficiary of Dolly's diversification into motion pictures was Reba McEntire. The unwritten law of country music was that a woman could not be both queen of country music *and* a pop megastar. Dolly's success meant that there was an opening for the job of queen of country music.

Reba had been making records since the late 1970s, but with little success. In some ways, she was Dolly's exact opposite. With her feisty red hair, she was distinctive like Dolly—and she was attractive like Dolly, though in more of a girl-next-door manner—but, unlike Dolly, she continuously tried to focus attention away from her simmering sexuality. That was a struggle because she didn't possess any of Dolly's skills when it came to manipulating men and their fantasies. Dolly is a brilliant, sophisticated woman who has made a career out of "talking" country. Reba is a brilliant country girl who desperately wants to be acknowledged as a sophisticated woman. If she ever "talks country," it is a slip of the tongue.

Throughout the 1980s, Reba released a new album each year. Some years the prolific singer released two albums. She never had a crossover hit during that time, but she was consistently successful on the country charts. In 1984 she won her first top female vocalist awards from the Country Music Association and the Academy of Country Music. In 1986 the Country Music Association honored her with its biggest award—Entertainer of the Year.

Reba had won the top honors from both the Nashville-based Country Music Association and the Los Angles-based Academy of Country Music, but when she received her first Grammy in 1987, both country groups started backing away from her, though the more conservative Country Music Association was the first to shut the door on her. When the 1997 Country Music Association award nominations were announced, country music fans were surprised to see Reba's name missing from the list. They should not have been surprised. Reba had not received a CMA award since 1987, when she was chosen female vocalist of the year.

Reba was said to have been hurt by the CMA snub, and who could blame her? She's had fourteen platinum albums, six double-Platinum albums, five triple-Platinum albums, and one quadruple-Platinum album. That represents sales of more than thirty-five million records. Her high-energy concerts, which often seemed more pop-oriented than country, were consistently among the top-grossing in the country. With that much success, why would the CMA stop giving her awards in 1987 and stop nominating her by 1997?

By 1987, Reba was perceived by the country-music establishment to be a woman with a bad attitude. Not content to record one or two albums a year, then to follow up the albums with promotional tours, she started poking around in areas where other women had not gone before. She decided to become a businesswoman. She purchased a building in Nashville across the road from the state fairgrounds. She hired a staff and set up her own management firm. She started up her own publishing company and decided to promote her own concerts. Most of the people she hired were women.

Independence is not a trait that is greatly admired by an industry that lives and dies by the motto, "you scratch my back and I'll scratch yours," especially when that trait is exhibited by the female of the species. Reba's genius is that she built an enormously successful career by going around some of the traditional roadblocks. Reba's true-blue fans know her song titles by heart, but few people outside that circle would be able to name many of her hits. That's because there are no monster hits that the public associates with Reba. By operating as a self-contained business and promoting her own work, she has been able to take her music directly to her fans, bypassing the industry and the media to create her own connection with the public.

By the 1990s, Reba had diverted her energies to a movie career. Had she forgotten that she had assumed the mantle from Dolly for precisely that same reason? Her debut as an actress came in 1990 as a survivalist in the thriller, *Tremors*. Then came acting roles in *The Gambler Returns: The Luck of the Draw* with Kenny Rogers and *North* with Bruce Willis and Kathy Bates. Concerned about what her fans would think about her new career interests, Reba told *The Saturday Evening Post* that she chose roles that were consistent with her image as a country-music entertainer. "I'm not going to strip off or do a sex scene," she said. "I'm not flirtatious and, goodness, I'm not an exhibitionist."

In 1995, Reba and her husband, Narvel Blackstock, decided to relocate her business operations, which operated under the name Starstruck Entertainment, from the fairgrounds to a newly constructed, three-story building on Music Row. The good ole boys who said she was standoffish when she set up shop near the fairgrounds would now get to enjoy her company smack dab in the middle of the sacred ground. Not much was said about her decision to move until it was announced that she was building a helicopter landing facility on top of her building. That was the last straw!

The country music establishment rose up in arms. Even the mild-mannered Chet Atkins came out against Reba and her helicopter pad. Music executives petitioned local government to stop her from going aerial. The idea of this redhead hovering over Music Row in a helicopter, stirring up the leaves and making a lot of racket, was more than the old boys of the Row could bear.

With that mischievous little grin she has made famous, Reba withdrew her request for authorization for a landing pad with an understanding that she could reapply at a later date. The men won. Or did they? To the men, the only thing worse than having a woman hovering overhead in a helicopter was a woman who kept them waiting.

◆◇◆◇◆◇◆◇◆◇◆◇◆◇◆◇◆

In the beginning, they called themselves the Bangs, a not-so-subtle word play on both a popular hair style and the sexual act as viewed from the male perspective. Annette Zalinakas played bass. Vicki Peterson handled lead guitar and her sister, Debbi, sat in on drums. Standing a foot shorter than the rest, was Susanna Hoffs on rhythm guitar and vocals. They enjoyed playing the southern California nightclub scene, where their hard-core audience was made up of horny high-school and college-age males who relished their in-your-face sexuality. When they wanted to put out a record, they pooled their savings and paid for it themselves. They did their own bookings and promotions. In short, the Bangs rode high without any males telling them what to do.

Then, along came Miles Copeland, the chairman of I.R.S. Records and manager of the Police. After hearing the Bangs at a Los Angles night-club, he told them he wanted to be their manager. He had a plan. They listened, but their first thought was, "Oh, no," because of his previous association with the all-girl group, the Go-Go's. The Bangs considered the Go-Go's, which were fronted by Belinda Carlisle, an uptown, bubble-gum exercise in feminine alter ego. They wanted no part of that.

Eventually, Copeland won them over. He booked them for a tour in Great Britain, and the girls quit their day jobs and made a dash for the airport. It was when they arrived in Europe that they learned another band already had established a reputation as the Bangs. No problem. They changed their names to the Bangles.

By 1983, the Bangles had released a self-titled EP, but they weren't exactly causing riots with their public appearances. Annette, the bass player, decided she had had enough. Singing was what she really wanted to do—and the Bangles already had a singer. It was about that time that Michael Steele heard that there was a room to rent in Vicki's house and a possible opening in the band.

Michael had played in lots of bands. The daughter of a commercial pilot (her mother) and a car-wash magnate (her father), she had grown up in Newport Beach in rich-girl isolation. Painfully shy, she preferred shut-ting herself up in her bedroom to read books over associating with her drug-using, high-flying peers. After high school, she tried her hand as an artist. "Then I realized as I got further into it that there are so many rules," she says. "I was really attracted to rock music because there is a lot of freedom and no particular rules, and I like that kind of situation better."

After learning to play bass, Michael discovered that rock bands had rules of their own. She played in many bands, almost too many to count—Boy's Ranch, Snakefinger, Slow Children, and she even served a brief stint in the Runaways with Joan Jett—but she never stayed with any one group for very long because she kept having problems with each group's unique set of rules.

By the time Annette made her decision to leave the Bangles, Michael had already moved in as Vicki's roommate. She auditioned for the job and was accepted, just in time, as it turned out, to sign a record deal with Columbia Records. The Bangles recorded their first album for Columbia and continued playing nightclubs; they were so busy that they barely even noticed that the album did not do well. It was not until 1986, with the release of their second album, *Different Light*, that it became apparent they had a future as a band. The first single, "Manic Monday," made it into the Top Ten and the second single, a novelty dance tune titled "Walk Like an Egyptian," caught fire and went to Number One.

With their sudden success came a change of audience. For the past five years, the Bangles had appealed to a mostly male audience. "Manic Monday" and "Walk Like an Egyptian" changed all of that. When Michael first heard the latter song, she knew it would either be a big success or a big failure. What she didn't know was that it would open the door to a new audience of female fans. When they arrived, she rationalized their presence by saying they had been there all along. They were "smarter than the guys, that's all, and they stayed on the back rows, where they wouldn't get smashed," she says.

Interviewed in 1987, at the height of Bangleonia, Michael spoke with pride of her newfound female fans. "When I go out now it usually is girls who recognize me," she said. "I've heard from some people that a lot of girls look to us as role models. I think that's great because we're basically well-adjusted people and we're doing what we want to do and there's nothing wrong with that."

The Bangles worked well together as a group when it was "us against them," but with success came internal cracks in their solidarity. Where once it was the girls against the guys, it soon became the girls against Susanna and vice versa. Susanna wanted to be a star and the more she wanted it, the less Vicki, Michael, and Debbi felt like a band. "Everyone in this band has to do what they want to do," said Michael in response to a question about the attention Susanna was getting for her movie, *The Allnighter.* "If people don't do what they want they'll start getting frustrated. Some of us are interested in films. It's a free country."

The Bangles charted with "Walking Down Your Street" in 1987, with "Hazy Shade of Winter" and "In Your Room" in 1988, and with "Eternal Flame" in 1989, but they ran out of hits by the nineties. They disbanded, and Susanna pursued a career as an actress and a solo artist. Michael, the quiet one, had seen the end coming as early as 1986, when she realized that the rules would decide their future. "All my life I've wanted to do this, but you have to be a realist," she explains. "You have to face the fact that rock 'n' roll is a loser's game. The people who set it up are the businessmen and they are the ones who profit in the end. Musicians are basically used and thrown aside. I don't mean to sound overly cynical, but you have to enjoy it while it's there."

◆◇◆◇◆◇◆◇◆◇◆◇◆◇◆◇◆

"You can't take sex out of rock 'n' roll," insists Ann Wilson, the raven-haired Heart sister who shares vocals with her blonde guitarist-sister,

Nancy. "If you do, you emasculate it. I suppose our image is largely visual at this point, but I think our success is much more dependent on our music. We can look like young love, perfect in every way, but if our music was bad, people wouldn't accept us. We can't just rely on looking good, looking the way young girls want the guys to look, and the way guys want Nancy and I to look. We just look the way we look and hope that's good enough."

Heart was the 1980s remake of the 1970s Fleetwood Mac, with Ann and Nancy playing the roles abdicated by Stevie Nicks and Christine McVie, but with a major difference: The three male members of Heart were glamour boys with long, well-styled shoulder-length hair. As a band, Heart pleased women record buyers at both hormonal and gender levels, the foundation of any good sales demographic. Explains Nancy: "There is a chemical balance, a sexual tension between the men and the women in the band. It makes the band more interesting, and we use it to our advantage."

When Heart first started out in the 1960s, the group was composed of Ann, Nancy, and four male musicians. Ann did lead vocals and Nancy played guitar. They had a number of hits in the 1970s, including "Crazy on You" and "Magic Man," but it was not until the mid 1980s, when the band was pared down to three males (with Howard Leese, the only survivor of the original group) that they extended their influence beyond the West Coast. Beginning with 1985's "What About Love?" and then moving on to "Nothin' at All," they stayed on the charts for the remainder of the decade, though they were never able to find a Number One hit. Their 1987 album, *Bad Animals,* gave them two hit singles, "Who Will You Run To?" and "Alone." They finished out the decade with two hits, "Stranded" and "All I Wanna Do Is Make Love to You."

Ann and Nancy are both serious musicians and songwriters, but neither has ever apologized for exploiting their sex appeal. Cleavage runs in the Wilson family, says Ann, who doesn't apologize for it. "I've always been lucky to know men who have encouraged us for that," she laughs. Nancy is content to leave the sex appeal onstage. It is her guitar that comes closer to being a constant companion. Picture Nancy onstage, dressed to the nines, blonde hair flying wildly in the hot passion lights, playing two hours a night before a live audience, then picture her returning to her hotel room to kick off her shoes to do more of the same in the privacy of her room, alone, without the fanfare. "I do a lot of playing after the shows," she says. "In my room I keep a tiny guitar, a tiny keyboard, and a tiny amp. I don't really practice, I just play a lot."

Nancy's guitar became important to her while she was in her teens when it became a substitute for a boyfriend. "I was kind of an unpopular girl, kind of fat, and my guitar was, like, my man. I really didn't have any friends in school. They were all Ann's age, about four years older than me. My guitar was my secret love."

Heart disbanded in the 1990s by mutual agreement. Nancy had married Cameron Crowe in 1987 and found herself thinking more about having children than making music, though she toyed with the idea of doing a solo album and writing scripts for movies. Ann was in perfect agreement. The months of being out on the road had taken their toll. "Nancy and I both want to have families," says Ann. "But I believe strongly in fate. I'm not getting desperate for it. I know it will happen to me, and then they (the children) will have a mother with a lot of experience to hand down to them."

◆◇◆◇◆◇◆◇◆◇◆◇◆◇◆◇◆◇◆

Janet Jackson's single, "Nasty," entered the Top Twenty in June 1986. It was her first taste of success and she was thrilled. If Madonna's "Live to Tell" had not been holding down the Number Three slot, "Nasty" probably would have entered higher. Unfazed, the promotions people at Janet's label continued to work the record, hoping to improve its position on the charts. The following month "Nasty" peaked at Number Two. There had been hope that it would move into the top spot, thus giving the eager new artist her first Number One hit, but Madonna's newly released "Papa Don't Preach" overtook Janet's record to top the charts.

In September, Janet released a new single, "When I Think of You." It entered the Top Twenty at Number Fourteen, but the next month it zoomed to the top, providing her with her first Number One record. Janet's label had hopes it would stay in the top spot, but with the release of Madonna's "True Blue," Janet's record sank like a rock, just barely staying in the Top Twenty. It was the second time in a row that a Madonna record had entered the charts like a heat-seeking missile, only to target Janet's latest effort.

In December, Janet released yet another single, "Control." It entered the Top Twenty at Number Fourteen, then the following month it peaked at Number Four. A month later, Madonna's new single "Open Your Heart" pushed it off the charts entirely. Janet fired back with "Let's Wait Awhile," which shot up to Number Two in March, only to be brought down In April by Madonna's "La Isla Bonita."

Janet sat out 1988, trying to avoid what she had come to believe was the Madonna curse. Perhaps she thought that if she waited long enough Madonna would vaporize into a blonde mist. She didn't return until late in 1989, with the release of "Miss You Much," which bounded over Madonna's "Cherish" and topped the charts. Knowing a good cat fight when they saw one, the music press nudged the two women into each other's face, like handlers taunting high-strung birds at a cock fight. Janet said this. Madonna said that. Word spread that the two women hated each other.

In fairness to Madonna, it must be said she was already an established artist when her 20-year-old rival entered the charts. At twenty-seven, Madonna was not exactly approaching retirement age, but she was more experienced and more focused on her career than Janet, even though Janet had been performing with her brothers since she was seven. The success of the Jackson Five, and then, in later years, of brother Michael Jackson as a solo artist, put a lot of pressure on Janet. The Jacksons were music royalty, of sorts. Janet was reminded of that on a regular basis. If she came out hissing and clawing at Madonna, it was because it was expected of her.

Janet had a lot going on for her. She was attractive, petite—although much was made of her oversized buttocks—with dark, soulful eyes that loved the camera, and when she was at her best, a voice that was as good as anything else around. On the negative side, were criticisms that she was vapid, had nothing upstairs. People said she was a shell filled with public relations goodies. Cruel, insensitive things were written about her. Janet responded by staying out of the public eye. She did as few interviews as possible, offering herself up to the public in carefully choreographed videos, which while effective did nothing to stifle the criticism. Often, when she did interviews—even with friendly supporters—her words seemed to work against her.

Janet's biggest contribution in the 1980s, aside from a few hit singles, was to give other African American female artists their freedom. Until Janet came along, black female artists were constrained by stuffy images of elegance and sophistication. It was a reaction to generations of racial prejudice that perpetuated the myth that black women were free and easy. The first female recording artists to emerge from the modern era felt they had to rise above that and set an example. It was a matter of black pride. They couldn't be sexy or casual, for fear it would reflect badly on their race.

For Janet, who had not been raised like that, all the old sexual taboos were ridiculous. Most of the black people she knew were millionaires. She didn't accept the old prohibitions set by the black community. Janet was a visual artist. Videos were an important ingredient in her success. To her way of thinking, Madonna had lifted—well, stolen—black rhythm &

blues to form the basis of her music. Madonna's edgy mixture of sex and music was undeniably effective.

Why, Janet wondered, couldn't she do the same? Convinced that she could, she threw out 200 years of racial caution. If fans wanted to see her belly button, they got their wish. If they wanted to be teased by quick glimpses of her breasts...well, here they are boys! Janet made videos that were unprecedented for a black artist by virtue of their strong sexual content. It was a bold, courageous, gutsy thing for her to do—and, by doing it, she not only set herself free, she freed the inhibitions of an entire new generation of upcoming black female artists.

As Janet was getting her first taste of the charts—and redefining sexual limitations on African American female artists—Dionne Warwick, Anita Baker, and newcomer Whitney Houston carried on the more conservative tradition of delivering rhythm & blues interpretations of sophisticated pop compositions. When Anita Baker's second album, *Rapture*, was released in 1986, it didn't generate a lot of hits—"Sweet Love" peaked at Number Sixteen—but it gave the black community a new heroine.

Rapture was packed with ballads—bluesy, clear-voiced vocals backed by real jazz-based instrumentation, not the synthesized substitutes that many black music lovers felt had sucked the life out of rhythm & blues in recent years. Anita eventually picked up a mainstream pop audience—not to mention a handful of Grammys—but her core audience remained in the black community, where older record buyers appreciated her devotion to the type of music earlier popularized by Sarah Vaughan.

Dionne Warwick had seemingly been around forever when "Then Came You," which she recorded with the Spinners, went to the top of the charts in 1974. Ten years earlier, she had made the Top Twenty with "Anyone Who Had a Heart" and "Walk on By," but for some reason she found success hard to sustain. Encouraged by the success of "Then Came You," Dionne thought she had turned a corner in her career, but that wasn't the case. Not until five years later, when she was paired with singer/songwriter Barry Manilow, did she again find a hit with "I'll Never Love This Way Again." She followed that up with "Deja Vu," which barely slipped into the Top Twenty.

Dionne's last hit—she eventually gave up music to create a profitable "psysic network" on television—came in 1985 with Elton John, Stevie Wonder, and Gladys Knight. "That's What Friends Are For," written and produced by Carole Bayer Sager and Burt Bacharach, peaked at Number Two, edged out of the top slot by Lionel Richie's "Say You, Say Me." Ironically, it was Stevie Wonder's last showing on the Top Twenty—in addition to "That's What Friends Are For," he had a solo single that peaked the following month at Number Fourteen—and Gladys Knight's next to last showing. Of the four artists who made up the "Friends" quartet, only Elton John was able to keep his recording career intact into the New Millennium.

Taking the baton from Dionne was her cousin, Whitney Houston—a slender, attractive woman with high-cheek bones and an expansive smile. Sex appeal was an important component in her persona, but it was the old-fashioned type—what you see is what you don't get—that fit into the African American tradition for female performers. Whitney first appeared on the Top Twenty charts in 1985 with two singles, "You Give Good Love" and "Saving All My Love for You." She picked up momentum the following year with two more Top Twenty hits, "Greatest Love of All" and "How Will I Know."

Her 1987 album, *Whitney,* produced three Top Ten hits, though you would never know it from the *Rolling Stone* review which called it "a mess of an album" and made references to the producer working within Whitney's "limited parameters." It was a scathing review that offered backhanded compliments—and it was typical of the reviews that female artists, especially African Americans, received at that time from the music press, which was published for a predominately male readership.

The women fought back by appealing directly to their fans, primarily through the electronic media. In 1986, despite all the hardships and roadblocks, women made history when Whitney, Patti Labelle, and Janet Jackson held the top three positions on the Top Twenty charts: Never before had three women done that.

✦◇✦◇✦◇✦◇✦◇✦◇✦◇✦◇✦◇✦

Managers are the glue that holds the music industry together. Without them, the people who create the product—the artists—would never be able to sit in a room with the people who manufacture and sell the product—the record companies—long enough to consummate a deal. Being a manager is a hapless job, for it means perpetually being in the middle of almost everything that affects an artist's life, good and bad.

Managers approach record companies on their client's behalf for the purpose of securing a recording contract; they help negotiate the contract, with the advice of an attorney; they assist in developing the marketing campaigns that will present the artist's work to the public; they decide who in the media their client will talk to; they relay the record company's suggestions to the artist and they provide the artist's response, translated into more palatable conversation, back to the record company; they break dates with romantic interests and notify spouses that their significant other wants a divorce; they hire and fire the artist's cooks and housekeepers, and they investigate why the artist's lawn was not mowed to his/her satisfaction. They seldom get credited for the success enjoyed by the artist, but they always get blamed for the failures. In short, it is a job that requires unique talents and a taut nervous system.

Until the mid to late 1980s, there were no successful female managers, other than a handful of wives of country music stars who managed their husband's careers from behind the scenes. Lib Hatcher is probably the first successful solo female manager. When she plucked Randy Travis from obscurity and transformed him from an insecure country singer into someone who had potential as a recording artist, there were no female role models for her to follow. She made it up as she went along, relying primarily on her instincts. Whether it was that inner voice—or old-fashioned common sense—she felt her best shot at landing a recording contract for Randy was with another woman. Since there were only two female A&R executives in Nashville at that time—Martha Sharp at Warner and Margie Hunt at Columbia—Hatcher didn't have a long shopping list.

Fortunately, Sharp liked Travis's demos and offered him a contract with Warner. From the beginning, Travis's career was the by-product of female engineering. It is as good an example as you can find of what can happen when women in the music business work together for a common goal. As Travis' career blossomed, extending to movies as well as music, Hatcher, who was old enough to be his mother, married her client when rumors of homosexuality threatened to torpedo his multimillion-dollar career.

On the heels of Hatcher's success, Columbia Records executive Bonnie Garner formed a partnership with Mark Rothbaum, Willie Nelson's manager. Rothbaum had dealt with Garner at Columbia, Nelson's record label, and when the opportunity arose in the late 1980s to make her a partner of the management team, he jumped at the chance. Until 1995, when Garner left the partnership to devote her full efforts to the management of Marty Stuart's career, they managed Nelson's career as Rothbaum and Garner.

Today, Rothbaum has nothing but praise for his former partner—and for the other women entering the profession. "The music industry is a small industry—and a young industry—and the male executives hang on very tightly to their authority—they give up nothing," says Rothbaum, who has been Nelson's manager for a quarter century. "For a woman to break in, they have to have extraordinary abilities. Those who do break in are extraordinary people."

Following in the footsteps of Hatcher and Garner was Pam Lewis, who, as Garth Brooks's co-manager until 1996, is considered one of the most successful female managers in music history. Her entry into management came through Bob Doyle, who had signed Brooks to a publishing and recording contract. Doyle knew he couldn't do it alone—he needed a partner, someone who had the creativity and media savvy to make Brooks into a star—so he asked Lewis to co-manage him. Lewis already had a successful public relations firm going and she agonized over Doyle's offer.

Once she decided to become Brooks' co-manager, she proceeded with a dedication and fervor that would have to be witnessed to be believed. At the time Capitol Records released Brooks' first album in the spring of 1988, there was a lot of confusion in the media over who Garth was; months earlier Capitol had released an album by a newcomer named Kix Brooks. Was everyone on Capitol named Brooks? Or were all that label's new artists named Brooks? All of which was not lost on singer Doug Brooks, who changed his name to Stone to avoid the confusion.

Brooks' first album was not well received by radio. The print media was slow to take to him because of the way he looked—slightly overweight, bland, a little too earnest in the face. During the first few months, it looked hopeless and Lewis wondered if she had made the right decision. "Everybody passed on him," she recalls. "I had people I thought I could count on and they didn't see it right away. They really saw him as sort of a Clint Black clone. . . . Journalists wanted to pit the two together. Clint had won all those awards and RCA had made him a priority. Everywhere you went, his albums were in the stores. Everywhere we went, there were no albums in the stores. It was ridiculous. Bob and I were going on a wing and a prayer. One time, Bob looked at me and said, 'You know what I feel like? I feel like I'm Mickey Rooney and you're Judy Garland and its like, let's do a play.' We were, like, so stupid that God smiled on us. I'm not saying we were dumb people, but there was a part of us that was so green. It was like—us against the world."

Doyle's strength lay within the industry. He did all his fighting on the inside, where his punches were never seen by the outside world. But it was the outside world that was holding up Brooks's career for examination. Doyle won his battle when he got Garth a contract with Capitol. Whether the hoped-for result of that contract, a hit album, ever saw the light of day was in Lewis' hands—and in her hands alone.

Shortly after the release of the album, Lewis called the producer of a syndicated radio program, "Pulsebeat—Voice of the Heartland." It was a small syndication, servicing only about seventy-five stations, but it offered a back door into the playlists of program directors who had been resistant to Garth's album. When you are trying to break a record, every station counts. Lewis pleaded with the producer, assuring him that Garth was the real thing and was deserving of a chance. Based on Lewis' recommendation, the producer agreed to devote an entire half-hour show to Garth and his debut album. Lewis had been right in the past. There was no reason to doubt her now. Garth showed up at the studio, which was located in a renovated house on Music Row, looking like anything but a country music star. He had on the jeans and the hat, but his eyes sparkled and he grinned from ear to ear like a teenager ready to negotiate his first deal.

The show went well. Garth was sincere to the ninth degree while answering questions asked by the announcer, Kim Spangler—the only female announcer doing country music syndication at that time—and the music, all chosen from his debut album, fit together into what the producer thought was a good show. Within weeks the show was pressed into vinyl and shipped out to the stations that subscribed to the syndication. Most stations played the program without sending comment back to the producer; but a couple of stations reacted negatively and canceled their contracts, saying Brooks had no talent and would never make it as a country artist. Said one program director: "If that is the type of music you're going to send me, then you can just go to hell."

Pam Lewis overcame that type of resistance by refusing to give up. She was absolutely relentless, tireless in her determination to get Garth the break she thought he deserved. She was everywhere, leaving no media stone unturned. She became his shadow, never leaving his side. "Out on the road, a lot of people thought I was Garth's wife or a fan-club president—it used to piss me off a little bit," she says.

Once the dust had cleared and Garth's success was assured by a string of Number One hits, Pam Lewis was approached by Ron Baird, Clint Black's longtime booking agent. "Can I ask you a question? How'd you do it? We were kicking your butts. How'd you do it?"

"I told him it was a grassroots thing," says Pam. "We didn't have any money. We didn't have a label that had the power [of RCA]. I started a 'hearing is believing' campaign. We did bumper stickers. We did advertising. I called all the radio stations every week. Did you add the record? Thanks a lot. Can we have a quote—oh, they love having their names in print. I sent the press clips out. We sent postcards out before everyone starting doing that. If we could get people to listen to the album, then we knew they would get it because he was so good. Garth never had a national radio tour. We set it all up ourselves. When the first single, "If Tomorrow Never Comes," went to Top Forty, the label was thrilled to death. We said, 'No, this can be a Top Ten record.' They were going to let it go. They thought that was fine. But we got on the phone and we got it to Number Eight."

Pam Lewis' efforts are now legendary in the music business. She is loved, hated, emulated, sought after, avoided, scorned, and worshipped for her pioneering efforts. "I'm not a monster, and I'm not a genius," says Pam. "It still bothers me that people who don't know me judge me so harshly. I feel really misunderstood and I get annoyed with myself for thinking that—it's wasted energy. I really want people to like me. I want people to think, 'You know, she's really normal.'"

◆◇◆◇◆◇◆◇◆◇◆◇◆◇◆◇◆

When Kathy Mattea was invited to be a contestant on "Celebrity Jeopardy," she jumped at the chance. How many country singers had been on the popular daytime television show? None that she could think of. Being on the show is not exactly analogous to winning the Nobel Prize in Physics, but it is a respected show, and its question-and-answer format can be intimidating to those not able to think on their feet.

In country music circles, Kathy is known as one of the "smart ones." When she's performing, the Grammy-winning singer doesn't make fun of those parts of her anatomy that are different from males. She doesn't sing songs that put women in unflattering or submissive positions. And she doesn't go for the cheap shots. She's a thoughtful, introspective "folkie" who is drawn to music that possesses a semblance of intellectual or legitimate emotional content.

In her own gentle, soft-spoken way, Kathy kicked ass on "Celebrity Jeopardy." Recalls Kathy: "I won my day, and at the end of the day I was close to having one of the top three scores for the week and having to come back and do the Friday afternoon show—but I didn't quite make it."

After the show, three women ran up to Kathy in the studio. "We work in the sound booth," they said. "My gosh, we were so excited when you won. Women never win!"

Kathy was stunned. Women never win! "It was like, 'You made us look good girl,'" she says. "I realized then that no one had told me to bring a change of clothes in case I won because no one in a million years thought I would win because I was female and because I was a country music singer. It never occurred to me that someone would not think I was smart, because I was the whiz kid in my family."

One of the interesting things about the direction female artists were taking in the 1980s was the fact that they approached success from different angles. For years, there were only two variations on the pop charts: One was black and the other was white. Gloria Estefan changed that by offering a Latino alternative.

Gloria and her band, Miami Sound Machine, debuted on the charts in 1986 with three high-energy, Miami salsa hits: "Words Get in the Way," "Bad Boy," and "Conga." They seemed to come from nowhere. Their catchy rhythms and Gloria's distinctive voice and sensual good looks touched a nerve with the public. More hits followed, with the twelfth-ranked "Rhythm Is Gonna Get You" and the group's first Number One, "Anything for You," which topped the charts in May 1988.

Also finding their way onto the charts were women like Aimee Mann, who after two years of exploring the punk/new wave scene in Boston with a band called the Young Snakes, regrouped with a new sound that wasn't exactly punk and wasn't exactly new wave. Aimee's new band, Til Tuesday, became an instant hit in Boston, with *Boston Phoenix* critic Joyce Millman describing it as "very much the band of the moment."

With her snow-white, punkish hair, Aimee seemed cold and untouchable on video; in person she was often standoffish and irritable. One way to annoy her was to suggest that she wrote from a woman's perspective. "I try to explore the way people feel toward one another, whether it's a man towards a woman or a woman towards a man," she told Dawn Baldwin. "I don't believe that there are certain feelings inherent in one sex more than in the other." Aimee said she had no patience with people who could not accept her because she is female. "When we're working with someone who is sexist, I just say, 'Get him out of here,'" she says. "They need to get over it." Aimee's attitude gathered steam as the decade progressed.

Rebecca Russell of Reba and The Portables, a popular nightclub band in the 1980s, said "Tina Turner really broke a lot of ice for women, but she was rhythm & blues, and Janis Joplin broke a lot of ice, too—but then she died. First the heroes come up and prove that women can be accepted, then we sort of infiltrate. But still it's hard because you get called a wimp by the guys. Or if you're in a bar singing and shaking your ass, you're called a whore. Now we're accepted. No one ever questions it now."

Vicki Tucker, the daughter of big-band singer Tina Brazil, had to learn how to be aggressive; it did not come naturally. When she followed in her mother's footsteps, forming her own band in the 1980s, she found the footing precarious at times. "When you're dealing in a man's world and you're female, you can't be soft-spoken," she says. "If you push, then you are called a bitch. I've been called a bitch. Okay, I don't care. If I'm a bitch, then I'm a bitch. But I'm going to voice my opinion."

"The guys are there to look at you—they hear you with their eyes before they hear you with their ears," says Russell. "They're the ones who come up and say you're great and all that, but it's the women who come up to you, maybe in the restroom, and say, 'Oh, I really admire the way you sing, and does your throat hurt?'"

◆◇◆◇◆◇◆◇◆◇◆◇◆◇◆◇◆◇◆

The place to be in America in 1987 if you were young, female, and had a little extra cash in your pocket was one of the thousands of shopping malls that had sprung up across the country. Teenagers, especially, found the air-conditioned enclosures a life-support system that provided everything they needed for survival: Entertainment, food, records, movies, cool clothing, and a place to hang with other teenagers.

Shopping malls were a natural place to break new recording acts. The fact that it had never been done before did not dissuade executives at MCA Records in Los Angeles. The previous year they had signed fourteen-year-old Tiffany Darwish to a multi-album recording contract. Teenage girls had recorded hit records before—and everyone agreed Tiffany was destined for stardom, but they knew they needed something different, something fresh and new, to get her name and face out before the public.

There were things going on behind the scenes at MCA that made it even more critical that Tiffany be successful as a recording artist. When Irving Azoff took over as label boss at MCA in 1983, the company was in big trouble. People jokingly called it the Music Cemetery of America. Of the forty-six recording acts on the MCA rooster, only Olivia Newton-John was bringing in money. Without warning, Azoff dropped thirty-nine of the company's acts. It was a musical massacre. As Azoff struggled to rebuild the label's roster, the company came under scrutiny by the feds amid allegations that organized crime had penetrated its operations. MCA was going under; it needed a hit—and fast.

Into this buzzsaw walked Tiffany, a pretty, redheaded teen who had a big, grown-up voice and ambitions to match. She was from Norwalk, California, a small town north of Los Angeles. She started singing at an early age and by nine was a backstage regular at Los Angeles's Palomino nightclub, where she won several talent contests. At that time, her specialty was country music. She would perform any place that would give her the stage—bars, country hoedowns, you name it. She just wanted to sing. Her biggest supporter was her stepfather, who was with her one night at the Palomino when they learned that country star Hoyt Axton would be performing.

"I'm gonna get you on stage with him," he told Tiffany.

When Axton showed up at the nightclub, Tiffany and her dad were waiting backstage. "My daughter here is nine years old and she's won most of the contests here, and if she could just get up and sing one song with you, that would be wonderful," he said. Tiffany looked up at Axton with that little-girl smile and he had nowhere to go but on stage with his new discovery. He wasn't disappointed. Together, they sang "Joy to the World."

The following year, Hoyt introduced Tiffany to his mother, Mae Axton, who knew a thing or two about the music business. Mae had started her career doing promotions for Colonel Tom Parker and his new discovery, Elvis Presley. As the co-writer of Elvis' first national hit, "Heartbreak Hotel," Mae went on to make a name for herself as a songwriter. Mae thought Tiffany had a future in country music, so she took her back to Nashville and worked with her for about six months.

Tiffany did interviews galore, including the major television shows on TNN. She even worked a booth at country music's biggest annual celebration, Fan Fair, where she signed autographs, and sold photographs and Tiffany T-shirts. "Mae really inspired me," says Tiffany. "She knew everyone in Nashville and she was a woman who had the key to the city, basically. It was wonderful being her student."

That arrangement fell apart when it became apparent that Tiffany's parents had different ideas on how to pursue her career. "I loved Patsy Cline and Loretta Lynn, but that was not what I really wanted to sing," says Tiffany. "I was a big fan of the Eagles and Linda Ronstadt. I wanted something edgier."

Tiffany and her parents returned to California, where Tiffany met publicist Jane Beaver, who helped her find a manager. She introduced twelve-year-old Tiffany to George Tobin, a former staff producer at Motown. He was producing a Smokey Robinson album at the time and it was during a break in that session that he first heard Tiffany sing. He was ecstatic. He told his friends that she had a voice like taffy—you could pull it in any direction and it would still be delicious. Tobin signed her to a seven-album exclusive production and management contract.

Once Tobin placed Tiffany with MCA—and her uptown country style had been pulled, taffy-style, into a pop format with a R&B groove—the problem of how to break her became paramount. For months, her albums sat in the warehouse. Radio was cool to her and the media was expressing burnout over the career of teen sensation Shaun Cassidy.

Finally, someone came up with the idea of a national mall tour. MCA approached Shopping Center Network, a marketing company that specialized in mall-based events; it already had a tour underway called

"Beautiful You: Celebrating the Good Life Tour." Tiffany was booked for ten malls, beginning at the Bergen Mall in Paramus, New Jersey. The routine was the same at each mall: Tiffany would sing on a small stage in a center area of the mall, accompanied by recorded instrumentals. Corporate giveaways and contests were also part of the package.

Put in charge of making the tour a success was MCA publicist Susan Levy. There was no handbook for her to go by; no one had ever had a successful mall tour because no one had ever undertaken a mall tour. Levy had to go by her instincts. Whether it was blind luck or creative genius born of quiet desperation, Levy succeeded in luring the local media to Tiffany's mall appearances, where photographers captured hundreds of screaming teenagers. "Susan and I used to hang out a lot during the down time—and we talked about clothes and stuff like that, things that interested me at the time," says Tiffany, adding with a hint of humor, "Of course, she was hanging out with a kid."

Most of the teens that turned out for the mall tour were female. In later years, Tiffany was always shocked when men approached her and said they had been fans. "I had some guys who came to my concerts, but it was mostly a sea of girls," she said in 1997. "Now, as time has gone on, guys come up to me and say, 'I had a big crush on you when I was sixteen.' I go, 'Really!' It embarrasses me. I didn't know guys thought I was attractive. Most of the guys who came to my concert, I didn't see them liking me as a girlfriend or anything."

The mall tour was successful beyond anyone's expectations. Part of that success was due to Tiffany's charismatic personality and her youthful energy; the other ingredient was Susan Levy's considerable skills as a publicist. "I Think We're Alone Now," the first single from Tiffany's debut album entered the Top Twenty in October and peaked at Number Three in November. The follow-up single, "Could've Been," peaked at Number Two.

As Tiffany's career rocketed upward, her personal life spiraled downward. In the midst of all her success in 1988—her debut album, *Tiffany,* had sold four million units—she hired a lawyer and filed for legal emancipation from her mother, who already had received a divorce from Tiffany's stepfather.

When seventeen-year-old Tiffany moved out of her mother's apartment, she was classified as a runaway by the Los Angeles County sheriff's office. Everyone in her life, it seemed, followed her lead and hired lawyers. Everyone wanted a piece of the action. It was a crazy time for her and it left a big scar. "All This Time" made the Top Twenty in 1989, but by then, Tiffany had had enough craziness: The fight with her mother, the pressure from Tobin, the constant media attention. She walked away from it all and disappeared from public view.

◆◇◆◇◆◇◆◇◆◇◆◇◆◇◆◇◆◇◆

As the 1980s came to a close, one of the most interesting and dynamic entertainers on the rock-club circuit was Melissa Etheridge. Her self-titled 1988 album failed to generate any hit singles, but several cuts on the album—"Similar Features," "Chrome Plated Heart," and "Bring Me Some Water"—were picked up for airplay by album-oriented radio stations. Her music was straightforward, high-energy rock 'n' roll, punctuated with tasty guitar licks—nothing fancy.

Shortly after the release of Melissa's first album, a male radio syndication producer went to a hotel to pick her up for a scheduled interview. The producer had already picked up two other guitarists—Stevie Ray Vaughan and Jeff Healey—both of whom rode in the front seat of the car with the producer. When the producer, thinking one guitarist was like another, opened the passenger door for Melissa, she sniffed, tossed her hair, and opened the door to the backseat herself and—without saying a word—jumped into the car. The surprised producer later swore to friends that he heard hissing sounds as she straddled the middle hump.

Once she arrived at the studio and saw that she would be interviewed by a female co-host, she relaxed and loosened up; she started cracking jokes and acting like one of the guys. Asked to perform live, she did so without a moment's hesitation.

On the way back to the hotel, perhaps sensing that she might have been unduly rude to her host, she invited the producer to her concert that night and to a backstage party after the show. Several hundred women showed up for the concert, but only a few men were in the audience. Once the music began, the producer leaned against the wall and watched with amazement as Melissa gave a frenzied performance that delighted the women in the audience. "I'll be damned," he muttered, as the realization came. "She's a lesbian." He looked around the roomful of women. "They're *all* lesbians."

After the show, the producer went backstage and was warmly greeted by Melissa, who was accompanied by a golden-haired female friend. Melissa extended her hand to the producer and asked what he thought of the show. Oddly, she did not withdraw her hand after the handshake. She talked to the producer, still holding his hand—tightly, the way politicians do in receiving lines.

The producer glanced at Melissa's companion, who glared at the lingering handclasp. Melissa was just having a little fun at the expense of her secret, sexual persona; a gesture that reflected what lesbian performers—and there were plenty, in both rock and country music—experienced on a day-to-day basis. "People think I'm really sad—or really angry," she said, explaining her music. "But my songs are written about the conflicts I have...I have no anger toward anyone else."

Melissa was well known in the underground gay community, which was why her concerts were always so well attended, but that did not become common knowledge until the 1990s were well under way. Not until she publicly acknowledged her sexual orientation did she obtain the level of success she deserved.

K.D. Lang went through the same sort of turmoil. When she first appeared on the country music scene, dressing like a man, looking a little *too much* like Elvis, music fans shrugged and attributed it to her exotic Canadian upbringing, as if all Canadians must be like that. Once country music insiders learned she was a lesbian, it didn't really affect her career since country music has always had a larger percentage of gay performers than pop or rock; a favorite pastime of Nashville songwriters is writing witty, sometimes cruel, songs about homosexual country performers.

Once K.D. publicly acknowledged that she was gay, her country music associations seemed to fall to the wayside, but that probably had more to do with the new direction her music was taking—more to the pop side—than to any backlash attributable to irate, homophobic country music fans.

What Melissa and K.D. went through was in some respects a crucial ingredient of the impending women's revolution. It's as if someone, somewhere, said, "Okay, we're all set to go—but first we gotta take care of that lesbian thing." None of the gay women who came out of the closet in the early 1990s suffered career-wise because of it; in some respects, their honesty opened new doors for them.

6 | Viva la Revolution! The 1990s

To anyone who lived through the 1950s, the 1990s were déjà vu—all over again, as the joke goes—but instead of guys singing about cars and surfing and making it with chicks on the backseats of Chevys parked on the levee, it was girls singing about menstruation, date rape, and making it with other girls. It was the same—and it was totally different.

Never known for their civic pride or cultural leadership, record companies looked for ways to translate the emerging girl pride into cold, hard cash. They began to make up for four decades of neglect. They actively looked for female musicians and artists. One of the female artists signed in 1993 by SBK Records, a division of the internationally powerful EMI Records Group, was Selena Quintanilla, a twenty-one-year-old Hispanic singer who already had a sizable fan base in the Tejano music community. "I don't like to compare artists, but Selena is the closet artist I've got to Madonna," said EMI head Daniel Glass. "She's definitely a pop star."

Nancy Brennan, vice president of A&R at SBK Records, had a dazzling track record with male artists, Jon Secada among them, and she was put in charge of guiding Selena through the musical minefield that lay between Tejano adoration and mainstream pop stardom. Brennan was sent to a showcase in Las Vegas, where an all-out effort was made on Selena's behalf. It was Brennan's first taste of Tejano music and she walked away from the showcase gushing with enthusiasm. "I was just so impressed," she told author Nick Patoski. "I think she has every element for international success: An amazing voice, a phenomenal stage presence, gorgeous looks, and a great personality."

Within three months of signing with SBK, Selena's album, *Live,* was topping the Latin American charts. In March 1994, she was awarded a Grammy for Best Mexican-American album. Two months later at the *Billboard* Latin Music Awards in Miami, she took home honors for Best Regional-Mexican album. For the remainder of the year, *Live* stayed at the Number One or Number Two slots of the Latin charts. By spring 1995, Brennan had Selena poised on the brink of pop stardom; everything was in place for her to make her crossover to a mainstream American audience.

If everything went as planned and Selena became the new Madonna, it would be a first for a Hispanic female and for a female A&R executive. Women had topped the charts for years, but never had a female executive been instrumental in guiding another woman's ascent on the charts. On March 31, 1995, all the hopes and dreams for Selena came to a sudden halt when the twenty-four-year-old singer was shot to death by Yolanda Saldivar, Selena's thirty-four-year-old bookkeeper.

Ironically, the publicity resulting from the murder and the subsequent trial sent Selena's album zooming up the charts. In life, she had never placed in the Top Twenty. By September 1995, *Selena* was the Number-One album on the pop charts. Selena became in death what everyone knew she was in life: A star. *Selena* is the first Number One hit ever achieved by a female with a female record executive at the helm. The fact that it was accomplished in death took some of the luster off the victory, but it did not lessen its importance.

The year before Selena's death, the music world had been shocked by Kurt Cobain's mysterious suicide. Throughout the 1950s, 1960s, and 1970s, sudden death had become a regular fate for rock musicians. Then, in the 1980s, the sudden death syndrome seemed to wane, as if it were no longer the popular thing to do. It returned in the 1990s, first with the fatal helicopter crash that killed Stevie Ray Vaughan, followed by Cobain's shotgun suicide, and then with Selena's pointless murder at the hands of another woman.

Rising out of that chaos was Courtney Love, who, in addition to being Corbain's widow, held the title of First Lady of Grunge as bandleader of a group named Hole. To the dismay of Cobain's fans, Courtney hit the road after his death, performing at every opportunity. Almost overnight, she replaced Cher as the woman America most loved to hate. She was crude, rude, overbearing, and disdainful of criticism. She was careless about her appearance, often seen with lipstick smeared over her face, unbrushed hair, and angry zits splattered across her face. In a move that was as surprising as it was brilliant, she played the role of Althea Leasure Flynt in the hit movie, *The People vs. Larry Flynt*. As a result of the success of the movie, Courtney underwent a temporary makeover, re-emerging as a serene, tastefully dressed (pearl earrings, for heaven's sake!), respectable woman any mother would be proud to embrace.

Courtney never really had a hit record, and was a rock star only by the loosest definition of the term, but she became one of rock's biggest female celebrities and she made the covers of every major magazine. She was the first visible evidence of the theory that American girlhood—*all* of

American girlhood—was beginning to think of itself in new terms. It was the new Rock 'n' Roll Bill of Rights: Each girl a star in her own right.

Hearing that clarion call was Liz Phair, who, like Courtney, was someone people loved to hate, although for different reasons. She was perceived to be a rich girl who wanted to play around at being a rock star. Her very existence was an affront to the tens of thousands of rock fans who took their music seriously.

When she wrote songs that had lines like, "I want to be your blow-job queen," there were those who were offended, not because of the ribald language, but because they sensed she might be insincere. To quell the rumors, *Details* magazine writer Rob Tannenbaum once asked Liz about why she wrote that particular line.

Liz admitted that she was in college—and good and drunk—when she wrote it. "I had this big crush on a younger man and I was so frustrated— I felt like a man dealing with a young fawn of a girl," she explained. "I'd been dancing around him in ways that he wasn't even aware of and all I wanted to do was get down and bone."

"Well, did you?" Tannenbaum asked.

"We never did," she said. "God, he even came over and slept in my bed one night and just snoozed there. It was ridiculous."

With her album *Exile in Guyville,* Liz established herself as one of the cutting-edge voices of the Girls of Generation X. She explicitly addressed the needs and wants of a new generation of women who felt they had gotten a raw deal. In 1993, *Rolling Stone* named her Best New Female Artist. *Newsweek* listed her as one of the twenty-five "must hear" voices of her generation. Toward the end of 1994, sales of *Exile in Guyville,* which had been released by a small, independent label, soared past 200,000, establishing Liz as a commercial success. Her second album, *Whip-Smart,* continued the momentum, spurred by the approval of feminist rock critics who saw her as the voice of the future.

Liz seemed to relish the attention, especially from her guy fans. The tables had turned and she marveled at the ease with which guys assumed roles formerly held by girls (she confessed to interviewers that she prefers to be called a girl since that's the way her fans think of her). "I know what I'm doing when I use the f-word, but I think it's termed explicit because I'm a girl," she told *Us* magazine. "The thrill of it is like, your little sister could be up there having these thoughts and you wouldn't know it. That's the titillation. It makes you look around at all the good girls and wonder what's going on in their heads."

Liz shocked her fans in 1996 by getting married and buying a house in Chicago. Then she shocked them further by becoming a mother. By midsummer 1997, she was spending her days at home in front of the television, rocking baby and watching the Weather Channel. Especially gratifying were the days when storm fronts marched up and down the American heartland spawning tornadoes and sending earthlings scurrying for cover. Liz's new album, *Whitechocolatespaceegg,* was released later in the year, surprising her fans further with tracks that had a distinctive country feel to them.

Equally prone to experimentation was Ani DiFranco. She had been performing forever, or so it seemed to her, without much success when she decided to shave her head. "Men don't smile at you as much," she explained to a *Boston Globe* reporter, "But at least when they do smile, you know it's genuine and not necessarily a come-on."

Ani grew her hair back after noticing that conversations stopped cold when she entered a room. That was a little more attention than she really wanted. Ani never made an imprint on the 1980s because she didn't fit; but the 1990s were a different story and she was embraced as the mirror image of disaffected womanhood. In 1994, after she had put in a good 12 years of barroom picking and singing—and released six albums on her own label named Righteous Babe Records—*Guitar Player* anointed her the hottest young performer in folk.

Ani once told an interviewer that she considered herself a vehicle through which women could project their own goals of self-empowerment. That image doesn't bother her until she considers her own self-described "goofyness," then she questions the entire system of offering up role models on the basis of a song. In truth, that tendency to waffle about the perimeters of reality is part of Ani's allure.

Her songs can be fierce, her stage persona can be unsettling (even to herself, she once admitted), but when she sets all that aside, she becomes the type of girl older men like to pat on the head. Because she writes and publishes her own songs, produces and sells her own records, uses a network of distributors, and has managed to sell over 100,000 tapes and CDs without the help of the majors, she is sometimes asked to wear her businesswoman hat and participate in dead-serious analyses of the music industry.

Once she was interviewed by the Financial News Network. They put her behind a desk with her guitar and bombarded her with statistics, until she reacted to one question with the observation that they were missing the point. The interviewer paused, as if hit in the face by a pie, then moved on to other statistical questions, ignoring her comment.

The point the FNN interviewer missed—and the one that all the statistics in the world can't address—is that Ani DiFranco's music, from the moment it is created until the moment it reaches the marketplace, is largely untouched by male hands (unless Ani so instructs). There are no Big Boys on the hill pocketing money earned by the sweat of Ani DiFranco's brow—and, to the girls on the way up, it just doesn't get much cooler than that.

If one thing was becoming clear, it was that the girls on the way up were not only learning the ropes, they were swinging on them like playground toys. "I'm just a girl—all pretty and petite," sings Gwen Stefani in No Doubt's hit single, "Just a Girl," continuing with, "so don't let me have any rights."

Newsweek probably spoke for a lot of people when it wrote of Gwen: "One of the most endearing things about Stefani is the way she simultaneously apes both feminist and bimbo stereotypes." With her bleached blonde hair, her bared midriff, her stripper whirls onstage, and her eat-your-heart-out-and-die smile, Gwen has tweaked the concept of sex appeal with a new post-feminist twist. She is the wild child who brings the teens in the audience to their feet with chants of "I'm just a fucking girl! I'm just a fucking girl!" She is the wild child who prances, skips, and whirls about the stage, taunting authority and social convention, only to go home that night to be with her parents. It is a contradiction her teen audience appreciates.

Strictly speaking, Gwen is not a solo female performer—she has actual guys playing the instruments in her band—but the guy profile of a No Doubt performance is so minimal it qualifies Gwen as a solo artist on a technicality. The guys in the band don't necessarily like that. Some of them have complained to inquiring reporters that the rock 'n' roll business isn't exactly what they expected. But they are, if anything, staunch California-bred realists. So what if they're not girls? They're making damn good money—their second album *Tragic Kingdom* sold more than five million copies—and they're raking in all the perks of being a girl, so who among them is going to rock that boat?

Besides, *someone* has to be the girl.

✦◇✦◇✦◇✦◇✦◇✦◇✦◇✦◇✦

WANTED:
Streetwise, outgoing, ambitious, and dedicated girls to play in a band.

With that newspaper ad, Bob and Chris Herbert—a British father/son team who thought the charts were primed for an injection of tag-team estrogen—set out to put together a super group of pop-savvy young women. They didn't care whether they played musical instruments; all that mattered was that they had to look damned good, and they had to be able to carry a tune.

Five women made the final cut: Victoria Adams, Melanie Brown, Emma Bunton, Melanie Chisholm, and Geri Halliwell. They came from varying backgrounds. Victoria's parents were wealthy, her father an electrical retailer who could afford to send her to school in a Rolls-Royce. Emma's father was a milkman, and her mother was a martial arts instructor who encouraged her to work as a child model. Geri's father was a car salesman and her mother a cleaning lady. By the age of nineteen, she had found her niche as a nude photographer's model. Melanie C's mother was a singer and her father worked as a travel agent. She has a tattoo on her upper right arm of a woman and the Japanese symbol for strength. Melanie B's father was a blue-collar worker and her mother was a department store sales clerk.

For months, the women worked together under the instruction of Bob and Chris Herbert, then, abruptly, the women broke it off. They spent the next year working together, writing, recording and trying out various dance steps; then in March 1995 they met Annie Lennox's manager Simon Fuller and signed a new management agreement. Five months later—calling themselves the Spice Girls—they signed a record deal with Virgin Records.

The Spice Girls' debut single, "Wannabe," went to Number One in Great Britain, making them the first girl group in history there to top the charts. The single eventually sold four million copies. Throughout 1996 and into 1997, they solidified their fan base in Great Britain, and then they set their sights on the most important market of all: America.

The Spice Girls' music was a mixture of dance, hip-hop, rhythm & blues, and smooth-as-silk pop ballads. Technically solid. Middle of the road. Nothing extreme. But music was not the foundation for the success the girls found in Britain: It was their sexy, bare-midriff attitude, their ability to give new meaning to the phrase "girl power," that made them instant celebrities. In many ways, the girls were caricatures of America's 1950s pin-up queen Betty Page; she was outrageous, naughty, totally devoid of sexual pretension, and she delighted in showing off her body. Once, when asked whom she most admired, Geri chose Margaret Thatcher. She called the former prime minister the "first Spice Girl."

Would "girl power" transfer to America? That was the question that echoed in the corridors of Virgin Records with the most nervous energy. The record label's first major decision for the American campaign was to put the Girls in the hands of another woman. It wouldn't do to have a man in a three-piece suit telling Americans what to think about Britain's newest export. Virgin turned to Suzanne MacNary, vice president of publicity at Virgin's New York office. It was her job to make the girls spicy, but not too spicy, to accommodate America's sweet-and-sour musical tastes.

MacNary knew it would not be an easy sell. In its March 1997 review of the Girls' album, *Rolling Stone* only gave it a star-and-a-half, calling the music a watered-down mix of hip-hop and pop. "Despite their pro-woman posing, the Girls don't get bogged down by anything deeper than mugging for promo shots and giving out tips on getting boys in bed," wrote reviewer Christina Kelly. The negative review didn't concern MacNary. *Rolling Stone* seldom gave good reviews to female artists. It showed her and other Virgin executives where they could and could not go with the Girls.

The Girls' strongest point was their video. Hip, colorful, sassy, sexy. MTV went for the Girls in a big way. Television in general embraced the Girls, but record executives knew they would have to be careful not to put the Girls in situations where they would be asked a lot of questions about girl power. Unlike the Brits, Americans don't have much of a sense of humor about feminism. Americans either embrace it, and don't see anything funny about it, or they despise it, and don't see anything funny about it. Either way, feminism was not a funny subject in America.

MacNary's campaign was based on accentuating the visual, and that meant high profiles for MTV, short interviews for television, and staged events where cameras could get passing glimpses of the Girls in controlled situations. What she positively could not do was put them in the hands of the print media. They would only ask embarrassing questions and then sit there, with the clock ticking, waiting for the Girls to answer. MacNary not only avoided setting up interviews with the print media, she refused to return reporters' telephone calls, with few exceptions. "She's not in—she's out with the Spice Girls," her assistant repeatedly told reporters. It was true—from the day the Girls arrived in America, MacNary stuck to them like glue, afraid to let them out of her sight.

By midsummer, it became apparent that MacNary's hide-and-run strategy was going to pay off. News magazines ran photos of the Girls in their people sections. David Letterman and Rosie O'Donnell had them on their shows. MTV went all out for girl power, showing the Girls' nipple-friendly video at every opportunity (it was banned in some Asian countries because censors felt it was too explicit).

In its July issue, *Rolling Stone*—the very magazine that had panned the Girls' debut album, practically slapping them silly with its catty review—ran a cover story on the group, with the headline "Spice Girls Conquer the World." The massive nine-page article, complete with ten photographs, told readers everything they could possibly ever want to know about the Spice Girls. Little was said about their music, but plenty was said about their private lives. Said Mel C to interviewer Chris Heath: "I haven't had sex since we've been successful. It's over a year. It doesn't bother me, though. I'm not really interested in sex and stuff. Not at the moment, anyway. I went through a phase where I had boyfriends, so I've kind of been-there-done-that kind of thing. Men bore me. I'm not saying women excite me, but men bore me."

The same month the Spice Girls were featured on the *Rolling Stone* cover, their album went to the top of the album charts. They were the Number One act in America, yet they had never played a concert, never played anywhere live except on the Letterman show—a performance most critics agreed was disastrous—and they had only given a handful of interviews, all to people hand picked by MacNary.

The Spice Girls could pontificate all they wanted to about "Girl Power." It was Suzanne MacNary who gave the term real meaning in America with her efficient, sometimes brilliant, management of their frequently unmanageable image. The Girls came, they conquered—and then they left. It was MacNary who stayed.

◆◇◆◇◆◇◆◇◆◇◆◇◆◇◆◇◆◇◆

Sheryl Crow grew up in Kennett, Missouri, a small town where entertainment possibilities are limited if you do not have the capacity to entertain yourself. Her father, a lawyer, played the trumpet; her mother, a music teacher, played piano. When she wasn't entertaining her sisters and brother, Sheryl led the football team in cheers, twirled a baton—one of the highest aspirations available to prepubescent girls of the South—and she learned all she could about music.

By the age of twenty-two, she had acquired a degree in education from the University of Missouri, and a day job teaching music to elementary school students in St. Louis. At night, she sang and played keyboards in the city's beer joints, leading a double life that would eventually send her packing to the bright lights of Los Angeles, where she waited tables for a while and then did radio jingles before she was hired as a backup singer for a Michael Jackson tour, the high point of which was a duet with Jackson on "I Just Can't Stop Loving You."

When Jackson's "Bad" tour ended in 1989, Sheryl was exhausted, uncertain about her future, and suffering from chronic depression. She had made it to the fringe of the big time, but her only celebrity came from tabloids that said she was Jackson's lover. Later that year she sang back-up on a Don Henley project, but nothing was working out the way it was supposed to and she lapsed into a long period of depression.

As a child, she had lain awake at night, afraid to go to sleep, afraid something dreadful would happen to her in the dark. She called it "sleep paralysis," an affliction she thought she had acquired from her mother. For three years she went day-to-day, singing backup, doing jingles. She even recorded an album for A&M as a solo artist, but the record company decided not to release it. Then she fell in with a group that eventually came to be called the Tuesday Music Club. The group included Kevin Gilbert, with whom she had a romance, David Baerwald, bassist Dan Schwartz, drummer Brian MacLeod, David Ricketts, and producer Bill Bottrell.

Despite a lot of bickering in the studio, when the Tuesday Music Club's debut album was released in 1993, everyone was optimistic: It just had that good sound. The first single, "Leaving Las Vegas," was an instant hit, earning Sheryl an appearance on "Late Show With David Letterman." During their on-camera conversation, Letterman asked her if the song was autobiographical. "Yes," she answered, to avoid having to explain more than she was prepared to explain. In truth, she had never lived in Vegas. The song had sprung from a friendship between Baerwald and his friend, John O'Brien, who had written the novel, *Leaving Las Vegas*. Everyone in the band knew the true source of the song.

When O'Brien and Gilbert heard Sheryl's comment to Letterman, they were furious. It was a guy thing that had to do with male honor, territory, and a sense of duty to one's friends. Sheryl wasn't opposed to any of those concepts. To her way of thinking, her comment was just a one-word answer to an unimportant question. Outraged, Gilbert telephoned Sheryl immediately after the show to express his anger, thus permanently severing his relationship with her.

O'Brien fumed and fretted over the incident for three weeks, then blew his brains out. O'Brien's family absolved Sheryl of any responsibility for their son's death—it had been a long time coming—but Baerwald wrote a piece for *L. A. Weekly*, accusing Sheryl of making him betray his friend. By the time "All I Wanna Do" was released, the group that had recorded it was history. The song made Sheryl into a star and earned her three Grammys, including Best New Artist.

Sheryl's problems were just beginning. The O'Brien incident became the betrayal that would not die. His novel was made into a motion picture starring Nicolas Cage and Elizabeth Shue. *Leaving Las Vegas* was everywhere she looked. She couldn't go outside her door or turn on her radio without being reminded of O'Brien's suicide. The saga took another bizarre turn in May 1996, when Gilbert was discovered dead at his home in Eagle Rock, California. He was wearing a black hood and a woman's skirt. The coroner listed his cause of death as autoerotic asphyxiation.

Later that year, when time came to begin work on her follow-up album, *Sheryl Crow*, only producer Bill Bottrell remained from the original group. Two days into the session, Bottrell walked off the job. Sheryl was stunned. She blamed it on bad communication. Rather than look for another producer, she produced it herself. When the album was released in 1996, it ran into immediate difficulties when Wal-Mart refused to distribute it. One of the songs, "Love Is a Good Thing," had a line that suggested that Wal-Mart sold firearms to children. It was just a line, another throw-away line like her "yes" comment to Letterman, but the chain store was not amused. Wal-Mart could have sued—songwriters sometimes forget that they are just as responsible for their words as any other writer—but instead, the retail chain was content to deprive the album of half a million or so in sales.

In an interview with *Newsweek*, Sheryl said, "I've said that it's really great for other female artists to look at me and know what not to do." Having said that, the backpedaling began and Sheryl retreated to a compromise. "Part of it was my own fault. I'm an accessible person. I'm willing to do whatever. Not for the fame, but I just kind of went along with it." Then came the comment the interviewer thought surely was a misstatement: "I'm not at all happy with the success I've had."

◆✧◆✧◆✧◆✧◆✧◆✧◆✧◆✧◆✧◆

When the smoke cleared from the 1996 musical battleground of the sexes, it was Alanis Morissette who was standing head and shoulders above the rest: Women had out-sold men by a ratio of fourteen to nine. It was the first time in history that women solo artists had out-charted their male competitors. As it became more and more apparent that Alanis Morissette was going to be regarded as the most successful female artist of the 1990s, people began to get a little uneasy about the Madonna factor.

Was Alanis a Madonna stand-in? Was the Material Girl lurking in a back room somewhere, calling the shots? Was Alanis a cruel joke the increasingly reclusive and isolated Madonna was playing on the public?

During an interview with radio station WHTZ in New York, Alanis was asked how involved Madonna was in planning release dates or song mixes. "I think, to her credit, she's more of a hands-off person," said

Alanis. "I think because she's an artist, that she appreciates the fact that we don't want people breathing down the back of our necks. So, if anyone would know how that feels, she would."

Alanis was asked if she had much communication with Madonna.

"Some," she answered, the tone of her voice indicating she was tired of fielding Madonna questions.

Rolling Stone asked Madonna the same question, though the emphasis was on how she thought Alanis was holding up under the pressure. "She reminds me of me when I started out: Slightly awkward but extremely self-possessed and straightforward," Madonna said. "There's a sense of excitement and giddiness in the air around her—like anything's possible, and the sky's the limit."

While Alanis was responsible for all the lyrics on her hit album, *Jagged Little Pill,* she had a male collaborator, Glen Ballard, who was responsible for much of the music. A Mississippi boy who had found success in Los Angeles as a songwriter and producer for Wilson Phillips, he was an unlikely partner for a ground-breaking feminist icon. Shortly after he took home three Grammys, along with Alanis, for his work on the album, someone in the Mississippi Legislature introduced a resolution praising him for his accomplishments. The resolution was killed after the lyrics of Alanis's songs were made known to the lawmakers. No one was surprised. Only recently had the legislature voted to ratify the Nineteenth Amendment to the U.S. Constitution, giving women the right to vote.

Alanis may have offended the Mississippi legislature, but she encouraged the loyalty of a very devoted fan base. Alicia Silverstone, Generation-X's most ambitious movie icon, was so impressed that she sent Alanis a fan letter. Even Alanis found it overwhelming at times. "It was like God's way of saying to me, 'You've been working your ass off, and I'm going to give this to you—enjoy it, please,'" she said to reporter Jeff Spurrier. She was talking about the mysterious process by which the inspiration for *Pill* landed unannounced on her doorsteps, but she might as well been talking about the revolution itself. If God was listening, *she* probably smiled.

◆◇◆◇◆◇◆◇◆◇◆◇◆◇◆◇◆

Kathy Mattea was sitting inside her tour bus at the Nashville fairgrounds. The bus was pulled up next to the stage at the 1994 Fan Fair celebration, a weeklong event that draws about 24,000 country music fans each June. Across the field and atop a hill was the old headquarters for Reba's Starstruck Entertainment. Fan Fair offers record labels an opportunity to showcase their rosters and it offers fans the opportunity to see and hear many of their favorite stars perform in an outdoor arena.

Kathy was scheduled to go onstage next. She likes to perform and the excitement showed in her eyes. "Sometimes I wake up and say, 'I live in Nashville and I'm a country music star,'" she says, breaking into a wide grin. "I want to grab someone and say, 'Is that a hoot or what?'"

Kathy is not your typical country singer. There is something terribly middle-class about her, despite her working-class, Italian-American upbringing in rural West Virginia. Something organized and efficient, despite her creative attraction to the fanciful. Something almost sisterish, despite her girl-next-door sex appeal. If you didn't know she was a country singer and you met her for the first time, you might think she was a bookkeeper or a physician or a schoolteacher. She has one of those unpretentious singing voices that critics love to rave about—and they have, lavishing praise in ways rarely offered for female country vocalists.

When Kathy moved to Nashville in 1978 at the age of nineteen to pursue a career in country music, she didn't have a clue—or a single contact in the music business. For several years she waited tables and worked as a secretary, wrote songs, and sang on demos and advertising jingles, hoping against hope for a break. Finally, she attracted the attention of Mercury Records, which signed her to a recording contract. Her first two albums, *Kathy Mattea* and *From My Heart,* earned her a nomination from the Academy of Country Music as New Female Vocalist of the Year.

Throughout the 1980s, Kathy released a string of singles that did well, but it was not until "Eighteen Wheels and a Dozen Roses" that she attracted major attention. In 1990 she won a Grammy for "Where've You Been," a song about a salesman and his wife and their final meeting in a nursing home. Two years later, she faced a crisis when a blood vessel in her vocal chords burst, threatening the end of her career; but after taking a little time off, she rebounded, her voice as strong and passionate as ever.

Kathy attributes the success enjoyed by female country artists in the 1990s to the fact that the record labels have given women more rope. "Women don't have as much pressure to conform," she said in 1997. "They leave us alone more than they do the guys. No one is breathing down your neck saying, 'You know, you have to wear a cowboy hat.' I've talked to more than one male artist who has gotten that kind of pressure from the labels. When I first started there were not very many women around. You would look at the Top Ten and there would be, like, one female, sometimes two, and that was it. It's much different now. I'm one of those people who, through all the changes in country music, has quietly done my own thing. I never had a huge spike in sales that a lot of people have had. I sort of quietly go Gold. I've never had a Platinum studio album, so my take on it is a little different because I haven't ridden that wave. There were times when I felt frustrated for not selling more, but for the most part I feel glad to have my own niche. I don't know if that is because I was taught not to expect more because I am a woman, or if it's just my nature as a person. It's hard for me to be objective about it."

There are areas where Kathy would like to see change. Little things, she admits, but things that would make life sweeter if they never came up. "If a guy walks out on stage in jeans and a T-shirt, no one says anything. If a woman walks out on stage in jeans and a T-shirt, people go, '…and she could be such a pretty girl, too.' There's more pressure on us to glam up. Part of that is cultural, but I think we feel more pressure to think about how we look. I would like to be able to walk out there in overalls, if I felt like it and it not become an issue."

Of course, image is an issue—especially when it comes to sex appeal. Sex is to country music what apple pie is to a Rotarian: Not the main course, but an essential component of the meal. There have been lots of sexy women in country music over the years, but most of them downplayed their sexuality in the belief that their fans wanted them to somehow raise themselves above sex. To their way of thinking, sex was common—it was what *everyone* did, rich or poor.

Shania Twain was the person who changed that attitude. With her skimpy outfits and her sensual song lyrics, she made sex seem uncommonly special—as if it were something only the chosen few could do really well. In 1996, if you asked country fans who the sexiest woman in country music was, most would say Shania Twain. Ironically, if you asked country music insiders who the most hated woman in country music was, most would give the same answer: Shania Twain.

Those who are down on Shania explain it by saying she alienated the Nashville music community by using her sexuality to sell herself as a performer. The real reason has more to do with the incredible success she has had, but the too-sexy-for-her-clothes criticism is easier to apply since it does not reflect nearly as badly on its user. It would be a fair criticism if it were true. It's not.

Talk to any male reporter who has covered the music scene since the mid-1980s and he will tell you a different story: Of all the female country music stars sliding up and down the charts in the mid-1990s, it was Shania Twain who least used her sexuality to her advantage. It was not unusual for other female stars to show up for interviews braless in tight-fitting T-shirts, or even in revealing aerobics outfits, but Shania was always well-dressed and well covered up. It is not unusual for female country artists to begin interviews by giving male reporters breast-to-chest hugs, but Shania would be mortified if anyone suggested that she should do that. Shania never dated music executives who could help her career—a common practice—and she has never come close to being tainted by scandal.

If Shania is due for some criticism, it would be for not using her sexuality enough. She made videos that displayed her board-flat abs, but that's nothing compared to what other women have done. Tanya Tucker once went to a restaurant near the Vanderbilt University campus and stripped buck naked and streaked through the main dining area. On another occasion, she went to a broadcasters convention, accompanied by NBC newscaster Stone Phillips, mounted the stage, whipped open her shirt and flashed her bare breasts to the audience. Deana Carter, whose "Strawberry Wine" was a Number One hit in 1997, once stopped a concert cold when she was asked to leave the stage to put on a pair of panties.

Not even Dolly Parton has been immune from the sudden urge to exert her sexuality. In her autobiography, she told of the time during the filming of 9 to 5 that she was riding past Tom Jones' house in a limo. "He was hotter than a firecracker at the time, and I said, 'I wonder how Tom would feel if I just got stark naked and streaked right through his front yard?'" she wrote. "Well, I was just talking, but before long people started to say 'dare' and 'double dare,' words like that make me lose control. . . . 'Jason, stop the car,' I said, and before I knew what was happening, I felt the cool grass of Tom Jones's yard on my bare feet. Of course, that was a perfect complement to my bare ass parading around in the swankiest part of L.A. for all to see."

Those feeling a tinge of moral outrage at the antics of Tanya, Deana, and Dolly, should know that they are no different from 99% of the other women of country music (Reba representing the remaining 1%). They've got the power and they know how to use it. In 1993, Playboy sent a talent scout to Nashville to scope out the potential for a major pictorial on the "Girls of Country Music." When he arrived at the hotel, he was greeted in the lobby by dozens of hopeful country music starlets. They formed a line a mile long to wait for interviews in the hotel suite, exchanging tips on the music business as they waited their turn. Some of the more interesting interviews, reports the scout, were with the big-name stars who pondered baring all for the magazine. He recalls one meeting in particular in which he sat on a sofa with one star, a Playboy magazine opened up across their laps to the centerfold section. "I could do that," the sultry star said, pointing to a photograph, "and that one—but, oh, not that one." The plug was pulled on the Playboy project after nervous label executives put out word that they thought a nude pictorial was more liberation than they could handle.

Shania Twain understands the sexuality inherent in country music as well as anyone. In the beginning of her career, by reversing the process—by being demure, almost puritanical, in her private life and then letting it all hang out in her public persona—she capitalized on an element of country music that everyone has known about and understood for ages. With the release of her third album in late 1997, *Come on Over*, Shania continued to stress the appeal of rock-tinged, high-voltage country music and the blinding power of womanhood (one of her favorite themes from day one).

"I spent my whole teenage life flattening my breasts, wearing triple shirts, always worried about those things," she told Associated Press. "Teenage girls, they need to learn to grow up confident about these new things that are growing on their chests. It's very important that girls grow up with a sense of confidence about the fact that they're women."

At the 1997 Country Music Association Awards, Shania introduced the first single from her new album, "Love Gets Me Every Time." It is an upbeat tune with a catchy hook that seems unintentionally reflective of her private personality. She sang it on live television, using a pre-recorded track, and she looked like a million dollars in formfitting knit that clung to her curves like wet paper. To everyone's surprise, she nailed the song, displaying polished dance moves that would have sent Patsy Cline into a tizzy.

When the song ended, the camera pulled back to show her onstage facing the audience. Polite applause, but no one rose to their feet. She was the hottest selling act in country music and the establishment could not bring itself to give her a standing ovation. After the show, local television reporters lined up the stars and trotted them past the cameras. Shania was nowhere to be seen. Feeling rejected, she was on a plane back to her farm in New York—and who could blame her?

◆◇◆◇◆◇◆◇◆◇◆◇◆◇◆◇◆

Deana Carter grew up in a musical household. Her father, Fred Carter, Jr., was one of country music's most sought-after session guitarists from the 1950s though the late 1970s, when he played with a variety of artists, including Willie Nelson, Roy Orbison, Bob Dylan, and Waylon Jennings. For Deana, that meant two things: First, there was never a shortage of music around the house (she tells the story that at family reunions she had the option of washing dishes or singing harmony). Second, music had a male scent to it. It was what her father did for a living, a male profession like truck driving or farming. She eventually changed her perception of what was male and what was female, but in the early years of her life music was pretty much something men did with other men for other men.

At the age of seventeen, Deana asked her father to help her get a record deal, and he did, taking her around to the record labels and studios, introducing her as his daughter. With Dean Martin as her namesake—her father once wrote a song for the crooner—she felt it was her destiny to be a major player in the music business.

When no one showed any immediate interest in her talent, Deana started having second thoughts about a career in music. At the time, her grandmother was suffering with a disabling illness and Deana, seeing what she was going through, decided to go to the University of Tennessee to study rehabilitation therapy. Part of it, too, was seeing the pain her mother experienced over her inability to help the grand-mother. "My mom was the Rock of Gilbralter in my family," she says. "She came from a generation when the female was, like, the mom. She is the biggest influence in my life and I love her with all my heart. If I could be one-fifth the person she is, I'd be happy."

After graduation, Deana got a job where she could help stroke and head-injury patients, but her interest in music eventually resurfaced. Anyone standing outside the door while she was caring for her patients would have realized that right away: One of the relaxation tools she used for her patients was the music of Fleetwood Mac.

At the age of twenty-three, she decided to give music another try. She left her job working with stroke patients and took a series of odd jobs— waiting tables, teaching pre-school children, and cleaning bathrooms— while she wrote songs and made demos to pitch to record labels. One of her demos made its way to Willie Nelson, who remembered her father. He was impressed with the tape and set up a meeting. They talked and sang and passed the guitar back and forth, a ritual as old as country music itself, and when the guitar passing was over, Willie asked her to perform with him at an upcoming Farm Aid concert.

Doors opened for Deana. Soon she had a record deal with Capitol Records, the home of Tanya Tucker and Garth Brooks. The first thing Capitol did was to pair Deana with its brilliant vice president of artist devel-opment, Susan Levy. Following her wildly successful Tiffany mall tour, she had moved to Nashville to head up MCA's publicity department. After six years at that job, she moved over to Capitol. As head of artist development, it was her job to oversee everything that influences an artist's image: Hair and makeup, photography, packaging, advertising, and video production.

Capitol's instructions to Levy were simple: Make Deana a star.

There was plenty to work with, but right from the start Deana made it clear she had a mind of her own. She co-wrote six of the eleven songs on the album. The first issue that arose was over the title. Deana wanted to use the title of one of the tracks she had co-written, "Did I Shave My Legs for This?"

"There was some thought at the label that people wouldn't take me seriously as an artist with that title—that people would think I was a comedian or a novelty act," says Deana. "But it was something I wanted to do. When we wrote that song, I said that if I ever had an album, that was what I wanted it called. That was before I was even signed with Capitol." With Levy's backing, Deana won the argument. "It wasn't much of a battle," says Deana with a laugh. "My argument was, well, come up with a better title—and that was kinda hard to do. As hard as I have worked to be taken seriously as a songwriter, I also wanted to show that I have a sense of humor. It's like swan diving. If people can do it well, you've got to respect it whether you dig it or not. That song said that about me, about my personality."

The first hit from *Did I Shave My Legs for This?* was "Strawberry Wine," a first-love reminiscence written by Gary Harrison and Matraca Berg. With that song, and Susan's Levy's guidance, Deana morphed from a pretty, earnest-to-the-hilt singer/songwriter with a sing-song voice, to a timeless beauty, a siren of lost love whose plaintive call was filled with promise. As music, the song was solid. As imagery, when paired with the video, it was masterful. With a female singer and songwriters (only one song on the album was not written or co-written by a female), a female label executive in charge of developing the concept, and, most important, female record buyers who bought into the premise, *Did I Shave My Legs For This?* was a female concept from start to finish.

By February 1997, to the surprise of no one, least of all Deana Carter, the album was in the Top Ten on the pop charts. The lesson was clear: Women reward women who tell it straight. It doesn't matter how they dress. Or how little they wear. It's not the medium; it's the message. "It's important to gain the respect of other women," says Deana. "Women have a very good sense of honesty and bullshit—not to be crude—so a woman knows when she's being snowed. Women have this checks-and-balance system, where they can communicate about their problems. Women like to cry. They *love* to cry. It makes them feel better."

To that, a male interviewer responded with, "We are different, aren't we?"

"Yes, but it's so cool to find that common ground," Deana said.

"That's why we get so excited when we connect," observed the interviewer.

"And why we get so frustrated when we don't connect," she answered.

Deana was appreciative of the work her label put into her project. Not all labels go to the mat for their artists, but she was especially appreciative of what Susan Levy did for her. "She's very talented," she says. "I'm fortunate to be on a label that has people like that. She has a vision for the artists—and she's been a good friend to me, too."

There was no doubt in Deana's mind that things are changing for women. She's living proof of that. She credits some of her success to men who had the courage to let women in the door. "Women will always have their perception of men, and men will always have their perception of women," she says. "As long as we try to understand one another and be respectful of one another, then I think it will be a better place. There were times when people were condescending to me because I was a young woman...or maybe it was because of my youth...I have tried to live my life non-genderized. It keeps you like one of the guys, but not threatening." Deana laughs, softly, almost teasingly, pausing in all the right places. "It's really important to accept people for what they are instead of what they *have*...physically or otherwise."

◆◇◆◇◆◇◆◇◆◇◆◇◆◇◆◇◆◇◆

Terri Clark is tall and slender, and she carries herself like royalty. Her sculptured face is flawless and her almond eyes are intense. She wears a T-shirt and rolls the sleeves up to show off her toned upper arms. Another time, another place, wearing a frilly dress and an uptown hairdo, she could be mistaken for one of those New York supermodel types, but she's not like that. She's a country singer and she wears cowboy hats and boots, and she lives in Nashville—and if you mess with her, she'll kick your citified butt all the way to New York City.

Like Deana Carter, Terri became an overnight sensation in 1997—after several years of hard work in the trenches. Her debut album sold over a million copies. Her debut single, "Better Things to Do," went to Number One on the country charts. Singles like "Poor, Poor Pitiful Me," "If I Were You," and "Suddenly Single," endeared her to a new generation of women who saw her as one of the new role models for the 1990s. The appreciation and respect is mutual. The first thing Terri looks for when she walks out on a concert stage is the faces of those women.

"They've got their fists in the air and they're screaming, 'You go girl! You go girl!' and they're holding up signs and they're wearing cowboy hats with their T-shirt sleeves rolled up and it's so flattering," says Terri. "They relate to me somehow. When I perform I never put myself on this pedestal because I could just as easy be one of them watching the show. Just because I sing doesn't make me any more different. I don't feel any better and I think they know that and I think they feel like I'm their best friend."

Terri arrived in Nashville by way of Medicine Hat, Alberta, where she grew up with big dreams of making it in Music City. She was eighteen when she pulled into town with her mother and strolled into Tootsie's Orchid Lounge, a famous country-music joint that has an open-door policy for performers: Anyone that wants to can take the stage and perform. When Terri arrived, there was a guy onstage playing for tips.

Terri asked the man if he minded if she did a little singing when he went on break. He didn't mind. Why would he? He had no time clock to punch. Terri, fresh and young and fearless, did so well that the management offered her a job singing every night. Terri thought she had it made. She didn't, of course. Eight hard years later, waiting tables, selling cowboy boots, and pushing thirty, she landed a recording contract with Mercury Records.

Terri found her image as a tough babe amusing. "I take it as a complement," she says. I do have another side to me. I have become known as the dirt kicking, aggressive, in-your-face, don't take no BS off of anybody—but there is a softer side there." She is amazed at the success that women, in general, are having in music. "They're kicking everyone's butt—I love it," she says. "I think that women are making some of the most unique music. They all sound completely different from each other. Women want to hear songs they can relate to. I've never been into doing male-bashing music. I've never been into bashing any particular gender. A lot of guys like my music, too. They turn it around with 'I've been there before.'"

No one in country music understood that sentiment better than Renee Bell, a woman that industry insiders say has the best ear in the business. Since 1995, she has headed up the A&R department of RCA Records in Nashville; before that she held similar jobs at MCA Records and Capitol Records. Since all the female A&R executives at major labels—indeed, all the female A&R executives who have ever worked at the majors—can be counted on two hands, she is a member of a select group that has no history of role models for second- or third-generation guidance.

By the mid-1990s, A&R was the next-to-last bastion of male domination in the music business, the last being production and engineering. The reason for A&R's supremacy is simple: While authority at a record label rests with the administrative head, the general manager or vice president in charge, the real power rests in the A&R department, for that is where the future of the label is determined. A&R executives are the people who sign new artists, monitor the progress of the older artists already on the roster, oversee what is recorded and by whom.

At the beginning of the modern era, the position attracted a certain type of male; typically, he thought of himself as someone who was a little hipper than his neighbor, someone who liked to live on the edge. A&R executives were always paid well, but accompanying the paycheck and prestige were certain temptations; if a man had a weakness for sex, dope, or gambling, then he could rest assured those weaknesses would be exploited by unscrupulous promoters and managers. Added to that were temptations to make money on the side by setting up secret production deals with recording artists who were signed by the A&R executive, with the executive as a "silent" partner. When critics bemoan the sleaze factor of the music business, they are primarily talking about A&R.

The women who have entered A&R in recent years—Renee Bell at RCA, Claire Parr at Curb, Kim Buie at Capitol, Susan Collins at Virgin, Margie Hunt at Sony, Jane Baintel and Laura Hill at Atlantic, Susan Levy at Capitol, Nancy Brennan at SBK Records, Paige Levy at Warner—have had a significant impact by making it more difficult for the sleazemeisters to weasel their way into the companies. It is difficult to know whether that has taken place because women have more integrity and fewer addictive vices than men, or because women, if they are prone to vices, are accustomed to indulging them outside the realm of business. Whatever the reason, they injected a sense of professionalism and class into an area sorely in need of an image makeover.

Renee Bell has a voice like actress Kim Bassinger (both are Georgia born, so it must be something in the water), the face and figure of a 1968-era Bobbie Gentry (some days she can be spotted in a mini skirt, other days she's all business in black pants and jacket), an energy level that has to be seen to be believed, and an incredible talent for hearing what's real in music. Former Decca Records senior vice president and general manager Shelia Shipley Biddy, who worked with Renee at MCA, says of her, "When she said, 'You better hear this,' you would rush to do it; she just has this passion for the song and the songwriter."

If you were to ask Renee the best way to become an A&R executive, she would probably advise you to work on your good luck. Her career began in 1983, when she volunteered to help organize a party in Atlanta for recording artists Steve Wariner and Lee Greenwood. One of the guests was Emory Gordy, an independent producer and A&R executive with MCA Records. "I was more excited about him coming than any of the artists, though I really didn't even know what A&R was at that time—I just loved music," says Renee. "During the party, Emory and I went out to my car and listened to music and he said I should work for MCA."

Within a year, Bell was hired by MCA label head Tony Brown as a receptionist. Soon she was asked to screen songs, then to dabble in A&R; it was after she discovered a band named the Mavericks that she was made director of A&R.

"I've been lucky because my superiors have not been chauvinistic males," she says. "I have never felt men were prejudiced against me because I am a woman. Women are used to working harder than men. We don't play golf, and if we do, we do it on the weekends because we would feel guilty doing it during the week. To get an edge [as a woman] you have to work three times as hard. If you are willing to do that you will get the respect of the men."

For all her success, Renee doesn't take compliments very well. Tell her she has a mesmerizing voice and her face will turn bright red. Ask her to speak in public and she will dance about the question, saying, "I'll really have to think about that—I don't like the way I sound." Ask about her success in A&R and she will look stunned that you think she is successful. She is as much in awe of the creative process as her peers are of her talent. "I'm still not sure I have an ear for music," she says with honest humility. "I just go with my gut feeling. I never really analyze anything. I never think about a song being rewritten. I either love it or I don't. Same thing with an artist. I would never take an artist and try to change them into something they're not—it's just a gut feeling I get."

Nancy Brennan, an A&R executive with SBK Records, also puts faith in her instincts. To *A&R Insider,* she said: "If I go to see a band or a singer, and if I can't take my eyes off of them, then I know that person has star quality." Nancy found her way to A&R by way of CBS Records, where she worked in the publishing division, discovering such talents as Miami Sound Machine, Toto, Jon Secada, Technotronic, and Desmond Child. Like Renee Bell, her interest in an act begins with a demo tape; if she likes what she hears, then she asks for a meeting or goes to a club to hear a live audition. If there's magic afoot, the would-be recording artist gets a contract.

Unlike Renee and Nancy, whose entry into the music business was dictated more by the fickleness of fate and the possession of old-fashioned persistence, Claire Parr's musical baptism was more or less genetically determined. Her father, Jim West, was a well-regarded musician in the 1950s that played bass with jazz greats such as Dave Brubeck, Count Basie, and Benny Goodman. In 1964, West was attending a broadcaster's convention in Chicago when he received word that his wife had given birth to a baby girl. "I think I was toasted at dinner that night by all the broadcasters, so I had no escape from the music business," says Claire. By then, West had put away his bass to start up a company in Dallas that provided pre-recorded programming to radio. As a child, Claire was treated to a constant stream of jazz musicians who stopped by their house when they performed in Dallas.

Claire was singing jingles for her father's company by the time she was a teenager, but the performance side of the business was not what attracted her. What she really wanted to do was become a sound engineer. While she was looking for a job interning with an established engineer, a friend asked if she would run sound for his band. She wrote out a proposal for a business loan on manila paper—she was only seventeen—and talked a bank into advancing her the money to buy a sound system.

"I wound up working with Elton John, Genesis, and a lot of jazz people as an engineer," she says. "I did that for about four years and burned out on it and decided I wanted to get into radio, so I went to my father and said, 'I see you teach everyone else this stuff, why don't you teach me?' He said, 'Fine, you can be my receptionist.' Well, that was a tough pill to swallow, but I took the job. Nepotism is not always so great on the inside as it looks to other people."

In time, she was able to parlay what she learned working for her father into a successful career, first in radio promotions, then in the record business. Stints at Geffen and Enigma led her to Curb Records in 1994, where as head of the pop and Christian divisions, she was responsible not only for A&R but promotion, media relations, and everything associated with the artists she signs. "I've been very lucky in that I've not had to deal with some of the prejudices that some of my cohorts have—but I know they exist," she says. "I don't think it's a man's world. I know it's a man's world, especially from a business standpoint. Still, there are more savvy females than anyone has any idea about. I have had a fantasy of starting a label run by women."

As a married woman, the biggest adjustment she had to make has been over separating those two parts of her life. "I don't want to take the person I have to be behind this desk home with me," she says. "That's something women struggle with—how to separate the two. You start to live this double life. As an executive, you have to be stronger, tougher than anyone else. As women, we are expected not to be that way at home. That is one reason so many female executives fail to keep their marriages. I don't want to be a man. I want to be a woman. But there are certain rules I apply in the boardroom that I don't apply to other parts of my life. I don't lose my cool. I don't start crying. I don't argue emotional issues. I feel an unspoken pressure that I have to work more than my male counterparts."

◆◇◆◇◆◇◆◇◆◇◆◇◆◇◆◇◆

It would probably come as a surprise to a lot of people, but it has been country-music singers who have worked the hardest to break down the gender barrier in production. One of the first was Reba McEntire. One day she was in the studio working on an album project for MCA Records. While listening to a playback, she suggested to the producer that the song would sound better with a fiddle on the track. She was told to mind her own business and "get back out there and sing." The next day she went to the MCA office to talk to label president Jimmy Bowen. She was distraught, in tears.

"This is my album" she said. "I should have input."

Bowen listened to her story, knowing that what she was asking was sheer heresy; but there was something about her, something about her passion for music that made him not want to say no. "You are right—absolutely right," he told her. "From this day on you will be a co-producer with me on your albums."

Reba took her new title seriously. She showed up at the studio with a notebook and asked questions about everything that happened in the control room. She made notes and learned it chapter and verse, and never again did she take a backseat on the production of her own albums. Kathy Mattea is another country artist who asked for and received co-production credits. By the late 1990s, female recording artists in pop, R&B, and rock were following the lead of their country cousins.

When an artist is in the studio, the producer is the captain of the ship and controls literally everything that happens. It is the producer who approves the musicians, the songs that are recorded, how they are recorded, and it is the producer who decides whether a track is acceptable. Most male producers are authoritarian by nature and when they are working with female artists there is a tendency for that authoritarian streak to be amplified.

Any artist, male or female, who is not co-producing his or her own work is subject to orders from the producer to "get back in there and sing it again." There are hundreds of instances in which female artists have been "broken" by unethical producers who got pleasure out of seeing stars reduced to tears. Being a co-producer on her own project gives an artist leverage with her producer in the control room; it gives her the right to say no and not be in violation of her contract.

The fact that she is the only woman in the business with a successful "public" track record is not lost on producer Tena Clark. She is listed as the sole producer and is given recognition for it by the industry. "It's sad to me," she says of the obstacles women face in production. "I see so many talented women who want to be producers and I hate it when I see them with a feeling that, 'Oh, my God—it's so impossible.'" The only reason she was able to get production credits, she concedes, is because she is a songwriter. It was her songs that enabled her to become a producer.

Tena was raised by her parents to believe she could do anything she wanted to do. She was never told there were things girls simply didn't do. At an early age, she developed a taste for rhythm & blues, the music that seemed to ooze from the red-clay hillsides and bottomland bayous of her native Mississippi in plentiful amounts.

By the age of fourteen she was writing songs and producing them herself in the low-tech studios that would allow her inside. No one told her music was for guys. It just never occurred to her that music had any connection with gender—not, that is, until she moved to Los Angeles and became one of the most successful female producers and R&B songwriters in the country, scoring hits in the 1980s and 1990s with Patti LaBelle, Dionne Warwick, and Gladys Knight.

One day Tena was ushered into a male record executive's office and the door was shut behind them. The gesture concerned her because in the music business a closed door is never good news. The executive was a vice president in charge of A&R; he was in charge of signing new acts and overseeing production of their records. He had final approval over the choice of producers and songwriters. Once the door was closed, he got right to the point. "Tena, you are pissing a lot of guys off," he said.

"What do you mean?" she answered.

"Look, you're white...you're female...and you're from the South," he said. "You're taking their gigs, and it's not setting real well."

Tena couldn't believe what she was hearing. It left her speechless. All she could manage was a lame "What?" It was issued more as a stutter than a question.

"You've got to think about it," he said.

Tena was thinking about it. It was a shock to her that being a white, female refugee from Mississippi would piss off anyone. With all the truly bad things happening in the world, was it possible that being a white female from the South would be enough to land someone on an enemies list? "I get a lot of flack for hiring you," the A&R executive continued. Then he paused, a smile inching across his face. "But you know what I think? I think you're the shits and I don't care what they say."

One of the things that baffled Tena about the record business is why it is so far removed from the standards set years ago by movies and television. "When I started working in movies and television, I produced everything I wrote," she says. "The first thing I got hired to do when I moved out to Los Angeles was to produce the title song for *Police Academy*. From there I went to television and everything I wrote, I produced myself. It was all very unsexist. Then, I got into records and, all of a sudden, it was like, 'Oh, no—you're a woman.' It was very frustrating for me."

Tena might never have broken the gender barrier in the record business if it had not been for R&B singer Vesta Williams, who had worked with her on several television projects. One day, she called Tena and asked her if she would write and produce three or four cuts on her new record. Tena was flattered, but said, "Yeah, that's really going to happen."

"Yes, it will," answered Vesta.

Vesta went to the A&R executive at her record label, A&M Records, and told him she wanted Tena Clark to produce three or four cuts on her album. "Won't happen," he said. "We already have someone to produce the entire album."

"Well, then I guess I will have laryngitis for the next five years," Vesta said, and walked out of the office. When production on the album began and Vesta was nowhere to be found, the record company executive capitulated. "Okay," he told Vesta, "Whoever this Tena Clark person is, you've got her...whatever."

What Vesta did took guts. Tena knows that and appreciates it. "She broke down doors for me," she says. "It's so rare that someone has the balls to stand up for what they believe in, and I will always be indebted to her for that. When they said, 'Whoever this Tena Clark person is,' it was so patronizing, so we knew our necks were really on the line."

Tena and Vesta responded with a song entitled "Congratulations," which went to Number One on the R&B charts; it was the biggest hit Vesta had ever had and it resulted in Tena receiving offers to produce other female artists. "There have been a lot of wonderful men in the business who have believed in me and given me breaks, but the person who opened the door for me was a woman," says Tena. "As a general rule, most men want to see women as artists and writers. They don't want to see them as producers or musicians. I have broken down those barriers and it is an old story to me, but I look at other women and I think, 'Oh, my God, if you only knew—and you will soon find out.'"

◆◇◆◇◆◇◆◇◆◇◆◇◆◇◆◇◆

Doug Supernaw couldn't figure it out.

Early in 1995, the country singer slammed into a stonewall of protest with the release of his record, "What'll You Do About Me." It was about a woman who invited a man into her life, changed her mind, and sent him on his way. Trouble is, the man didn't want to leave. Women's groups came out in force to protest the song because they considered it pro-stalker. Supernaw's record label, BNA Records, heeded the protests and wrote out a statement of apology for Supernaw to sign.

"I got really upset when they did that," says Supernaw, who balked at signing the apology. "It was like nothing I would have said. I said, 'That's bullshit.' They said, 'We don't want you to talk about it because you'll make it worse than it is.'"

As a result of the controversy, Supernaw and BNA severed their relationship. Supernaw said he thought the song was humorous and reaction to it was unfair. "It's sad when just a few people can dictate what the rest of the country can hear," he says.

What Supernaw learned—the hard way—was that country music was changing. Women reacted to his song in a negative way, and it was their economic clout that mattered more than his pride or even his career.

By 1997, women artists were busting out all over—not just in country music. It was like a virus sweeping the country. As a movement it was very different from the feminism of the 1960s and 1970s in that it had none of the rough edges. For all its false starts, it was a fascinating event to observe from the sidelines.

Janet Jackson released her seventh album, *The Velvet Rope,* and was thrilled to see it debut at Number One on the Top Twenty album charts. Her previous album, *Janet,* released in 1993, had also debuted at Number One, and it ultimately sold more than six million copies. But it was obvious from the start that *The Velvet Rope* was about more than money. It was about Janet setting herself free, not just in a creative sense, but in a personal way. In her previous album, she toyed with her sexuality like a giggling schoolgirl flashing her class and then running away to hide in the gym.

With *The Velvet Rope,* we have Janet standing stark naked in the spotlight singing the hip-hop equivalent of "It's My Party." It's about girl-fun with sex, the nastier the better. When she sings about screaming and moaning in "Go Deep," she's not referring to the effects of deep-sea diving. For its review, *Entertainment Weekly* used a headline that asked the question, "What's a (relatively) nice girl like Janet doing on the erotic *Velvet Rope?* She's making sex sound brazen—and beautiful."

Janet had not spoken to her brother Michael since 1993, according to some published reports. If true, who could blame her? Sex scandals are nothing new to a business that thrives on rumors of who's doing the nasty to whom. But rumors of sex scandals involving children are something else. How is a sister supposed to feel when the media is publishing stories that call her brother a pedophile? By exerting her own sexuality—the nasty-girl kind—Janet drew an imaginary line, not just with her fans, but with her own family. She needed some distance. No one could empower Janet but herself; it took courage, but she did it.

Janet also seemed to have set herself free from her obsession with Madonna. In 1994, *Vibe* magazine asked her if it was true that she hated Madonna. "Hate is a strong word," she said. "I never said 'hate.' But if I did hate her, I'd have valid reasons."

The new millennium is not likely to bring further comments from Janet about Madonna. As Janet's popularity has risen, Madonna's has fallen, at least as a sex-symbol recording artist. Her future seems more as a business executive and as an actress. Despite all the media hype over her 1996 movie, *Evita,* the next few years were not kind to the Material Girl.

Madonna is a true pioneer, not just in music but in the arena of women's rights. She's made lots of money, and she's influenced popular culture in myriad ways, yet she has few friends and is often viewed by the women of the 1990s as something of a public nuisance. She can't figure it out. "There's a whole generation of women—Courtney Love, Liz Phair, even Sandra Bernhard to a certain extent—who cannot bring themselves to say anything positive about me even though I've open the door for them, paved the road for them to be more outspoken," Madonna told *The Face.* "[Liz Phair] doesn't have the power I have, so people are amused by it. But none of these women would want to recognize that. In fact, they slag me off any time anybody asks what they think of me or compare them to me. It's kind of like what a child does to their parent, they denounce you. They want to kill you off because they want their independence from you."

As Madonna's influence waned, two unlikely women stepped into the spotlight: Mariah Carey and Jewel. They were unlikely replacements for media attention because they projected images of strength through sweetness. If they gave out an award to the 1990s diva with the most moxy, it would have to go to Mariah. In 1997, she not only celebrated the release of a new album, aptly titled *Butterfly,* she celebrated the end of her marriage to Sony Music head Tommy Mottola. In some ways, the two events were related.

When Mariah and Tommy first met in 1988, she was an eighteen-year-old waitress who had hopes of becoming a singer, and he was the thirty-something head of Sony Music. He was looking for a pop star, someone along the lines of Whitney Houston, and she wanted to be a star—any kind of a star—so it was a perfect match. Tommy's vision for Mariah's success had her playing the role of the virgin next door, the squeaky clean, velvet-voiced angel of every man's wildest dreams. It was a vision that easily translated into big bucks. Her 1990 debut album, *Mariah Carey*, went to Number One, as did her 1995 album, *Daydream*. By 1997, her albums had sold over eight million copies and brought in over 200 million dollars.

Mariah's working relationship with Tommy turned into a romance during the production of her first album, then evolved into marriage. When Mariah and Tommy announced in 1997 that they were separating, the music world was stunned, not so much because they were surprised that the marriage didn't work out—that was pretty much a sure thing from the start in the eyes of most people—but because they naturally assumed neither Mariah nor Tommy would ever do anything to jeopardize their working relationship.

With the release of *Butterfly*, the public was treated to the new Mariah. Gone was the sweet little girl image. Replacing it was the startling image of a thirty-year-old woman in her sexual prime. There was lots of flesh in her personal appearances and in her first video, and lots of nasty talk and sexual references in her music. She was seen darting about New York on the arms of young, black rappers and models, wearing next to nothing. It was all deliberate, calculated to win her independence.

With the exception of Mariah and Celine Dion—and newcomer Fiona Apple—Sony Music had little success with solo female artists during the 1990s. In fact, it probably had the worst track record of any of the majors when it came to women artists. Mariah Carey *was* Sony Music at that time. If Tommy were to fight the divorce Mariah wanted, or if he were to tamper with her career, it would be professional suicide. Mariah was aware of that. By airing the dissolution of her marriage in a very public way, she gave Tommy only two options: He could accept her newfound freedom and back away, or he could challenge her declaration of independence and set her free to move on to a new record label (and him to find a new job). It takes courage for a woman to play that sort of game, but Mariah did it—and she won.

Jewel Kircher didn't have a typical upbringing. Her parents, Atz and Nedra, were folk singers who raised Jewel and her two brothers on a ranch in Homer, Alaska, where milking cows and riding horses were as much entertainment as chores. Jewel was eight when her parents divorced. She stayed with her father when her mother moved to Anchorage and often accompanied him to seedy barrooms, where they sang together to earn a living. Male patrons sometimes put dimes in her hand, with the suggestion that she give them a call when she turned sixteen. She knew what that meant.

By the time she turned sixteen, Jewel had moved in with her mother. She stayed in touch with her father, and once took her black boyfriend home to meet him. Her dad broke out into tears at the sight of the rapper. At first, Jewel didn't understand. She thought that maybe he was racist. Then he explained that he was crying out of pride that he had raised such an open-minded daughter.

Jewel wasn't in Anchorage long before she and her mother moved to Seward, a small town about two miles away. The move was prompted, according to Jewel, by the sudden appearance of FBI agents who were investigating the business dealings of her mother's business partner. When the agents started showing up at her school, Nedra figured it was time they got a fresh start somewhere else.

Mother and daughter eventually ended up in southern California, though they arrived at different times from different directions (Jewel had taken a detour to Michigan to attend an art school). Jewel sang in coffeehouses and, for a time, lived with a guy who operated an escort service out of his house.

By the time she was nineteen, Jewel had landed a deal with Atlantic Records. The album, *Pieces of You,* was recorded in the Innerchange Coffeehouse in San Diego, where she frequently sang. When the album was released in 1995, it was largely ignored by critics. It was an acoustic, folk-influenced album by an unknown girl from Alaska. How much further out of the mainstream could you get?

With Nedra's help—by then Nedra and a friend, Inga Vainshtein, had signed on as her managers—Jewel stayed out on the road, promoting the album with a fierceness that could only be understood by someone who has lived in her car (as Jewel did on more than one occasion). Atlantic followed up with a series of videos that capitalized on Jewel's extraordinarily cool beauty. Her face seemed flawless, as pure as an Alaskan stream, and she projected an air of sweet accessibility.

It took a year-and-a-half, but by the end of 1996 there was a definite Jewel buzz on the music pipeline. Jewel, Nedra, and Inga accomplished the impossible. In April 1997, *Pieces of You* peaked at Number Four on the Top Twenty charts, making Jewel a contender for stardom and Nedra a contender for manager of the year. It was a girl thing from start to finish, with Jewel's success largely untouched by male hands. It also set a record for Atlantic: No artist had ever taken longer to break.

"The creative process is not just about writing songs," Jewel told

Acoustic Guitar. "It's about approaching your life creatively, so that you are not a victim of circumstance; so that you are creating your life and it's not creating you."

◆◇◆◇◆◇◆◇◆◇◆◇◆◇◆◇◆◇◆

One of the most important breakout R&B artists of the 1990s was Toni Braxton. Women have been the backbone of R&B, almost from the beginning, but they have been expected to find success within the conservative, gospel-influenced traditions of the black community. Until Toni Braxton came along, that meant downplaying their sexuality and femininity in favor of more traditional role models.

Toni was studying to become a teacher when she was discovered by Babyface in 1991 and signed to his Atlanta-based LaFace Records. With Babyface writing songs for her and producing her projects, no one was surprised to see her self-titled debut album rack up sales of ten million and earn the singer three Grammy Awards. Babyface supplied his protege with lush, synthesizer-laced ballads that pushed her R&B intonations into the realm of pop acceptance, but it was Toni's break from R&B tradition in the area of her personal image that ensured her long-range success. "She may be the daughter of a preacher man, but R&B's sultry new star is definitely no choir girl," said a headline atop a profile of the singer in *Us* magazine.

"You're Makin' Me High," the first hit single from her second album, *Secrets,* was all about sexual desire and masturbation, two subjects entirely foreign to traditional R&B. When Toni first heard the Babyface-penned song, with lyrics about her lover being inside her all night, "doin' it again and again," it made her uncomfortable at first, and she worried about what the black community would think of her. "I'm very comfortable with my sexuality, but the lyrics in that song are so overt," she told the *Los Angeles Times.* "There were times when I was singing it when I felt I was letting the whole world know my thought about that subject."

Toni not only broke R&B ground with explicit lyrics, she allowed herself to be photographed in her bare feet (a longtime no-no for black women) and in revealing clothing that displayed her body. She let her hair down, literally, and she wore a wig that accentuated her silky smooth sexuality.

What Toni did for R&B, other women such as Queen Latifah and the rap trio known as Salt-n-Pepa attempted to do for that most anti-female music of all—gangsta rap. Sometimes called the "Queens of Rap," Salt-n-Pepa turned heads with a debut album, *Hot, Cool & Vicious,* that sold over one million copies.

For more than a decade Salt-n-Pepa turned out a series of rapper hits, causing more than a few critics to scratch their heads. Why would women participate in an art form that is synonymous with unrepentant misogyny? The short answer was that their songs did not attack or berate women. The long answer is that the genre just got to them. In 1997, they broke away from the man who had discovered them and produced their work for eleven years, in order to self-produce a new album, *Brand New,* that reflected the gospel influences that had been a part of the group all along. The women called it their declaration of independence.

Gangsta rap itself raises interesting questions about how women perceive themselves. The irony is that the first rap hits were released by Sugarhill Records, an independent label owned by Sylvia Robinson, an African American, and her husband, Joe. Their 1979 release "Rapper's Delight" was the first rap hit. Another rap record, "White Lines," was the first to deal with drug use. Yet another, "The Adventures of Grandmaster Flash on the Wheels of Steel," was the first to use a DJ's "scratch 'n' cut" skills. Without Sylvia Robinson, rap might never have gotten off the ground.

The answer to why women seem attracted to gangsta rap can be found in the larger question of why some women pursue self-destructive relationships. The reality is that a sizable percentage of women are attracted to the danger that accompanies bad-boy behavior. Women, for all their healing and nurturing attributes, are not without their disciples of the dark side. So it is with rap.

◆◇◆◇◆◇◆◇◆◇◆◇◆◇◆◇◆

Tiffany had been living in Nashville about a year when her husband came in from work one day—he was a makeup artist and was frequently called out on location for video productions—with the news that he had run into someone who knew her.

"Who was it?" she asked.

He didn't know, but if she wanted to find out she could go with him on location, since whoever it was would be certain to return. Tiffany accompanied him to the video shoot, but the mystery woman wasn't there when she arrived, so she waited. She had plenty of time; it had been nearly ten years since her last hit record.

When the mystery woman arrived, she walked in the door, paused and looked at Tiffany, and excitedly said, "I remember you." It was Susan Levy. It had been a decade since they had hung out together at the mall and Tiffany had been America's star of the moment. In the years since,

Levy had turned her fortuitous association with Tiffany into a career that, at the time of their meeting on the video location, had blossomed into a high-flying display of executive acrobatics that required her to perform without a safety net. It was now her job to hoist new acts such as Deana Carter up onto the high wire—and to keep others such as Garth Brooks from falling to a certain death. As Levy had assumed new responsibilities, so had Tiffany found new direction by signing a management deal with Garth's former manager, Pam Lewis.

"I didn't realize how hard it would be to get back into the business," says Tiffany of her decision in 1997 to jumpstart her career, this time in the direction of her first love, country music. "It's so easy when you're working to get burned out and to say, 'I'm going to take a break.' I was young and it was a little overpowering. Even if you are on top, if you take two or three years off, that could really set you back, no matter who you are."

At first Tiffany was not sure putting her career in the hands of another woman was the right thing to do. The only manager she had ever known was male. All the people associated with her career, with the exception of Susan Levy, were males. A part of her questioned whether she would be able to work with another woman.

To her surprise, when she and Pam got together for an introductory meeting, they clicked and formed an instant bond. It was a female thing, an experience she had not shared with her male manager. "There are times when she may be struggling through something and I can lift her up," Tiffany says. "Same thing for me. Just to know that she's there and believes in the project."

Pam feels the same way. "I feel very alone at times," she says. "I don't feel I have very many close friends. I am like Garth in that way—I don't trust that many people, and I have been burned and I have been hurt and I have had people I don't even know be mean to me. But I'm a fixer—I gotta nurture. I'm surprised there are not more women managers because they are naturally suited."

◆◇◆◇◆◇◆◇◆◇◆◇◆◇◆◇◆

Brenda Lee marvels at the progress women have made during her lifetime. "Women have pretty much come into their own, haven't they?" she said in a 1997 interview. "When I started out, we were not starring in our own road shows. It was always a male star. We were on the bill, but we were not the stars—and there were no women executives then that I knew of. Now you have women heading up publishing companies. Women in top jobs in every facet of the music industry. Being a woman,

I always want to see women do well. Right now women are at the creative edge of everything they are doing—I think women are doing fabulously."

In early 1997, Brenda performed with the newest teenage sensation on the pop and country charts—LeAnn Rimes, whose hit, "Blue," had made the fourteen-year-old an overnight superstar. If anyone had been there, done that, it was Brenda Lee. She used the occasion to talk to both LeAnn and her parents about success at a young age. "I told LeAnn I think it is important to have a life apart from [the music]," says Brenda. "You have to be a child. I think it's important to go to school with children your own age and she's not having those experiences. When you have a hit record, you have to get out there and be seen—and when you do that you are missing out on precious time you could be spending with people you love. That's one of my big regrets. If I had it to do all over again, I would spend more time with my brother and sisters, the people who are precious to me—because I can't bring those times back. I look back and wish I hadn't done it the way I did."

On the night that Brenda Lee was inducted into the Country Music Hall of Fame, LeAnn Rimes was awarded the Country Music Association's Horizon award. When she accepted her award, Brenda thanked the audience and all the people who had supported her throughout her nearly forty-year career. LeAnn thanked the same audience and her mother and father for "being behind me one hundred percent."

Backstage, Brenda and LeAnn stood side by side for a joint television interview. LeAnn smiled and was gracious, especially toward Brenda, but she seemed subdued and there was a look of sadness in her eyes. Earlier that day, LeAnn had learned that her parents had filed for divorce. The young singer's personal life was about to undergo radical change—and she understood that.

Throughout the television interview, Brenda glanced at LeAnn, her face sympathetically reflecting the pain she sensed the teenager was feeling. If anyone could understand the lonesome sigh of the moment and the ultimate price of the long, hard road ahead, it was Brenda Lee. The television interview ended with the announcer speaking loudly above the noise of the gathered crowd and Brenda looking at LeAnn with the "look"—the one known to every mother and grandmother who ever lived.

◆◇◆◇◆◇◆◇◆◇◆◇◆◇◆◇◆

The women who captured the charts and hearts of America in 1996 were all media-savvy entertainers who understood that imagery, whether expressed in print photos or on television, was critical to their success.

Their images, sometimes haunting, sometimes seductive, sometimes daring, were splashed across the media until they were recognizable to consumers who felt that they knew them, even if they did not know their music. Stardom is a measurement of what is received by the public, not what is offered by the artist: Stardom is always in the eyes of the beholder.

While the public is familiar with the names and faces of the women who made history in 1996—and will, in time, come to define the revolution in terms of the women who made the charts—they are not so familiar with the women in the trenches who made the revolution possible. Was it a fluke that women outsold their male competitors in 1996 for the first time in history? Was it some sort of gender-based fate? Was it luck?

Or was it the result of decades of hard work?

If you examine the bigger picture, it is hard to escape the conclusion that the revolution of 1996 was the inevitable by-product of a lot of ambitious, goal-directed women who had been working for years behind the scenes of the music industry. For every female recording artist who scored in the Top Twenty, there were other unseen, unheralded women developing strategies, pulling strings, all harmonizing to chants of, "Go, girl, go!"

Of the fourteen women who made the Top Twenty charts in 1996, it is probably Alanis Morissette who delivered the deadliest punch to the male dynasty. She seemed like an unlikely slugger: Small, fashionably thin, and soft-spoken in conversation, the twenty-year-old downplayed her looks and consciously tried to develop an air of intellectual curiosity. The further she went down that road, the more interested male record buyers became.

The lyrics of her songs are most unflattering to men. Often they bristle with hostility. Other times with a curious blend of sexuality and hostility. "I hate to bug you in the middle of dinner," she sang in "You Oughta Know." "It was a slap in the face how quickly I was replaced. Are you thinking of me when you fuck her." Then in "Right Through You," she sings: "You took me out to wine dine sixty-nine me/But didn't hear a damn word I said."

In 1995, Alanis told *Rolling Stone* that she had been told she did not look like her songs. "People expect me to have purple hair and a pierced nose and boobs," she explained. "Then they meet me, and I'm just...me. I hate to let any one down, but I'm not the cleavage sort of aesthetic babe."

The more outraged Alanis became in her lyrics, the more women flocked to her. That outrage had a similar effect on men. The tougher she talked, the more they wanted her. Those same men who could never figure out how nice girls could take up with gangsters and bad boys were being given an insight into that attraction, only in reverse. Men were figuring

150

out something women have known for centuries. Sex with successful people has an added edge. Throughout the 1990s, men discovered that sex with successful women, even if they were bad girls, or at least talked like bad girls, was superior to sex with stay-at-home submissive sunflowers. Men bought Alanis's CD for the same reason women bought Elvis' albums: They wanted to have sex with her. Women bought her album because her message was on target for the times.

Unlike Shania Twain, the other flagbearer for the revolution, Alanis did not have a female manager. Nor did she come under the guidance of a female producer. It would have been a statistical improbability for her to have a female producer. In 1984 British writer Bert Muirhead published a directory of rock album producers entitled, *The Record Producers File*. To compile the book, which covers the period between 1962 and 1984, Muirhead examined the album covers of approximately 75,000 albums. He was able to list 1,016 record producers, along with the titles of the albums they produced. Of those, only three—Emmylou Harris, Suzi Jane Hokom, and Laurie Lathan—could be identified by their names as being female. That's three out of 1,016!

Males oversaw Alanis's career and her music. What Alanis had that worked to her advantage was a savvy record company owned by a woman. Unfortunately, despite Madonna's ownership, Maverick Records was not headed up by a woman. By late 1997, there were only two females heading up major record labels: Sylvia Rhone at Atlantic in New York and Shelia Shipley Biddy at Decca Records in Nashville. They are the only two females ever to head up a major record label.

Rhone is a behind-the-scenes player who avoids the public spotlight and seldom returns calls to reporters. Her area of expertise is music; it may be that she is uncomfortable exerting a public persona, or it may be that she feels the corporate stakes are too high, that she has everything to lose and nothing to gain by becoming a more vocal spokeswoman for female advancement in the industry.

Not so with Shelia Shipley Biddy. Accessible, thoughtful, articulate, she is as comfortable dealing with the public as she is boardroom strategists. That may be because, like Frances Preston, she came up through the ranks. When she moved to Nashville in 1972 from Kentucky, she was married and had a two-year-old son, but she had a dream of becoming a television journalist. Without a college degree, her prospects of entering that profession were practically nil; the closest she came was getting a job with a local television station tabulating election returns. It was during that time that she heard about a receptionist job at Monument Records.

She interviewed for the job—seven times. Each time she was turned down. Finally, after about a year-and-a-half of rejections, she was hired at $70 a week. The job did not turn out to be the glamorous introduction to show business she expected. "In those days, you were treated like a servant," she says. "I was told, 'you are nothing but a secretary, how dare you ask for anything this company does.' I was cursed at for pushing too hard, when all I wanted was credit for what I did."

After three years at Monument, she moved over to RCA Records in 1979; it was at a time when the label was at its heyday under the leadership of Joe Galante. "I believe there are crossroads in your life," she says. "I stayed in the music business instead of following the dream I thought I wanted and each crossroad after that led me in a different direction." Her job at RCA was similar to the one she had at Monument, but she knew she could do more than secretarial work. "I'd get so depressed," she recalls. " I would think, 'I can do that.' I'd think, 'I just can't go in there and be beat up again. I wasn't just a secretary. I was making calls to radio stations—and I was taking work home at night. I went in at eight and left at six or seven. I knew in my heart, I was more than just a secretary."

After five years at RCA, she heard that MCA Records, under the direction of Jimmy Bowen, was restructuring and was looking for fresh, new talent. She made a few calls and landed an interview with Bowen himself. "I went in there all prepared to talk about my career, but Bowen did all the talking—his philosophy of music, things like that— and every once in a while he would throw me a question which I would answer and then he would take off again. I thought, 'Well, I'm probably not going to get this job.' Then he said, 'Is there anything you want to ask me?' I said, 'Don't you want to know about my career, how I've handled certain situations?' He said, 'I've checked you out—I know all about you. You make me feel comfortable and you'll make my artists feel comfortable.' Then he said, 'If you want this job, you've got it.' I thought, 'Wow!'"

Shelia's first job at MCA was as promotions manager. "All my male counterparts were betting I wouldn't last a year, but I was okay with that," she says. "They had a right to question that. You can't demand respect. You have to earn it." Soon, after piling up a string of Number One hits, she was made senior vice president of national promotions, a job she held for ten years, until she took over leadership of MCA-subsidiary Decca Records.

Shelia's experiences have influenced her approach to the music industry as a business, but not the way she views herself as a woman. She wears conservative dresses, which while feminine, do not detract from the authority of her position. She is an attractive woman and she does not attempt to hide her good looks. She has learned that she can be female and authoritative at the same time. As far as sexual harassment is concerned, she says, "You learn to either laugh it off or walk away." She sees it as a game that has its own peculiar set of rules. "For those women better endowed than others, you don't go into work in a turtle neck and no jacket. You're asking for it. I came up [the corporate ladder] at a time when literally there were leers and jokes. It is still the same today. There comes a point where you have to draw the line. You can't help what they are thinking, but you can help how you react and how you encourage them. If a woman goes in as a business person with a business attitude and keeps it on the up and up, then no matter what happens, she will come out unscathed.

"I was blessed in that I never had a bad, bad situation where I was in a corner and couldn't get away. I had a couple when I thought I wouldn't get out, but I did. I've counseled other women about that. It's hard to be on the road with radio guys and a lot of times you're taking them back to your car late at night or to your hotel. If you want to be successful, you just swallow your pride and go on. You say 'no thank you' and walk away.

"One time I had three breakers [hit records] at RCA and thought that was quite an accomplishment. It was the first time it had been done there. I had a guy say, 'Why don't you come down to my office tonight and we'll celebrate and I'll thank you for your hard work.' "I said, 'I'm looking for praise, not punishment.'"

As head of Decca Records, Shelia received more than her share of praise, as the record label reclaimed its place as a country music leader. She had every reason to be optimistic about the future, but toward the end of the decade, Universal, which owned Decca, merged with PolyGram. In early 1999, the doors at Decca were closed and all the employees, including Shelia, were terminated. Decca artists were told they were free to look for recording contracts with other labels.

Shelia, the first woman in history to head a country music label, was shown to the door, with no offer of work in the corporation's other companies. Rather than apply for work with Decca's competitors, she hung out her shingle as a manager.

Having better luck as a record executive was Sylvia Rhone, who left Atlantic Records to become chairman/CEO of the Elektra Entertainment Group. It was a historic appointment because it made her the only African American and the first woman to ever attain such a title in the music industry.

✦◇✦◇✦◇✦◇✦◇✦◇✦◇✦◇✦

You can't have a decent revolution without a party afterward.

In the case of the women's revolution of 1996, it seemed only fitting that the victors let down their hair and throw a whiz-bang of a celebration. They could have called it anything they wanted, but they called it Lilith Fair. It began the day after Independence Day, July 5, 1997, and continued for six weeks, offering nearly forty coast-to-coast concert performances featuring more than sixty female artists.

Participating in the series of concerts were some of the founding mothers of the revolution: Indigo Girls, Pat Benatar, Emmylou Harris, Suzanne Vega, Tracy Chapman; field commanders, such as Sarah McLachlan, Joan Osborne, and Sheryl Crow; and flower-child newcomers who were the future of the movement: Fiona Apple, Abra Moore, and Jewel. Some women played a few of the dates; others played a dozen or more. The line-up was always different, but the essence of the concerts was the same: Female artists, female musicians, female stage crew, and, for the most part, female audiences. It was an enormous success, artistically as well as financially.

Lilith Fair was the brainchild of Sarah McLachlan, the twenty-nine-year-old Canadian-born daughter of American expatriate parents who moved to tranquil Nova Scotia, Canada, during the crazed, violent years of the Vietnam War. Since so many of the big guns in the revolution were Canadian—Shania Twain, Alanis Morissette, K.D. Lang—it was entirely appropriate that a Canadian plan the victory celebration. Sarah chose the name Lilith because, according to Hebrew folklore, Lilith was Adam's first wife. She tacked "Fair" onto it because "it means beautiful, it means equal, and it means a festival or celebration."

Sarah was discovered at the age of seventeen, fronting a new-wave band named October Game. She was offered a recording deal by Nettwerk Records, a Vancouver-based record label, but she waited two years before accepting it because she knew it would mean relocating to Canada's West coast. Her first album, *Touch,* was released in 1988 in Canada by Nettwerk, and by Arista Records the following year in the United States. The follow-up album, *Solace,* marked the beginning of her working relationship with producer Pierre Marchand, who encouraged her in her songwriting.

Over the years, Sarah discovered to her dismay that no matter how hard she worked, or how well she performed, she was restricted in her achievements by radio programmers who followed the "we already have a girl" system of putting together playlists. Sarah thought that was unfair. The success of the 1996 revolution proved she was right; what better way to celebrate than to throw the biggest girl party ever held?

When the Lilith Fair tour began, Sarah was a well-regarded singer/songwriter, a ten-year veteran of the club and concert scene, but she was not a major star, even though she had a strong, cult-like following and her most recent album, *Fumbling Toward Ecstasy,* had sold over two million units. Two weeks out into the tour, her fifth album, *Surfacing,* was released. Like the three previous efforts, it was produced by Marchand. Unlike the other albums, *Surfacing* took off during the summer at blazing speed, finally peaking at Number Two on the pop charts in September 1997.

Sarah began the Lilith Fair tour a devout believer in the power of the feminine mystique and she ended the tour a recording star of the first order. "You know what the bottom line was?" Sarah told the *Hartford Courant.* "I just thought it would be really fun to put a whole bunch of women on stage—all the women I loved. To be able to play with them on the same stage and be able to put on a show like that—for us and for the audience."

For Pat Benatar, who played two dates with the tour, it was "the best 48 hours" she had ever spent. "These women were totally empowered, as we were not. It was remarkable. There is a total difference between their generation and our generation. We didn't have that feeling of friendship. We felt like we were competing against each other. We were terrified to let our guard down, of being gentle, kind, any of those things—because it wasn't about that. It was about being as strong as you could to get through it.

"These women are the product of what we did to get through it," Pat continued. "It was so amazing to see the difference. It was like a toddler trying to learn to walk. Then, the toddler at three-and-a-half refining her motor skills. That was what those women were doing—refining their motor skills, because they did not have to run through the gauntlet. It was so emotional for me to be there. For them, it is not a question of, 'Do we deserve it, can we have it?' In their mind, it's, 'Yeah, we deserve it,' and, 'Yeah, we want to have it.' I was just so proud of them. It was amazing."

◆◇◆◇◆◇◆◇◆◇◆◇◆◇◆◇◆

As the decade ended, twenty-year-old Fiona Apple and twenty-nine-year-old Abra Moore were two of the strongest contenders for leadership into the new millennium; both are inventive songwriters who looked up from their interpersonal travels to find themselves in the "strangest places" imaginable.

Abra adopted Austin, Texas, as her home, but she arrived there by way of a circuitous route that took her from her childhood home in

Hawaii to New York, where she studied piano in her teens, then on to Europe, where she performed in small clubs along the coast of England, then back to Hawaii, where she became one of the founding members of Poi Dog Pondering, only to leave just as the band was about to ink its first recording contract.

With guitar in hand, Abra became the metaphorical wanderer. Perhaps because her mother died when she was four and her father was an artist in the Beat Generation mode—and her childhood was filled with the music of Bob Dylan, Billie Holiday, and the Beatles—finding herself was not easy for the five-foot-six, waif-thin brunette with a face like a Generation-X fashion model and a lifelong penchant for fearless introspection.

For a time she settled into a folkie acoustic style, her playful, lighter-than-air voice reminiscent of 1980s artists such as Edie Brickell and Rickie Lee Jones. She released a critically acclaimed album, *Sing,* on a small, independent label, but despite enthusiastic reviews, the album never found radio airplay and quickly disappeared from store shelves. It did attract the attention of Arista Records, which signed her to a recording contract and sent her back into the studio with producer Mitch Watkins, who encouraged her to pursue a harder, more contemporary sound.

Abra emerged from those sessions with a string of songs that suddenly made sense of her life and her wandering. When *Strangest Places* was released in 1997, "Four Leaf Clover," the first single, attracted immediate attention from alternative music radio stations and the video fell into heavy rotation on MTV. In addition to the success of her album, she made an impact on the movie industry by contributing songs to three motion pictures: *Excess Baggage,* starring Alicia Silverstone; *The Matchmaker,* starring Janeane Garofalo; and the *Newton Boys,* starring Matthew McConaughey and Ethan Hawke. Abra even made a cameo appearance in *The Newton Boys* as a chanteuse who croons the blues classic "Millenburg Blues," in a seductive barroom scene.

"My introduction into the music business has been in baby steps," says Abra, her early morning voice as breathy and melodic as the recorded version. "As far as feeling like I had to prove something, I may have felt that a little bit on the latest record because of all the hype on the female …so I came into it feeling like, 'Oh, well, here comes another one, but give me a chance.' It's a good record aside from being from another girl."

Abra is delighted with the success of the women's revolution, but she thinks people who focus on the femaleness of it all are missing the point. "Maybe it's just about the music," she says. "Know what I mean? I think women are having success because they are making really nice records and people are appreciating them. People go, 'I wonder why there are so many? What's the deal? It must be some sort of fad!'"

Just hearing herself say the "fad" word makes Abra break out into laughter. "Maybe it's just balancing out. You know? I think if there's a good record out there, it deserves to be heard, whether you're a boy or a girl." Abra is like many other female singers and songwriters who have spent a lifetime suppressing the influences of their gender on their music and concealing their appreciation of other female performers, only to suddenly be told that it's all right to be female—all right to appreciate the work of other women.

As a veteran of the 1997 Lilith Fair, Abra was astonished at the reception the tour received. "There was a balance of people—a lot of boys, too," she says. "And backstage—everyone was rooting the other one on, you know. It was nice meeting Sarah (McLachlan). She's a very inspiring, steady, supportive person, and Jewel, she's great…and Emmylou Harris, she's the queen."

Fiona Apple was one of the shining stars of the 1997 Lilith Fair tour, but at nineteen she was so overpowered at discovering her own identity that she was barely able to appreciate the depth of womanpower that surrounded her. Six months before the tour, she was the opening act for Counting Crows. She had toured for a year in Europe and released her first album, *Tidal*, but her career was still in the very early stages … and she was still ever so green. Critic Kristin Whittlesey, writing for the *Nashville Banner*, was at one of Fiona's performances with Counting Crows: "It was truly jarring when she opened her mouth between songs. That's when you realized that, yes, she really is all that young. Her stage demeanor was girlish, slightly goofy, and clumsy. Her apparent lack of stage experience was all the more jarring because of her polished, professional performance."

By year's end, Fiona had grown up, as girls are apt to do, and her album had cracked the Top Twenty, spurred by the success of the haunting single, "Criminal"—in which she sings about being a "bad, bad girl" who has been "careless with a delicate man." If she was still "slightly goofy," it was as endearing in its own way, as was the dark, brooding power of her music. That contradiction was one of the fascinating things about Fiona, for it intimated that she would either become one of the biggest stars in pop music history, or that she would self-destruct and vanish, James Dean-like, in a puff of smoke.

Fiona herself seems to understand that. Once, while out on the road, she read a scathing review of one of her concert performances and went back to her hotel room and scratched her hand until there was no skin left. Her cries of *listen to me but don't hurt me* can probably be traced back to the time she was raped at the age of twelve in the hallway outside her mother's New York apartment. "How much strength does it take to hurt a little girl?" she asked a reporter for *Spin*. "How much strength does it take for the girl to get over it? Which one of them do you think is stronger?"

Fiona answered that question with her work, which offered a blend of musical sophistication and existential detachment that was sometimes staggering in its complexity. How is it possible for a young girl, who just the year before had never worked with other musicians, to write such powerful, jazz-influenced songs? And how is it possible for a young girl who still lived at home with her mother to be so savvy to the gender battles that made the Women's Revolution of 1996 possible?

If you have to ask, says Fiona—then please don't. "A lot of people who are saying that [I'm too young] just don't know today's world," she told Associated Press. "I've been in therapy my whole life—and it's the same with a lot of kids today."

With her oversize blue-grey eyes, her long, blonde hair, and her awkward body that sometimes seems torn between childhood and adulthood, Fiona has been made into a sex symbol, one that takes well to television's hit-and-run mode of operation. Brave and defiant, she paraded about in her underwear for the video of "Criminal"—a video some critics said bordered on child porn—but she was quick to defend it by telling interviewers that walking about in her underwear is something she would never do at her own home because she *hates* the way she looks in her underwear. Get it? She was *acting!*

Fiona promised herself that she would give her fans, the record label, the video makers, the entire world what it wants, even if it means showing herself in a bad light. That's only fair, she reasoned—she owes them that. But she knows that there will come a day when the prettiness, the bare skin and the pouty looks, will get lost in the power of the music—and that's when she will twist the knife.

In 1999, Fiona followed up her debut album with one that had the longest title in music history: *When the Pawn Hits the Conflicts He Thinks Like a King What He Knows Throws the Blows When He Goes to the Fight and He'll Win the Whole Thing 'Fore He Enters the Ring There's No Body to Batter When Your Mind is Your Might So When You Go Solo, You Hold Your Own Hand and Remember That Depth Is the Greatest of Heights and if You Know Where You Stand, Then You Know Where to Land and If You Fall it Won't Matter, Cuz You'll Know That You're Right.* Critics simply called it *Fiona II.*

The album received excellent reviews, but they all seemed to end with the same wish that Fiona would hurry and grow up. "Like any proper tortured artist, Apple hasn't gained much in psychic confidence following the success of *Tidal*," wrote David Browne in *Entertainment Weekly*. "On [this album] Apple presents herself as a mental shambles, and she's more than happy to tell us about it."

When she went out on tour she did more than sing about being a mental shambles, she had a meltdown on the stage of the Roseland Ballroom in New York, when she lost her cool over what she called a bad sound system. "I can't fucking hear myself," she screamed. "Please forgive me. Let's just fuck it and have fun." She performed three songs, then left the stage for a "five-minute break" that was extended until... well, somewhere that audience is still waiting.

The following day, she appeared on "Late Night with David Letterman," where, to everyone's relief, there were no sound problems; she gave a stellar performance and the evening passed without incident. Later, she apologized for the way she acted at the Roseland Ballroom, saying "Speaking selfishly, I'm glad I walked off, because if I hadn't, the sheer mediocrity that that show would've become, would've absolutely killed me. So I'm sorry, and I'm not sorry, and I'll make it all up."

Once the tour ended, Fiona took a two-year break, during which she did little more than take walks, play with her dogs, ride her bike, and write songs. Once she had enough new material, she started on a new album in 2003 with producer Jon Brion, only to discover that she had problems concentrating. Finally, the album was completed, but her record label put it on ice because executives said they couldn't find a single on it and didn't know how to promote it. Brion told *Rolling Stone* that the record label would "take whatever amount of time they'll take deciding how to promote it. And who knows? Those things are a black hole."

◆◇◆◇◆◇◆◇◆◇◆◇◆◇◆◇◆◇◆

"The type of change that is happening now could not be realized overnight—it has taken two generations," says Pat Benatar. "The first generation—they were the pioneers. The next generation were the people who got the benefits. For second and third generation females, this is law for them. They look back at what happened to their mothers and say, 'How could that ever have happened?'"

Pat laughs with the confidence of a battle-scarred veteran of many hard-fought campaigns. "Well, they weren't there," she explains. "My mother was a working mother at a time when everyone else stayed home. That is one reason I was so open to the women's movement. It was the way I was raised."

As women have assumed increasingly larger roles in the music industry, they have begun to question the rules of the game. Are boardroom and marketing aggressiveness male qualities or are they gender-free qualities defined by the nature of the work itself? "I think they are male qualities, because when women work together, they don't work under the same rules," says Curb Records executive Claire Parr. "When I work with a team of female executives who are secure in what they do, they are more team-oriented. There is a loss of the sense of 'I' and more of a team attitude. They are more willing to help other women succeed. I have had men be incredible mentors to me, but the men who have been mentors have at times been threatened by me."

One of the troublesome facets of the debate about women in music is the realization that men and women do have well-documented differences when it comes to music. They look for different things when they select music—and they hear different things when they listen to the music.

"I was at a panel discussion in New York on the sonics of music," said former Decca Records head Shelia Shipley Biddy. "They had done research and found that the female ear is different as to how it hears sounds sonically. They used the example of a man and a women together in a car. The music is playing loud and the woman will take it down a notch because it vibrates her eardrum differently. The researchers speculated that females, brought along genetically to hear children cry, hear lower and higher frequencies better. Men hear the middle range better and they'll listen to it real loud. Women listen to lyrics first, melody second. Men listen to the melody and rhythm and beat—and that catches them first. They might have listened to a song six or seven times, and you ask them something about it, and they will say, 'What?' They might not get the lyrics until they have listened many times."

It's a subject that prompts laughter from Renee Bell. "I think women are *so* different," says the RCA Records executive. "I still don't know how we ever got together. Women are very complicated creatures. It is incredible that men can write songs about what women are going through and don't have a clue how to deal with women. I'm sure that most of the [successful] songs written by men are by happily married men who have been in long relationships."

7 | Country Divas Reshape Pop Music

Eileen Twain came to Nashville from her native Canada in 1991 to record a demo, armed with little more than raw singing talent, a dazzling natural beauty, and a manager named Mary Bailey who shared her client's drive for success. It was hardly a potent arsenal with which to do battle with the grandfather of all good-ole-boy networks, the country-music establishment. The twenty-six-year-old brunette resembled a feisty magazine covergirl more than she did a country singer. Elegant. Reserved. Above the fray. She didn't look like someone about to step into the vanguard of a music revolution.

With two notable exceptions—Pam Lewis, Garth Brooks' co-manager, and Lib Hatcher, Randy Travis' manager—female managers were a rarity among successful recording artists on either side of the pop-country fence, but what did a country girl from Timmins, Ontario, know about the gender politics of stardom?

Mary Bailey, herself a well-known country singer in Canada, had discovered Eileen in the Canadian North Country about 400 miles north of Toronto, where she had been singing since childhood in restaurants and small-town nightclubs. Eileen sang mostly pop and Top Forty material, but she was no stranger to country music and it was well represented in her repertoire.

As a teen, Eileen worked in the Canadian bush planting trees with her stepfather, Jerry Twain, a full-blooded Ojibway Indian who had married her mother when Eileen was two. She had no memory of her natural father, Clarence Edwards, a man of French-Irish decent. As far as she was concerned, Jerry was her father—her only father. Jerry's crew went into the bush in teams of a dozen or more, with Eileen the only female. That didn't seem to bother her since she had grown up a tomboy, with no real concept of gender differences. The only concession she made to her femininity was the large wash tub she loaded into Jerry's pickup when they headed out to camp. She filled the tub with water and parked the truck where it would receive direct sunlight while she was away at work.

When she returned to camp at sunset, the water was warm enough to bathe in, and she stripped and climbed into the tub and unselfconsciously bathed under the open skies. If anything, her tomboyish bravado made her more trusting of men than was perhaps the norm for her age. She thought of herself as just another one of the guys.

If it was Jerry who helped Eileen define herself as a woman, it was her mother, Sharon, who helped her develop her musical talents. Sharon was a tall, no-nonsense woman of Irish stock who had an eccentric "British air" about her. "She couldn't sing a note, but she was such a wonderful, wonderful lady," Eileen says of the woman she nicknamed Angel. "Everywhere she walked, she was definitely going somewhere. She was certainly not the sort of person to kinda' saunter around."

Sharon instilled a sense of self-worth and confidence in Eileen at an early age. Just as Jerry taught her she could do anything a man could do and could work alongside any of them with a sense of equanimity, Sharon convinced her she could sing as well as any of the women she heard on the radio. Sharon just knew her daughter could be a star. Eileen grew up believing stardom was her destiny.

The Twain family was poor by middle-class American standards, but so were most of the working-class families in northern Ontario. Although there was not always enough food to eat, according to Eileen's recollections, the family managed to scrape together enough money to send her to Toronto for voice lessons. After years of county fairs and local talent contests, Sharon finally got the break she dreamed of for Eileen and booked her on the "Tommy Hunter Show," a nationally broadcast variety show. It was that booking that brought Eileen to the attention of Mary Bailey.

Unfortunately, just as it appeared Eileen's career was about to move to another level, Jerry and Sharon Twain were killed in a car accident when their Chevy Suburban slammed head-on into a logging truck. Eileen was devastated. Since her older sister, Jill, was married and had children of her own, Eileen took responsibility for her three teenage siblings—two brothers and a sister—and became their surrogate parent. They moved to Huntsville, Ontario, where she found work as a singer at a resort lodge. She did three shows a day, seven days a week, singing everything from Broadway show tunes to country ballads. As Eileen became a parent to her siblings, so did Mary Bailey become a parent to Eileen, replacing Sharon as her primary dreamweaver.

For three years, Eileen worked as a cabaret singer, supporting her siblings and making a name for herself in the resort communities of northern Ontario. Finally, in 1991 Mary arranged a meeting with

Nashville attorney Dick Frank, who put her in touch with Norro Wilson, a successful Nashville producer/songwriter, and Buddy Cannon, the head of A&R for Mercury Nashville Records. Mary paid Wilson and Cannon to record a three-song demo, something she could pitch to the record labels. Soon Eileen had a contract as a singer/songwriter with Mercury Records.

It was a fortuitous union, though just how fortuitous Eileen would not understand right away. Mercury had signed Kathy Mattea several years earlier and was gaining a reputation as a female-friendly label for new-wave country artists. The main reason for that was label head Luke Lewis, who didn't share the traditional view that women artists couldn't sell records. Another reason was Sandy Neese, the head of media relations. Sandy had gotten into the record business by way of radio following a stint as a reporter at the *Nashville Tennessean*.

Sandy had a reputation for giving her all to her work. She worked as hard for male artists as she did for female artists, but it is the latter that had a special place in her heart. Unknown to Eileen, Sandy was a member of a loosely organized "good-ole-girl network" in Nashville that years ago had pledged its membership to give breaks to female artists who were deserving of a helping hand. In time, Sandy would have a profound influence on Eileen's career, though the singer would never quite understand why.

The first thing Eileen did upon moving to Nashville was to change her name. She adopted the name Shania, an Ojibwa name that means "I'm on my way." She took the name out of tribute to Jerry and led reporters to believe it was a product of her Ojibwa heritage. Later, when the truth came out, she was roasted by the press for "lying" about her Indian heritage. In fairness to Shania it must be said it was a heritage with which she had come to identify totally. She had no memory of her natural father and considered Jerry to be her father. What possible interest would the media or music fans have in disassociating her from the man she considered her father? She would learn that the media and music fans have a penchant for tearing down people they build up, but at that point in her career it simply never occurred to her that her family life would be of interest to anyone but herself.

Most people who move to Nashville from New York or California experience a certain amount of culture shock, but it is based largely on the laid-back, rural folkways of the city. Not so for Shania. Her introduction to Nashville was her introduction to the United States. Her culture shock was of a different type. When working out in the bush with Jerry, they lived in a camp similar to what hunters call home in the States. They killed deer for food and butchered the animals on the spot. Because they had no refrigeration, they buried the meat in the cold tundra while they worked in the bush. That had the effect of preserving the meat and protecting it from wild animals.

"There's a big difference, just in the culture," says Shania. "When I first moved to Nashville, going into the grocery and everything was real different because of the labeling and things like that. There were thirty or fifty different types of beans. It was, like, 'Where do I start? What kind of butter do I buy?' Just going to a restaurant was different. If you ordered a tea and didn't specify that you wanted hot tea, they would give you an iced tea. I'm not used to that, you know. I ordered a country-fried steak one time, because at home country-fried steak would be a piece of ham. Here it's deep-fried steak that's battered. I couldn't believe it. I said, 'I can't eat this. What is it?'"

Mary Bailey was almost as shocked as Shania, but not so much at the southern cuisine as at the overall business climate. "Because there was a male dominance, they didn't necessarily take women seriously, as equals," she later recalled. "I found that was very difficult to overcome. It was a serious boys' club in the music industry in general. You are walking into a strange land and you have to be very careful and know what you are doing."

Bailey had a marketing plan from the very beginning, based on her observations of Shania's Canadian performances. Apart from a unique voice, Shania possessed a sex appeal that never failed to impress her resort audiences. "Shania is beautiful—let's not kid ourselves—and she's a very sensual woman," says Bailey. "But what she brings to the table is that instead of being a threat to the female audience, she is someone they want to be like. She gives them a sense of values and worth. Up to that point in time, there were no females [in country music] who had a class type of sex appeal, in conjunction with the phenomenal talent she possesses. Dolly was the closest, but she used her sex appeal in more of a fun way. Shania's sex appeal was very classy. Where other artists would use their sex appeal in a very slutty way, Dolly and Shania did it in a positive way."

While Bailey worked on Shania's image, the singer worked on her songs. Since she had been signed as a singer/songwriter, she turned in a slate of original songs for her first album. All but one of the songs were turned down by co-producers Wilson and Cannon. She was crushed. Those songs represented her unique view of country music.

Wilson and Cannon felt more comfortable with the traditional songs penned by Music Row tunesmiths. It represented a male view prevalent at the time: The records that female artists recorded that sold well were all variations of the "he done me wrong" theme. Shania's songs didn't fit into that genre. They were all about strong women taking charge of their lives. They weren't feminist in point of view, but they were unmistakably from the heart of a woman who had not been brought up to feel she had been put on earth to please the male of the species.

When the self-titled album was released in 1993, it didn't do well on radio or in the stores. The two singles, "What Made You Say That" and "Dance With the One That Brought You," never cracked the Top Fifty. Shania was sent out on tour with two of Mercury's new male artists, Toby Keith and John Brannen. By the end of the tour it was Keith—not Shania—who emerged as the star. Despite the disappointing public reaction to the album, it was not a total loss, for listening was rock producer John "Mutt" Lange. He liked what he heard and called Mercury to get Shania's phone number.

After several telephone conversations, Shania and Mutt met for the first time in June at that year's Fan Fair. Mutt, who had grown up in his native South Africa listening to country music, suggested they collaborate on her next album. That sounded like a great idea to Shania—and to the label executives who signed Mutt on as producer—but the singer and the producer collaborated on more than music and ended up getting married before work on the album was completed.

This time around, Mutt told Shania that, as her producer, he only wanted to record songs she had written herself. He asked her to go through her catalog and choose ten songs that she felt defined her as an artist. All ten of the songs she chose were keepers. All of the songs had been submitted for her first album and then rejected as being unsuitable. Mutt wrote one song himself for the album and Shania added a twelfth, a song fragment sung without accompaniment.

When the album was turned in, label executives were stunned. They had previously turned down the songs, and the album didn't sound like anything else on the country market. It was an upbeat, instrumentally potent collection of songs that expressed a fresh approach to country music. Luke knew it was special, but was it too special? He asked for confirmation from the Mercury staff that his gut instinct was right. Sandy Neese knew in her heart it was a hit album.

The first problem was what to name the album. Recalls Shania: "Mutt and I went through everything possible for the title. Then Sandy came out one day and said, 'The Woman in Me' should be the one. Just the way she said it, I said, 'Yep, that's it.'"

"Whose Bed Have Your Boots Been Under?" was the first single released from *The Women in Me*. Radio wasn't sure what to do with the record. It was an upbeat, aggressive record that had the female narrator telling her unfaithful man to hit the road. "So the next time you're lonely, don't call on me," sang Shania. "Try the operator. Maybe she'll be free." It was a far cry from Tammy Wynette urging women to stand by their man.

"We really had a struggle with that first single," recalls Sandy Neese. "Radio didn't want to play it. It was too pop. It was too this, too that. Luke went back and pounded week after week on the promotion department. 'I know this is a hit. I know we've got something phenomenal going here.' He wouldn't let go. So what we finally did, we went to, oh I don't know, maybe six stations, who had given her some support on her first album and talked them into airing it enough to get reaction from the listeners. When the phones started blowing off the wall, then that's when they woke up and listened."

Those callers, for the most part, were women. Unknown to Shania, the good-ole-girl network fell in behind *The Woman in Me*. If there was one album that could rally the troops, it was *The Woman in Me*. Behind the scenes, women worked hard to make the album a success. Their hopes were riding high on Shania.

Soon it became clear that the success of the album was due to female record buyers. Promotions targeted that audience like never before. Shania didn't want to do a concert tour to promote the album because she felt she didn't have enough songs to merit a full-scale concert performance. Instead, she performed on television and focused on the media, doing hundreds of interviews. In a throwback to pop star Tiffany's wildly successful mall tour in the late 1980s, Shania made appearances at malls where large numbers of women could be expected to gather. At the Mall of America in Minneapolis, more than 10,000 fans gathered to meet her. She didn't sing a note. She simply appeared.

The success of *The Woman in Me* was a dream come true for Shania, but for women in the music industry it was one of the early warning shots fired in the quiet revolution taking place in American music. By September 1995, *The Woman in Me* had peaked at Number Six on the pop charts, putting Shania in the same company with hitmakers Alanis Morissette and Natalie Merchant. By 1996, *The Woman in Me* had sold over 12 million copies. The women's revolution was under way.

◆◇◆◇◆◇◆◇◆◇◆◇◆◇◆◇◆

Before Faith Hill was ever a star, she was a statistical footnote. Born on September 21, 1967, in Jackson, Mississippi, she was one of 8,344 children born to unwed mothers in Mississippi that year. Adopting Faith were Ted and Edna Perry, a Jackson couple that already had two sons in the family. They were devoted parents and raised Faith with the same love they showed their natural sons, but Faith did not grow up exactly like her brothers, for she had a wild streak in her that marked her as different.

In 1977, after Faith got into trouble with the police over a rock-throwing incident at an abandoned house, Ted and Edna moved the family to Star, Mississippi, a small town south of Jackson, where they felt that their ten-year-old daughter could grow up in a community with old-fashioned values. That was very much the case, but Faith did have to wrestle with her wild streak from time to time, like the times she played "chicken" with the fast freight train that sped through Star three times a day on its way to and from Jackson, or the time she "rolled" her English teacher's lawn with enough toilet paper to accommodate a battalion of dysenteric soldiers. Inspired by that late-night adventure, she also rolled the lawn of the music director at the Star Baptist Church.

No one in Star was surprised when Faith dropped out of college and moved to Nashville, where she hoped to break into country music. Ever since she had attended an Elvis Presley concert at the age of seven, she had felt destined for a career in music. Unfortunately, no one in Nashville agreed with her. The only music-related job she could find was at Fan Fair, working in Reba McEntire's T-shirt booth.

Frustrated by her failure to interest anyone in her singing abilities, she married music-publishing executive Daniel Hill, a man twelve years her senior. The marriage took place four months after her arrival in Nashville. "She moved to Nashville to sing, but at times she would get frustrated with the music business, and her priorities seemed to shift toward more domestic pursuits, such as cooking and decorating our home," Hill told *Good Housekeeping*. "She even considered enrolling in interior-design school. I always tried to steer her back toward music, where I knew her true talent was. The interior-design industry doesn't know what it missed!"

With Hill's encouragement, Faith plugged away at her music career, but without much success. Four years later, unhappy in her marriage and despondent about her career, Faith loaded up her 1989 Toyota Camry with her possessions and left her husband, not at all certain about her future. Luckily, she attracted the attention of Martha Sharp, one of only two female A&R executives in Nashville. She had made a name for herself in the 1980s by signing Randy Travis to a deal with Warner Bros. Records, moving up from secretary to one of the top executives at the record label.

Sharp first heard Faith sing at the legendary Bluebird Café. There was something about her singing, indeed, her very look, that mesmerized Sharp, but she left that evening without introducing herself to Faith. Two months later, Sharp ran into Faith at a barbecue and asked her if she had a demo she could send her. If there was one thing Faith had plenty of, it was demos, so she wasted no time delivering a tape to Sharp, who was equally time-efficient in offering Faith a recording contract with Warner Bros. Records.

In 1992, women were a tough sell to radio program directors. It was the Garth Brooks era, a time when male singers dominated the country-music charts. Sharp knew that Faith would not be given second and third chances, so she took her time developing her as a recording artist. She paired her with producer Scott Hendricks, who had produced hit albums for Alan Jackson, and Brooks and Dunn. He had no track record working with female artists, but Sharp had confidence in his studio savvy and she felt that his easy-going personality would be a good match for Faith.

Working together, Faith and Hendricks turned out an album titled *Take Me as I Am*. The first release, "Wild One," went to Number One on the country charts and held that position for four consecutive weeks. The second release, "Piece of My Heart," also went to Number One. The same week that "Piece of My Heart" peaked on the charts, *Country Weekly* published a story about Faith under the headline "From Secretary to Superstar."

Despite her success that year, the Nashville music industry was slow to warm up to her as a performer. Some people felt she was too glamorous to be a country singer. They mistakenly thought that female record buyers were too countrified, too gritty and blue collar, to go for a woman as striking as Faith Hill. To her surprise, she was nominated for the Horizon Award, given out each year by the Country Music Association to the most promising newcomer in country music. Also nominated were Martina McBride, John Michael Montgomery, Lee Roy Parnell, and Tim McGraw.

That fall, when the award was presented, Faith was passed over in favor of Montgomery, whose album, *Kickin' It Up*, had sold two million copies. Faith didn't know it, but she never had a chance to win the award. In the fourteen years the award had been presented, it had gone to female singers on only three occasions. Country music was viewed by the establishment as a manly pursuit, unless, of course, women wanted to sing about standing by their man or that sort of thing.

Faith Hill was anything but manly. With her ultra-feminine stage presence and her feminist approach to song content, she was an enigma to anyone who could not understand the thought process of a twenty-something woman—and, let's face it, that included almost all the men working the front lines of the industry.

As Faith's career took off, so did her love life. She fell in love with Hendricks and filed for divorce from Daniel Hill. Over the next several months, the tabloids seemingly followed her every move, at one point reporting that she was having an affair with Dallas Cowboys quarterback Troy Aikman. The football player was so disturbed by the rumors that he telephoned Hendricks to tell him there was no truth to them.

The rumors hurt both Faith and Hendricks, but they figured that was the price they had to pay for success. Anyone who lived in Nashville in the mid 1990s, as did this author, knows that a favorite pastime was gossiping about Faith's imagined love life and how it had affected her success. There were also rumors that she was nothing more than a musical pawn, a bimbo creation of Scott Hendricks.

One reporter, noting that the record label had put together a glamour calendar to promote her CD, one that focused, literally, more on her face than her music, asked her point-blank if she was afraid of being labeled a "bimbo." Faith protested: "I'm not a bimbo! I think that's a really embarrassing question for me to answer."

By 1995 Faith and Hendricks were viewed as country music's newest power couple, a distinction that was made even more apparent when Hendricks was named head of Capitol Records' Nashville office. By Christmas, they were as much in love as a couple could be—or so everyone thought. Hendricks had asked her to marry him and she had accepted his engagement ring. That month, the happy couple celebrated Christmas and counted their blessings as Faith prepared for her upcoming concert tour with the current Bad Boy of country music, Tim McGraw.

Faith began 1996 with doubts about her career. Her first album had spawned a couple of hits, but it had not sold as well as expected. Her second album, *It Matters to Me,* was selling well, but not well enough to catapult her into superstar status. She had been in Nashville for nine years, and her career was still not going as well as she had hoped. Hendricks pressed her for a wedding date, but she put him off, making excuses.

By the time she left Nashville (and Hendricks) to go out on the road opening Tim McGraw's *Spontaneous Combustion* tour, she was looking, desperately some would say, for something or someone to believe in. She found it in McGraw, with whom she had an instant physical attraction. The emotional attraction grew as the tour progressed, fueled to no small degree by the fact that he had been raised in a home without his father— a distinction that complemented her own sense of familial displacement over being abandoned by her birth mother and father.

Faith saw a kindred spirit in McGraw, someone who would under-stand her quest for self-expression in music and her sense of longing for a family of her own. Tim was the first man in Faith's life who did not tell her to "get over" her issues about being adopted. She loved him for that. In Faith, Tim saw someone who could understand his own abandonment issues with his father. Faith was the first woman in his life who viewed him as "special" because his mother kept him and did not abort his birth or give him up for adoption. He loved her for seeing special worth in him.

During one of their Nashville layovers, Faith broke off her engagement with Hendricks. Before the year was over, Faith married Tim in his hometown of Rayville, Louisiana, and seven months later gave birth to a daughter they named Gracie Katherine. By the time Faith got around to recording a new album—it had been three years since the release of *It Matters to Me*—she was at a crucial point in her career. If her next album was not a success, then she knew her career was pretty much over.

By the time Faith released her third album in 1998, a great deal had changed in the music industry. Shania Twain and Alanis Morissette had spearheaded the women's revolution in music, opening doors for women like Faith Hill. Twain's album, *The Woman in Me,* sold more than twelve million copies its first year out and by 2000 it had sold over seventeen million copies, making Twain the biggest-selling country-music artist, male or female, in history. Her success made Faith Hill more attractive as an artist.

When *Faith* was released in 1998, the album received only a tepid response from country-music critics—the *New York Post* described it as "listenable"—but CD buyers had a different reaction, embracing the first single, "This Kiss," with such affection that the song zoomed to the top of the charts. Encouraged, Faith returned to the studio and the following year she released the album that would make her a superstar: *Breathe.*

When *Breathe* was released in November 1999, the album debuted at Number One on the country charts, providing Faith with the credibility she had sought for nearly a decade. More importantly, the single "Breathe" debuted at Number One on the pop charts, and the video went into heavy rotation on both Country Music Television and VH1, establishing Faith as a major force in the music industry.

Incredibly, Faith became a multi-Platinum artist without the support of the male-dominated Nashville music industry. The most objective measure of the industry's hostility toward her can be found in the awards given out by the official voice of the industry, the Country Music

Association. During the first eight years of her career, she was nominated for CMA Female Vocalist of the Year four times, but she only won the award once.

Not so reluctant to recognize Faith's talent was the National Academy of Recording Arts and Sciences, which awarded her the first Grammys of her career in 2001: Best Female Country Vocal, Best Country Album, and Best Country Collaboration With Vocals for "Let's Make Love," a duet she recorded with Tim. When Faith took the stage for the final award, she was hurried along by producers and urged to wrap up her speech. Instead, she stamped her foot in defiance. "I've waited a long time for this award," she explained, then concluded with "...I love *everybody!*"

Shortly after taking home the Grammys, Faith became pregnant with her third child, Audrey (she and Tim had their second child, Maggie, in 1998). Although she was at the top of the pop charts and had a joint income of an estimated $100 million a year, she shocked her fans by announcing that she was going to put her career aside to focus on her children. She issued a press release that made it clear that she would return to music when Audrey was ready for her return—and not a day before that.

Tremors shook the Nashville music industry, but her supporters praised her decision. Bill Whyte, a morning announcer at Nashville's WSM, longtime home of the Grand Ole Opry and probably the most important country station in America, did not see a problem with Faith taking time off. "I think she could take two years off, especially as well as she sings," he told a reporter. "I think she will come back and have Number One songs immediately again. Faith is one of those artists that we all knew could sing when she first came out, but through the years I think her singing has just improved and improved and improved. She's just starting to touch what she can do."

One of the radio stations that got behind Faith in the beginning of her career was Miss 103, the leading country station in her hometown of Jackson, Mississippi. "I don't think there will be any long-term effect (on her career)," explained Rick Adams, the program director and one of the morning announcers. "I know she is doing the right thing in supporting her values as a mother and raising the kids that she has always wanted to have. So we applaud her and support her in her family values and her willingness to put her career on the back burner for a while."

When Faith returned to music in late 2002, with the release of a new album titled *Cry,* it appeared that her supporters were correct in predicting that she could rebound from a long layover. The album debuted at Number One on both the country and the pop charts and sold an incredible

427,000 copies its first week in stores (twice what *Breathe* had sold). In a press release Faith said: "*Cry's* debut is especially gratifying because it is the most direct validation of an artist's work by his or her fans. The loyalty that they have shown me, from day one, is something that I will never take for granted."

Unfortunately, *Cry's* impressive debut was based on her fans' anticipation of the album's contents and not the reality of the music it offered. When critics and fans actually listened to the album, they became more subdued. It only sold two million copies, down considerably from the seven million copies that her previous album had sold.

By 2004 it was apparent that Faith had peaked as a recording artist. Disappointed, she fell back to Plan B and threw herself into fulfilling her second goal of becoming a motion-picture actress. She auditioned for a role in *Cold Mountain,* staring Nicole Kidman and Jude Law, but the part went to Natalie Portman instead. She had better luck when she auditioned for *The Stepford Wives,* a remake of the 1975 classic. She landed the role of Sarah Sunderson, joining a cast that included Kidman, Bette Midler, and Glenn Close.

Whether Faith will be able to duplicate her singing success in cinema is not something that odds-makers would embrace, simply because the statistics are mixed. Movies did nothing to enhance the music careers of Johnny Cash, Willie Nelson, or Elvis Presley, but they did no apparent harm to the careers of Dolly Parton and Cher.

Faith Hill has an almost spiritual belief in her destiny as a shining star. Although declining album sales since 2002 indicate that her career as a major recording artist may be over, and her skills as an actress are as of yet largely untested, only a fool would count her out, simply because she has an irresistible, down-home charisma and an inner drive that is unforgiving of failure.

◆◇◆◇◆◇◆◇◆◇◆◇◆◇◆◇◆◇◆

In the beginning, there were four Dixie Chicks: Sisters Martie and Emily Erwin on fiddle and guitar, Robin Macy on guitar and vocals, and Laura Lynch on bass and vocals. To reflect their Texas backgrounds, they dressed as retro-cowgirls: Colorful jumpsuits decorated with sparkly fringe, cacti, and iridescent stars; cowgirl hats; and Texas-sized boots, all calculated to present a familiar, almost cartoon-like, image.

In the late 1980s and early 1990s, their music was unlike anything else circulating in Texas: A mixture of bluegrass and country, all performed with pop sensibilities that attracted a loyal following of men attracted to their good looks, women who identified with their no-nonsense lyrics, and teenage girls that were mesmerized by their playfully irreverent attitude.

The Dixie Chicks were so different that no record company would give them the time of day. Unfazed, the Dixie Chicks traveled across country, playing county fairs, corporate events, and county-western bars, building a loyal fan base that grew year by year. They lived on the road for much of the year, traveling in a mileage-weary van that creaked with each turn in the road. Despite the hardships, they reveled in that gypsy lifestyle, the only downside being that they had no recordings to sell to their fans.

In the fall of 1990, when it appeared that their dreams of becoming recording artists would never be realized, they were the recipients of a small miracle. Penny Cook, the daughter of Senator John Tower and an enthusiastic fan of the Chicks, as they often were called, knocked on Laura's door one day and asked her what it would take for the group to make a record. Stunned by the question, Laura answered, "I think it would cost about $10,000."

Without another word, Penny whipped out her checkbook and wrote the Chicks a check for $10,000, the only condition being that the women "pay it back when you can." The Chicks took the money and ran—all the way to the nearest studio, where they laid down fourteen tracks for an album titled *Thank Heavens for Dale Evans* (a reference to king of the cowboys Roy Rogers' loyal cowgirl wife).

They recorded the songs live, the way Elvis, Scotty Moore, and Bill Black had done at Memphis Recording Service. "If we ended the song at the same time, we'd say, 'that's a keeper,' and then move on to the next song," recalls Laura. "We didn't do any dubbing or any of the rigmarole. We did it the way that was the most efficient and economical."

Thus began one of the wildest rides in music history.

Thank Heavens for Dale Evans did not help the Chicks land a record deal in Nashville, but the CD sold well at their concert venues, allowing them to pay back the loan from Penny Cook. Encouraged by their success with the first album, they returned to the studio in 1992 to record a second album, *Little Ol' Cowgirl.* It was a departure from the predominantly bluegrass influence of the first album in that a drummer was added to provide them with a more contemporary sound. Robin was unhappy with what she saw as a sellout to their bluegrass origins, so she left the group to pursue a solo career.

With Robin gone, Laura stepped up to handle the vocals. The Dixie Chicks were a democracy, which meant that it only took two members to change the group's direction. As expected, fans were enthusiastic about the group's "new" sound. Still unconvinced were the Nashville music executives who saw no future for the women in country music.

"Early on, when they were doing more of the cowgirl stuff, Nashville did not have a clue about what to do with them," says drummer Tom Van Schaik, the only male to travel with the group. "They looked at the Chicks and said, 'That's not what we're doing now.' I kept scratching my head because they were selling so many CDs."

A third album, *Shouldn't a Told You That,* followed in 1994. Nashville music executives gave a thumbs down to it as well, but a Sony Records executive offered them a contract with an understanding that Sony would put out an album as long as he was allowed to produce it. The Chicks couldn't believe their good fortune. After all the years of struggle, they finally had a contract with a major record label.

The Chicks began 1995 by performing at the inauguration of Texas Governor George W. Bush, after which they hit the road for a long string of performances in Texas, North Carolina, and Tennessee. That summer they went into the studio with their new producer, but to their disappointment none of the tracks they recorded were approved for release by Sony. So they kept trying.

Meanwhile, while struggling to come up with ideas that would be acceptable to Sony, Martie and Emily wrote a song titled "You Were Mine," which they decided to record on a demo. Laura was out of town, visiting her daughter, so the sisters asked Natalie Maines if she would be interested in singing it for them. Natalie was the daughter of steel guitarist Lloyd Maines, who had performed with the Chicks on occasion. The sisters had heard tapes that Natalie's dad had sent them and they thought her voice would be a good match for the song.

The demo went so well that the sisters decided to exercise their majority vote to cut Laura out of the group and add Natalie as the new lead singer. On October 30, 1995, Martie and Emily went over to Laura's house and told her that they wanted to buy her out, effective that day. Stunned, Laura asked, "Do you have a replacement in mind?"

"Yeah, Natalie Maines," they answered. "She's been working up the material."

Laura saw that the women had their minds made up, so the only remaining question was the terms of the split-up. They gathered together in a circle, with notepads on their laps, and agreed that each woman would write down what she thought would be a fair buyout price. On signal, each woman held up her notepad. "It was almost the same thing," Laura later recalled. "It was amazing how close to the same number we all came. We just worded it differently. All along we knew we thought alike—and in the end we did."

The three women parted friends, and Emily and Martie returned to the studio where, working with Natalie, they recorded an album titled *Wide Open Spaces*. Even with a new lead vocalist, Martie and Emily had a difficult time making the album come together; it took an additional two years for them to convince Sony to release it.

Less than a week after the first single, "I Can Love You Better," was released in early 1998, Sony Records issued a press release under the headline: "Dixie Chicks Make Dazzling Debut/Texas Trio Are Highest Debuting Group in Seven Years." *Wide Open Spaces* debuted at Number Seventeen on the album charts and went on to sell more than nine million copies, making it the biggest-selling album ever by a country group. It also earned the women two Grammys and two Country Music Association awards.

Dixie Chicks fans were elated by the album's success, but their happiness was tinged with a hint of bittersweet remorse. Noted Robert Wilonsky in the *Dallas Observer:* "No band in town ever worked harder to get further; outsiders will write of their overnight success, but the Chicks know better. So do Robin Macy and Laura Lynch, women who defined the band's sound from the beginning...Macy and Lynch were sacrifices made on the altar of country-music success."

Macy and Lynch reacted differently to the group's success. Macy withdrew and declined to speak to reporters, while Laura praised her former bandmates, Martie and Emily, when talking to reporters, and kept in touch with the sisters. Taking the high road, Laura went to hear them perform when they returned to Texas. Backstage, she was greeted with enthusiasm by all three band members, who embraced her as their spiritual sister. "I'm so happy for them," Laura later said. "I will always love that band and will forever support them. We had ups and downs, but we did it together, holding hands."

The Dixie Chicks brought a new dimension to country music. Young girls who previously listened only to pop and rap artists found themselves drawn to the Chicks' plucky, sometimes irreverent, style of music. The good ole boys of country music, who had dominated the charts for so long, were ushered to a back row, where they were instructed to sit quietly and behave themselves. Martie, Emily, and Natalie not only energized country music at the creative level, they brought new money into an ailing industry that worships nothing quite so much as it does cold, hard cash.

Soon after the release of *Wide Open Spaces,* the Dixie Chicks started work on a new album, a decision that both pleased and horrified their record label. The conventional wisdom dictated that they should continue to promote an album that everyone knew was a winner and not risk failure with a sophomore effort, since few new artists with monster hits have been able to achieve the same level of success with a second album. The Dixie Chicks were told that they simply did not understand the business.

As Sony Records struggled to arrange interviews for the women to promote *Wide Open Spaces,* they ran away from the bright lights and set up shop in a series of rented cabins, where they composed new songs in isolation. Although they were criticized for going to a writers' retreat, the women stood their ground. "I think we were wise to go on these retreats, because it was the only way to really get time to write," Martie insisted to *Billboard.* "I think that gave us a head start, and the writing flowed more freely."

Once again, the Dixie Chicks proved that they knew what they were doing. When their second album, *Fly,* was released in September 1999, it was greeted with acclaim. *Time* magazine music critic Richard Corliss confessed that he had wondered if they would be able to duplicate the success of *Wide Open Spaces,* but his conclusion was that *Fly* was a "big leap forward, ornery and urgent." He went on to describe the album as offering "prime, primal, high-altitude Country." The *Nashville Tennessean* described the album as "brimming with confidence—an amazing amount of confidence."

Fly was not a typical country album. Instead of urging their fans to "stand by your man," they indulged in a level of apparent male bashing that was unheard of in country music. In one song they sing that they need a man "like a hole in the head." In another, "Goodbye Earl," they tell the story of an abused wife who slips poison into her spouse's black-eyed peas and then dumps his body into a lake. There was such an uproar from the conservative country media that the Chicks had to point out a disclaimer in their liner notes: "The Dixie Chicks do not advocate premeditated murder, but love getting even."

Fly produced six Top Ten hits, including "Ready to Run" and "Without You," and went on to sell nine million copies. At the 2000 Grammy awards, the Chicks performed "Goodbye Earl," much to the displeasure of male radio executives that had pulled the song off the air, and then took home a Grammy for Country Album of the Year.

The following year, the country-music establishment, already shocked at the women's refusal to bow to authority, was stunned when the Chicks announced that they were terminating their contract with Sony Records because of alleged accounting misdeeds by the record label. In a "60 Minutes" interview with Dan Rather, the women said that Sony Records, according to their math, had made $200 million from their first two albums, but they had yet to gross seven figures individually.

Nashville shook in its alligator boots. The record industry had a long history of shucking and jiving its artists, but none of the male artists, despite their outlaw, tough-guy public images, had ever had the courage to stand up to the record labels. Sony Records sued for breach of contract and the Chicks counter-sued, claiming the label had engaged in "systematic thievery"—tough talk from three very stubborn women.

Explained Martie: "Everyone in the country industry kept telling us, 'Keep your mouths shut. Why don't you appreciate what you have?'" That argument didn't register with the Chicks for the simple reason that they had worked too hard for their success to have it tempered by a false sense of gratitude. Emily was only seventeen when she started playing with the Chicks, and Martie was only twenty; now in their thirties, it was the only life they knew and they had no intention of surrendering their hard-fought success to people they felt were cheating them out of what was rightfully theirs.

As the lawyers slugged it out, the Chicks packed up and returned to Texas, where they started work on a new album titled *Home*. It was different from the previous two albums because it was stripped down to the basics: No drums, no studio tricks, only old-time country music tinged with bluegrass.

Meanwhile, Sony Records settled with the Chicks, offering them their own label to be called Wide Open Records, a reported $20 million signing bonus, and an astonishing 20% royalty on all future records. One other thing: The men who had signed them and produced their first two albums were banished from the Chicks' sight. From that point on, they would deal directly with executives in the New York office—and no one else.

When *Home* was released in 2002, it proved to be an instant success, with hits such as "Long Time Gone," "Travelin' Soldier," and a cover of a 1975 Fleetwood Mac hit, "Landslide." Stevie Nicks, who wrote that song, said, "If I were younger, I would at this minute be convincing them that I should be the fourth Dixie Chick."

By that point, the Chicks had sold twenty-five million albums and collected four Grammys and ten Country Music Association awards, making them the most successful country group in history. Throughout it all, Martie married, divorced and remarried; Emily married for the first time; and Natalie married, divorced, and remarried. When babies started appearing on the arms of Natalie and Emily, the music industry let out an audible sigh of relief. Were the Chicks, finally, going to drop their reckless, outspoken ways and settle down and become down-home mamas?

The answer came in March 2003 at a concert in London, when

Natalie told the audience that she was "ashamed" that George W. Bush was from their home state of Texas. The comment was an expression of her opposition to the United States' invasion of Iraq for the stated purpose of saving the world from weapons of mass destruction. When the Chicks returned to the States, they did an interview with Diane Sawyer for ABC's "Primetime Thursday," at which Natalie clarified her statement by saying, "We support the troops one hundred percent.... There is not a correlation between not wanting a war and not supporting the troops who are doing their job."

Natalie went on to apologize for "disrespecting" President Bush, but stood firm in her opposition to the war (by 2004, it would be obvious to everyone that Bush had misled the public on his reasons for invading Iraq). Nonetheless, the country-music industry turned a cold shoulder to the Golden Girls of country music. Country radio stopped playing their music. The Chicks received death threats and had trash dumped onto their lawns. Male country singers, who had been weaned on the redneck credo that the "boss" was always right (in this case, President Bush being the boss), saw an opportunity to retake the chart momentum they had lost to the Chicks—and they took out after the women like half-starved dogs on a deer hunt.

The Dixie Chicks responded to the attacks by posing nude on the cover of *Entertainment Weekly*. They showed contempt for their critics by having the names they had been called stenciled onto their bodies: "Dixie Sluts," "Traitors," "Saddam's Angels," and "Opinionated." James White, the photographer, later told the magazine that the women were "bashful" during the shoot but not with the language they wanted painted onto their bodies. Said White: "A lot of names they wanted to put on their bodies their handlers wouldn't allow, because they thought it was too extreme."

Some country-music stars voiced support for the Chicks' antiwar position—Rosanne Cash, Emmylou Harris, and Steve Earle, to name a few—but most attacked the women for speaking their minds. Travis Tritt called Natalie's comments "cowardly." Toby Keith, one of the first male casualties of the women's revolution in music, began a public feud with the Chicks over his support of the war, best expressed by a jingoistic song titled "Courtesy of the Red, White, and Blue." Keith had begun his career in the early 1990s with a concert tour with Shania Twain; she went on to fame and fortune, totally overshadowing his career, which receded to honky-tonk bar status.

Standing up for their convictions initially cost the Chicks sales on the country charts. Their single "Travelin' Soldier" dropped from Number One to Number Three, but the album actually moved up on the pop charts, from Number Six to Number Four, proving once again that the country-music establishment had misjudged Chicks fans.

The Chicks' conflict with the country music establishment was about more than free speech. More at issue was the right-wing territory the industry had staked off for its artists. It was a no-[wo]man's-land in which war was extolled as a national birthright, redneckism was viewed as a God-given virtue, and women were expected to support their men folk, right or wrong. It was in direct opposition to the women's revolution that Shania, Faith, and the Chicks had spearheaded in an effort to take country music to a higher level.

As the 1990s ended and the new decade began, Shania had fled to Switzerland, Faith was eyeing a new career in Hollywood, and the Chicks had dropped any pretense of returning to Nashville. They spent the remainder of 2003 touring, playing seventy-nine shows in all, and then began 2004 with the release of a two-CD set titled *Top of the World Tour Live*.

Martie told reporters that she no longer felt that they were part of the country-music scene. "We feel let down by our industry," Martie told *Entertainment Weekly.* "Alienate Shania. Alienate Faith. Alienate us. You're driving away the top artists in your format. How can that be good?"

8 Into the New Millennium

At the end of the twentieth century, the women's revolution in music was well under way and assured of success. Women dominated the charts, their closest competition coming from male rappers. Set free by the events of 1996, the women of the new millennium each went their own way, sometimes taking surprising routes to stardom. The women who had laid the groundwork, the 1990s veterans, didn't always approve of the tactics and personas adopted by the new wave, but they supported the upstarts, both publicly and behind the scenes, and they cheered them on at every opportunity.

The artist who had the greatest influence on music during the first half-decade of the New Millennium was Britney Spears. No woman generated more media heat or more fan adoration. Raised in the small town of Kentwood, Louisiana, Britney had stars in her eyes at a very young age. Not long after she started walking, she was singing and dancing about the house, displaying an aptitude for music that often startled her parents.

Convinced that Britney was destined for stardom, her mother, Lynne, took her to Atlanta when she was eight so that she could try out for "The Mickey Mouse Club." Told that Britney was too young for the show, Lynne then took her to New York, where she enrolled her in three years of study at the Off-Broadway Dance Center and at the Professional Arts School. She also found Britney an agent, someone who believed that she had potential.

At the age of ten, Britney landed her first professional job as the understudy for Laura Bundy in *Ruthless,* a play based on the movie *The Bad Seed.* It was about a demonic preteen named Tina Denmark, a personification of evil, who is sent to reform school after she commits a murder to win a starring role in a school musical. Laura Bundy and Britney were alike in a number of ways: Both girls were born in the South, and both girls possessed that precocious sense of femininity that is peculiar to prepubescent girls in the South. Perhaps because of that, whenever either girl stepped out onstage, they projected a breathless presence that was felt by the audience.

After almost a year of playing the lead role, Laura left to pursue other interests, thus allowing Britney to replace her full time. Britney's promotion meant that another actor had to be moved into the understudy's position—Natalie Portman, who later went on to fame as Queen Amidala in the *Star Wars* trilogy. The two girls became fast friends, despite being fiercely competitive. Sometimes when Natalie was onstage with her, Britney turned her back on the audience to make funny faces at Natalie in the hopes of cracking her up.

Eventually, Britney moved on to other things, dropping out of the play when she learned that she had been accepted, finally, by "The Mickey Mouse Club." She was a Mouseketeer for two years before making an all-out effort to land a record deal. She was seventeen when Jive Records signed her to a recording contract and teamed her with Swedish producer Max Martin, who had forged hits with Backstreet Boys and Ace of Base, and songwriter Eric Foster, who had written hits for Whitney Houston.

The resulting album, *Baby One More Time,* was released in 1999, just weeks prior to Britney's eighteenth birthday. In its review, *People* said that Britney was "peppy and enthusiastic," but not "precocious enough" for major stardom. In disagreement were legions of teen fans that made the album a smash hit, with sales eventually reaching ten million units.

Britney's manager, Johnny Wright, who also represented the boy group 'N Sync, told reporters that her success did not surprise him in the least. "People were tired of grunge and songs about people doing drugs or getting shot. There was a big void for uplifting, up-tempo, positive music."

Maybe—but the video that accompanied the release of the single, "Baby One More Time," took advantage of Britney's physical attributes by depicting her as a much younger girl wearing an unbuttoned white shirt, a sexy black bra, and a mini skirt. The song was positive all right, in a bubble-gum sort of way, and despite its undeniably solid musical hook, it was also naughty in its dark appeal to adolescent sexuality.

Shortly after the single's release, Britney appeared in a *Rolling Stone* cover story that offered titillating photographs of America's newest "overnight" star. According to Geoff Boucher of the *Los Angeles Times,* some music executives half-jokingly described the photographs as "child pornography."

America had produced a long line of teen girl stars—Tiffany, Brenda Lee, Tanya Tucker, and Debbie Gibson, to name a few—but Britney was unique in that she showed no hesitancy in playing the "sex card." Teenage girls have sexual lives of varying degrees, whether real or imagined, and the music of the past fifty years has found creative ways of exploiting that without appearing naughty; Britney was the first teen pop sensation to make sex an equal partner to her music—and without apology.

In 2000, Britney released her second album, *Oops!...I Did It Again.* The accompanying photographs showed Britney wearing slacks, slightly unzipped, with a top that displayed a bare midriff. Commenting on the album, a reviewer for *Entertainment Weekly* wrote: "It's as if Spears herself is veering between good girl and bad, and at this point she could go either way."

As if to drive home that point—and the fact that she had turned eighteen—Britney had her navel pierced and had a small black-winged fairy tattooed onto her ass. "I still feel like a teenager in some ways," she told *USA Weekend.* "But there is something about being eighteen. You feel like you're more of an adult."

In 2001, Britney did another provocative cover for *Rolling Stone* to promote her third album, *Britney.* Asked by the reporter whether she thought baring her navel would encourage little girls to become "underage vamps," the singer said, "I think it's not that deep. I like wearing those clothes. I like, when I'm onstage, to be an entertainer....I put on my cute clothes, and I go onstage, and I do it. If the song calls for me to wear something a little voluptuous or sexy, I like to go there."

By that point in her career, Britney found it difficult to do an interview in which sex was not mentioned by the reporter. The message was clear: The public liked Britney's music just fine, but they liked her sexuality even more. The first real criticism she received for exploiting that sexuality came from *Rolling Stone,* the same magazine that had so eagerly encouraged her to push the envelope for their photo sessions. Sniffed Barry Walters, the reviewer that gave *Britney* only three stars: "Spears is one month away from entering her twenties and clearly needs to grow up. Her Lolita shtick is nearly past its expiration date, and the growing pains presented throughout the album too often come across as contrived."

Soon Britney's life was imitating her art. She began a romantic relationship with 'N Sync's Justin Timberlake, only to have it fall apart in full view of the entire world. Emotionally scarred by that misadventure, she hit the nightclub circuit, smoking and drinking Malibu rum cocktails, generating a new image that was startling in its commonness. The same media that had egged her on when she was younger turned against her and depicted her as an out-of-control rich girl. Britney responded by announcing a six-month recess from her career, a decision that encouraged *Us Weekly* to declare that Britney was "on the brink" because of the failed relationship had turned her life "topsy-turvy."

Britney bounced back in 2003 with an *Entertainment Weekly* cover story, the headline of which described her as "Nobody's Angel—On the Rocky Road with Pop's Sexiest Bad Girl." Britney was not doing anything in her private life that was not on the list of things to do of other twenty-two-year-olds, but because she was a "star" the public seemed to hold her to a different standard. She began her career as a virgin pretending to be naughty. Now it seemed the public wanted her to be a whore pretending to be a virgin. The confusion of it all was sometimes more than Britney could handle, but she played along and gave the public what it demanded.

Throughout it all, she smiled and swished her hips in that awkward manner that women who have not had a lot of sexual experience do to suggest that they have had a lot of experience. And, whenever possible, she shocked audiences with revealing costumes and suggestive dance moves, packaging her sexuality with a sort of clinical detachment that slyly intimated that the joke might not be on her after all.

By 2003—the year more than one critic has called Britney's "wild year"—it appeared that the pop star had run out of material with which to shock her fans. Was she suffering from a failure of imagination? Inquiring minds wanted to know. The suspense was lifted at the Video Music Awards, when Britney and Christina Aguilera smooched with 1980s sexpot Madonna at the conclusion of the older woman's song. The audience went wild, especially at the sight of Britney's open-mouth kiss with Madonna. At last, imagery that everyone could understand: A faux-lesbian bridge between the generations.

Britney followed that incident with her most explicit photographs yet for *Rolling Stone.* Still, the "kiss" buzzed the Internet and the airwaves, even CNN's political show "Crossfire," where Britney went head-to-head with bow-tie-clad Tucker Carlson. Britney said no, she had never kissed a woman before—and yes, she would do it again, but only if Madonna was her partner. Carlson seemed impressed by Britney, but he must have wondered if life, as he knew it in his starched-shirt world, was coming to an end.

Toward the end of the year, Britney released her fourth album, *In the Zone.* It sold 609,000 units the first week, less than the 746,000 units that *Britney* sold, but it was enough to allow the album to debut at Number One on the pop charts, despite mixed reviews. Under the hilarious headline "Spears Explores Her Erroneous 'Zone,'" *Boston Globe* reviewer Sarah Rodman gave the album a good skewering. Calling it "robotic and chilly," Rodman wrote, "Ultimately, what is jarring about the album is that for all her newfound freedom, Spears never really sounds like she's enjoying this new 'zone.'"

✦◇✦◇✦◇✦◇✦◇✦◇✦◇✦◇✦◇✦

If Britney Spears is the gold standard for women pop stars of the 2000s, then Christina Aguilera is the silver standard. In a career that has paralleled Britney's since the release of her self-titled album in 1999, Christina has come close to passing her competitor on several occasions, but something always seemed to get in the way.

Like Britney, Christina got her start in "The Mickey Mouse Club," where the two preteens hammed it up with Justin Timberlake for top Mousketeer status, and like Britney, she released her first album in 1999. The album gave her two Number One singles, "Genie in a Bottle," which had a five-week run at the top of the charts, and "What a Girl Wants." Despite the differences in their music—Christina has a rhythm & blues subtext to her hits, whereas Britney sticks to a pop formula—music writers compared the careers of the two women at every opportunity, sometimes in the hope of instigating a media cat fight between the two teen divas. "I get a lot of the Britney questions," Christina told *Entertainment Weekly.* "'Is there a rivalry? Is there catfighting?' I'm like, 'Nooooooo.' If anything, we'll probably do a collaboration."

Technically, Christina has the stronger voice, but her songs have been weaker, if only by a bleached hair, and that has put her at a disadvantage. Early on, she opted for the same teen sex-queen image patented by Britney, but she always seemed to come off second best, primarily because her Latin background gave her a darker, blue-collar look that does not sell as well with Britney's bubblegum brigade. Later, when Christina tried on the "slut" label, people believed her, while Britney had to practically beg her fans to suspend their disbelief that she could be the baddest bad girl of them all.

Incredibly, the sex label was taken to absurdist lengths when headlines questioned whether either woman's breasts were real or manufactured. Both women acknowledged their changing bust lines, all the time thinking how weird it was that boob questions sometimes dominated their interviews, but both women denied getting implants, and attributed the changes in their bodies to the fact that they were simply "growing up." Of course, no one believed them.

Just as they had done with Britney, the tabloids launched "Christina Aguilera Is Spinning Out of Control" headlines that charged her with various misdeeds. She didn't help her case when she accompanied MTV's Carson Daly to an Atlanta strip club called Cheetah. Christina protested that she went to the club without knowing what it was and only discovered the truth when she was escorted to a VIP room, where she joined members of 'N Sync, 98 Degrees, and the Backstreet Boys. "I'm totally tattling," she admitted, "but it's the whole double standard."

In 2000, Christina went to court to stop the release of an album titled *Just Be Free*. Composed of songs she had recorded when she was fourteen and fifteen, the album was put together by producers who had worked with her on her first demos. Failing to block the album's release, she also filed a lawsuit against her longtime manager, Steve Kurtz, for fraud and exercising "improper, undue, and inappropriate influence" over her career. He returned the favor with a countersuit claiming breach of contract.

Meanwhile, her relationship with dancer Jorge Santos fell apart, causing Christina to feel even more alienated. She began a relationship with a producer that she refused to name, only to have it end in disaster as well. "I felt like I was nutty," she explained to *Blender*. "I didn't want anyone to get close to me. I had put an imaginary box around me. I would literally scoot away from a person. It was bad, bad, bad."

Throughout the chaos of 2000 and 2001, Christina worked on a new album with an assortment of producers and co-writers, including Eminem and Glen Ballard, who produced Alanis Morissette's biggest-selling album. *Stripped* offered a range of musical styles, from rants such as "Make Over," directed toward those who tried to control her image, to syrupy ballads such as "Beautiful."

Stripped debuted at Number Two on the pop charts, but it sold a disappointing 300,000 units the first week. Critics praised it, generally, but her fans seemed somewhat put off by the album. The title was meant to portray her emotionally stripped condition during the two years it took to record it, but the nearly topless photograph of her on the CD jacket suggested something else entirely.

From the start of her career, Christina went from squeaky clean to fallen angel in her imagery, but with *Stripped* she stepped out of the box with a new campaign that depicted her as a tease. She went from blonde to raven-haired, and she practically begged her fans to see her as a mature woman. What she didn't seem to understand was that her fans enjoyed her previous images as virgin and tramp because both images suggested that she was accessible to them. You can have a tramp, and you can dream about having a virgin, but a tease, by definition is off limits. By becoming a tease, she removed her protective cloak of accessibility, the real strength of her previous success.

Still, her fans stuck by her, if begrudgingly—all the more so in 2003 when she toured with Britney's old flame, Justin Timberlake. During the tour, Christina talked about the former couple at every opportunity, sometimes offering predictions that Justin and Britney would someday reconcile. The tour was her smartest move yet, for it not only enabled her to introduce her music to Justin's fans, it allowed her to tap into Britney's fan base. Before the year ended, she racked up an estimated $30 million in album sales, product endorsements, and concert revenues.

Christina did a number of interviews in 2003, and they always seemed to focus more on her sexy image than on her music. Finally, in response to a question about her appearance, she told *Rolling Stone:* "I'm unapologetic for the things I do, the things I wear, the things I say. You know, it seems like they all want this pretty, perfect little America's sweetheart.... I love my curves.... The media should say something freakin' nice about someone that's trying to step out of the boundaries. And, no matter what, I'm just going to keep on doing what I'm doing."

Christina received confirmation, finally, that her career was falling in place at the 2004 Grammys, when she won an award for "Beautiful." It was a much-needed validation for the emotional torment she had endured while making the record. Christina knew what others must have known but forgotten: That sex appeal has been an integral part of the rock and pop experience ever since the day Elvis Presley first stepped out on the stage. The Grammy was needed confirmation that the music mattered, too.

♦◇♦◇♦◇♦◇♦◇♦◇♦◇♦◇♦

Eyeing Britney and Christina's success was former teen queen Tiffany, who released her first album in over a decade. Titled *The Color of Silence,* the pop-friendly album featured several songs co-written by Tiffany, a departure from her teen hits. *Billboard* generously described the album as "thoughtful and intelligent," and suggested that it could be to 2000 "what Alanis Morissette's Grammy Award-winning *Jagged Little Pill* was to 1995."

Unfortunately, Tiffany's former fans did not rally to her new cause. The album got off to a good start in Asia, where the teen queen still resonated among older fans, but fans in the United States were slow to embrace it and the album ultimately withered on the charts. In a gallant effort to revive it in 2002, Tiffany did the unthinkable for a former teen queen: At age thirty, she posed nude for *Playboy.* "I'm not interested in resurrecting Tiffany from the past," she told the magazine. "I feel confident standing on my own two feet as an adult, a woman, a mother, and a musician."

MTV asked Tiffany if she thought that a nude pictorial would be the next step for Britney. "I don't think Britney would have to pose nude in *Playboy*," she responded. "She is doing what she does in her videos and stage shows and has already established a sexy image." The reason for showing her stuff in *Playboy,* she explained, was to drive a stake in the heart of her old teen-queen image. She was convinced that her album did poorly because her old image kept getting in the way, preventing concert promoters and CD buyers from giving her new music a chance. She used her sex appeal as a tool because it seemed to work for Britney and Christina. In Tiffany's case, it didn't work; her body parts were impressive, but not impressive enough to breathe new life into her album.

There is no denying the effectiveness of sex as a marketing tool. Sex most definitely sells. But it has a downside in that it raises expectations in an industry that has a horrendous track record on gender equity, and that is what has made older women in the music industry uncomfortable about the new generation's blatant use of sex.

For decades, women have been asked to trade sex for record contracts, songwriting deals, private secretary jobs, entry-level positions at record labels—you name it, and women have been asked to put out to get it. The familiar line is, "If you don't want to put out to be a star, then you must not want to be a star bad enough to do what it takes." In some instances, women have even instigated the notion of a trade. For some women, the prospect of spending a few nights in the sack with an asthmatic old geezer seems a fair trade for potential stardom and all the financial trappings of success. Those women are in the minority, but they arrive in sufficient numbers to feed the beast.

It is hard to imagine what the music industry would be like today if the situation had been reversed: If male wannabes had been told that stardom—or even an ordinary career—required them to strip naked, bend over, spread out, and otherwise "be nice" to certain people in the business. Most men would have a difficult time even imagining a work environment like that, much less submitting to one. They would probably find the suggestion itself laughable.

Not laughing are the many women who have fought back in recent years with sexual harassment lawsuits and public accusations of wrongdoing in the workplace. Penny Muck, a secretary whose 1991 lawsuit against Geffen Records brought national attention to the issue of sexual harassment in the music industry, received an estimated half-million dollars in an out-of-court settlement with the record label. At the time the alleged wrongdoing took place, Geffen Records was an industry leader, with a roster of "bad boy" acts such as Guns n' Roses and Aerosmith.

In her lawsuit, Muck alleged that her boss, a high-ranking male general manager, masturbated in front of her over a two-month period, forced her to touch his penis, fondled her breasts and buttocks, and once jammed her face into his crotch. "I couldn't believe it," Muck told the *Los Angeles Times*. "All of a sudden, he just starts doing it [masturbating in front of her]. He's got this crazy look in his eyes... and he's saying, 'Watch me! Watch me!" After he ejaculated, it was so weird. Like something out of Dr. Jekyll and Mr. Hyde. He just walks back into his office and it's like business as usual. As if nothing ever happened. I thought to myself, 'Right, like who's going to believe this?'"

Former Geffen promotions director Christina Anthony believed it. After Muck's allegations became public knowledge, Anthony gave an interview to the *Los Angeles Times* in which she alleged that the same executive who had harassed Muck also had harassed her during her time of employment at Geffen between 1984 and 1990: "I was sexually harassed, intimidated, and terrorized. I personally told three top executives under David Geffen of the abuse and nothing was done about it. In order to maintain my self-esteem as a professional, I was forced to resign."

Muck's allegations sent a shock wave through the industry. Boardrooms were suddenly filled with reports on the extent of "the problem" and proposals to protect the corporate purse. Of course, what happened at Geffen was less a product of corporate management than it was a product of the industry's mindset. Wasn't rock 'n' roll supposed to be the voice of adolescent sexual fantasies? Weren't all rock 'n' roll acts, male and female, selling sex appeal as much as they were selling music? Hadn't rock 'n' roll stars occasionally masturbated in public during concerts to express their sexuality and their disdain of the uptight, straight "system"? Had rock 'n' roll become its own worst enemy?

Of course, Geffen Records wasn't the only offender and there was no evidence that the offenses reported by Muck and Anthony were systematic of a corporate policy. On the contrary, one month before she left Geffen, Anthony handpicked her own successor. Her choice was Claire Parr, a hot-shot promotions person who recently had been given the pink slip from Enigma Records. "One day I got a call from a friend who said, 'Don't take that job at Geffen until you talk to me,'" recalls Parr. "I said, 'What job at Geffen?' In half an hour I got a phone call from a woman who said she'd like me to come to work tomorrow. Her name was Christina Anthony. I had met her at record conventions, but I didn't really know her very well. She said she had a person on maternity leave in adult contemporary promotions and wanted me to take that position temporarily. I didn't know Christina was leaving Geffen. She brought me in to that position as her replacement and so about a month after I came in, she resigned and I found myself the director of promotions for Geffen without ever going through the normal biting and scratching. Christina was my guardian angel."

Despite her anger over her treatment at Geffen, Anthony apparently didn't blame the company; otherwise she would not have been so conscientious in finding a replacement for herself. Whether because of the negative publicity or because the alleged harassment was due to that one executive, Parr never reported any similar problems at Geffen. By the late 1990s she had moved on to Curb Records, where she became a vice president in charge of the pop and Christian divisions.

As word of the Muck case spread, other lawsuits emerged. A secretary at Warner Brothers Records filed a complaint against her male boss. By the mid-1990s, what had once been one of the industry's darkest secrets suddenly became its most widely discussed problem. "I'm afraid to let a woman come into my office alone," confided a high-ranking male executive with Columbia Records. "It's just not worth the risk."

BMI's Frances Preston is among those who worry about a backlash. "There are too many people who sit around reading books on how to sue for sexual harassment and try to create such a situation," says Frances. "It is hard to believe that people do that, but they do and it ruins it for people who have real cases for sexual harassment. With some people, it's, 'He screamed at me!' Or, 'He said I was a high-school dropout.' They say that to men, too. There are a lot of women who try to sue for harassment and they do it on the basis of, 'He screams at me.' No one should scream at anyone, but sometimes people do lose their cool and you have to, in a way, say, 'Well, he had a bad day.' And if someone makes the statement, 'Were you a high-school dropout?' that could be said to a man, too.

"When you work with people, you see them more than they see their families sometimes, and sometimes they have bad days. But that doesn't mean they are out to harass you. They didn't say that morning, 'I'm going to harass this woman to death.' Plus, you can create a lot of [problems for] yourself. I've seen some girls in our business who have invited it. If you go to work in a halter top and a skirt that barely covers your panties, I'm sorry—you have invited it. You just don't go to work that way."

Debe Fennell is a marketing executive who has had experience in most areas of the music business. She has worked as an editor with *Radio & Records* magazine, a booking agent, an assistant to singer Randy Travis, and in the promotions departments at Curb Records, Magnatone, and BNA Records. Sexual harassment is a way of life at some businesses, she says, adding that she was abused physically and verbally at one record label. "[My boss] was always touching people," she says. "I was on the phone talking to a radio station and he wanted to talk to me and he took the phone out of my hand and slammed it down. Another time, he grabbed my boobs. That only happened twice. The second time, I grabbed him back. It scared the hell out of him. He got the message, but I got squeezed out my job. Two weeks after I left, I was at a music seminar and he walks up and says, 'Well, there's one good thing that came out of this, Debe.'

"I said, 'What's that?'

"He said, 'We can see each other socially now.'

"I said, 'After a bad dream,' and I walked away. I could have sued the record label, but I wanted to continue working in this business."

Debe acknowledges that progress has been made in recent years, but she feels it has been slow developing. "There are lots of women succeeding," she says. "How they do it is another matter. But you can find that in any walk of life. If you weigh everything out, women are gaining. Does the good-ole-boy network still do the glass-ceiling thing? Yes. Do they gang up on women? Yes. Is it inequitable? Yes. Am I going to change it? No. In every situation I have been working in for a record label, the guys in charge have always been looking over their shoulder, going, 'God, she's aggressive.' And I'm saying, 'You'd better watch out, I want your job.' It makes them nervous and they will do whatever. It is the survival of the fittest. It took me a while to figure that out."

There is no question that women have been preyed on by unscrupulous men in the music business, but for every woman that has been harassed there are others that have not. Is it the luck of the draw? Or is it something the women themselves do to forestall potential trouble? Country singer Terri Clark is a tall, willowy woman who wears cowboy hats and T-shirts with the sleeves rolled up to reveal lean, well-defined biceps. As a woman, she has striking facial features and a warm conversational manner that smacks of big-time femininity. As an entertainer, she has a reputation for aggressive, ass-kicking, foot-stomping performances that smack of no-nonsense in the first degree.

Terri has never encountered sexual harassment. "I've been lucky in that I never had the casting couch thing happen to me," she says. "I've never had anyone get out of line, not people that I've been professionally involved with—and that's nice to know. They see talent and they hope to cash in on it and they're not going to screw it up. I think, being a female, you have to be on the lookout for things like that. It is a man's world and sometimes you have to act like a man to be taken seriously. And I don't mean that in a negative way. I mean it in a confident, aggressive way. You have to come across that way. A lot of it is how you carry yourself and your attitude. You've got to come across like you mean business. It's important that you maintain that male attitude in the way you go about it."

The problems women have encountered over the years have not all been of a sexual nature, nor have they been confined to the creative side of the industry. There are certain areas of the business where gender hostility has been longstanding. Radio is one area. Another is concert and event promotions. Liz Gregory owns her own concert-promotions agency that concentrates on large public events such as county fairs. She started doing that type of work in the early 1980s while living in Oregon. "When I started, it was tough," she says. "The men tried to run me out of the business. I've had them tell stories about me and not take me seriously." By the late 1990s, attitudes had changed, she says, but she still felt it was "a man's world."

One way to get around that, says Debe Fennell, is to fight fire with fire. "As you get older, you learn what battles to fight and which ones not to fight," she says. "There is a group of us women who a few years back decided to form a good-ole-girl network—and we're not the only ones [to do that]. It was very loose. A tacit agreement we wouldn't hurt each other. If you can't beat them, emulate them."

Marilyn Arthur has been in the music business since the late 1960s and has worked as head of publicity for RCA Records in both its Nashville and Los Angeles offices. She hasn't seen many gender-related problems because "most of the media departments are women," except in the area of compensation: "I don't know if women will ever get to where men are with salaries." The women's revolution in music has not surprised Arthur. "Women are doing great and will continue to do greater and greater things," she says, pausing for a laugh, "...and take over the world." There is not a department at a record label, she says, that a woman could not walk into and head up.

"The old style of management really doesn't work anymore, not in today's world," says Sandy Neese, the former head of publicity at Mercury Records. "Most females are not going to put up with someone being condescending to them. That is an old male mentality that doesn't work anymore. They are liable to wind up with the president of a label being female, so they better be canning all the sex jokes and all the leers."

It is that changing world which Neese considers with a sense of pride and occasional nostalgia. "Without divulging my age, I will tell you that I'm middle aged and I do have grown children," she says. "I just feel so fortunate that I am in my generation as opposed to my mom's generation. Because she never would have been able to do what I have done because in her time no one had come along to really kick doors down in massive numbers like my generation did. Life's just more interesting now for females than it ever was." With that, Neese pauses, smiling at her male interviewer, then breaks out into laughter. "Because the world doesn't belong just to y'all anymore."

As a baby boomer and a product of the turbulent and creatively chaotic 1960s, Neese traces the line of progress of equality over more than four decades of struggle. The enormous success enjoyed in the mid-1990s by women did not happen overnight. "Until we hit Vietnam, life was just a dadgum breeze, man, just a breeze. That was the first thing that just really began to rock our world. That was like our defining moment. It was what spawned the flower children and the peace and love and all of that. If all that hadn't happened, who knows, maybe things just would have breezed along like they were. Maybe we'd still be sitting in the suburbs getting sloshed every afternoon, playing bridge—and trashing our husbands.

"I really think that the women of today are benefiting from the doors that we had to bang and pry open. Today's young woman is very different because she had us as moms, and we didn't want to bring our daughters up under the restrictions that we had. Get out and do it! Don't depend on a man for anything—for your income, for your happiness! Be capable of doing it on your own. If you have a relationship, have it out of want and not need! When Terri Clark sings 'If you think I'm gonna be sitting around broken-hearted over you, I've got better things to do,' today's woman can relate to that. That's the way they're thinking…Now they have music models they can identify with lyrically.

"Look at Shania's 'Any man of mine had better walk the line.' Could you have had that song recorded [twenty] years ago? I don't think so. Radio would not have played it. Not with lyrics like that. That would have been a man's lyric. You know, 'Shape up or I'm outta here, babe!' Today you have women who were reared like I reared my daughter—and they are going to be singing those kinds of songs."

◆◇◆◇◆◇◆◇◆◇◆◇◆◇◆◇◆

Besides sagging CD sales, one of the biggest problems the record industry faces is what to do with all the artists displaced by the new talent that just keeps coming, year after year. Does having a hit record guarantee an artist career security for life? Obviously, the answer is no. There is a limit to how many CDs will sell in a given year. When you have new artists competing with older artists for their share of that market, it usually turns out badly for everyone involved. It's Economics 101, but most artists have a difficult time accepting that concept—or the reality that hit records are not a license for a career.

By 2000 it had become clear that in order for the music industry to accommodate all the artists making records there would have to be a great deal of career rotation. That meant that the market could sustain half a dozen super artists over a given period only if all the other artists took longer breaks between albums.

Two influential artists from the 1990s that took breaks from their careers in order to roar back in the 2000s were the relentless Alanis Morissette, one of the Founding Mothers of the women's revolution in music, and Jewel. When the numbers tapered off on her CD sales in the late 1990s, Jewel diversified and published two books, one of poetry and the other a memoir. A smart move, as it turned out, because it provided her with an engine to keep her career moving forward.

In late 2001, Jewel released *This Way,* an album that was more upbeat than previous efforts (if you don't count 1999's Christmas CD, *Joy: A Holiday Collection*). It didn't catch fire with the teen-heavy buying public, but the following year a remix of one of the tunes, "Serve the Ego," went to Number One on the dance charts. Buoyed by that success, she spent most of 2002 writing new material. The result was the 2003 release, *0304,* a major departure from the folk-based tunes that had made her a star in the 1990s. This time around, she went for a techno-pop sound, the sort of dance music that required her to glam-up and do the one thing she had refused to do in her previous life—use her sex appeal as a sales tool to hawk her CDs.

Apparently using Britney and Christina as role models, she toned her twenty-nine-year-old folkie body, stripped down, pushed up, and sighed her way through one interview after another, vamping her image with a determination that often crossed over into parody. *Blender* magazine did a feature under the headline "Girl Gone Wild" in which the reporter asked her what was still old-fashioned about her. Jewel deadpanned: "I like to serve a man. And I like to be served. I love belonging to someone. I've never really liked being a flirt about town. The sexiest thing you can be is breakable."

Critics were glad to see her again, sort of. *People* said that the results of Jewel's musical makeover were "mixed," but gushed: "Move over, Madonna. There's a new club queen on the scene." Brian Hiatt wrote in *Entertainment Weekly:* "Sellout move or not, *0304's* unexpected dance-pop vibrancy makes it Jewel's best album—or, for detractors, her least unbearable."

Taking a different road on her return was Alanis Morissette, who had stripped naked, literally, to promote her 1998 album, *Supposed Former Infatuation Junkie.* It was successful, though not as big as *Jagged Little*

Pill's twenty-eight million seller. Both albums had been produced by Mississippi's Glen Ballard, and Alanis found it hard to shake rumors that he was the real creative force behind her music.

After her *Supposed Former Infatuation Junkie* tour ended, Alanis retreated to her native Canada and took stock of her life. By that point, her first two albums had sold over forty million units and she had garnered seven Grammy awards. You would think that would be validation enough for her, but she was troubled by her success, not certain what it meant in terms of her future. She decided to sever her relationship with Ballard and spend some time with herself in an effort to explore her own musical talents.

Four years after the release of *Supposed Former Infatuation Junkie,* Alanis emerged from her self-absorbed cocoon with her third studio album, *Under Rug Swept.* Because the album represented her innermost thoughts, she demanded control of the production process, which meant that, unlike her previous albums, she co-engineered the album. That is a little bit like representing yourself in a court case—not recommended. To Alanis's surprise, the album was a huge disappointment, offering only one major hit, "Hands Clean." That same year she released a second album, *Feast on Scraps*—a CD/DVD package that offered live concert video and unreleased tracks. It, too, faltered.

Alanis rebounded in 2004 with *So Called Chaos,* which she recorded in collaboration with longtime friends Tim Thorney and John Shanks. She used her touring band instead of studio musicians to obtain a more familiar sound. The songs continued her awkward probing of her own feminine consciousness, but unlike earlier efforts she seemed more willing to accept the possibility that she might not be the center of the universe. "I do tend to explore both sides of an argument on some of the songs," she says. "Either that interests me as a person and a writer, or I'm schizophrenic. Of course, both may be true."

Done with exploiting her own sexuality, the thirty-something Alanis put her focus on more immediate concerns—entering middle age. The mechanics of relationships now seemed of more concern, as in "Knees of my Bees," a love song written for her boyfriend. "The title was something I actually said to him several times in conversation: 'You make the knees of my bees weak.' So that line is very precious to me."

Alanis' repudiation of sexuality as a marketing tool for her music was an aberration that made her seem vaguely old-fashioned, an oddity, especially when compared to the in-your-face sexuality of *Jagged Little Pill.* Going the other direction was former Go-Go's singer Belinda Carlisle, who joined Tiffany in posing nude for *Playboy* (the headline read: "Go, Go, Girl! Belinda Carlisle Rocks Naked"). Pink posed topless, with only a few strands of beads covering her breasts. Beyonce left Destiny's Child to strut her stuff as a solo entertainer, stripping down to the bare essentials to generate a level of sexuality steamy enough to give Britney and Christina serious competition. And, of course, there was Courtney Love, who actually worked as a stripper before becoming a rock star. She flashed her breasts throughout the first half of the decade, her appearance on CBS's "Late Night With David Letterman" creating controversy when she jumped up on his desk with her back to the audience and lifted her shirt.

The women's revolution in music had reached a critical point by 2005, making it clear that the only barrier not yet breached was the previously forbidden world of the Total Sex Star. Was it just a matter of time before hit records were made by women willing to release videos of them actually having sex, thus merging the music and porn industries? It seemed unlikely until Hilton Hotel heiress Paris Hilton became a celebrity with the unauthorized release of a video showing her having sex with her boyfriend. Paris' video made everyone realize that it was just a matter of time until total sex became just another marketing tool for the music industry.

Curiously, running counterpoint to the sex boom, was a movement devoted to that most durable of all American icons—the Virgin Blonde. Brunettes can be good, bad, or anything in between, in the eyes of America pop culture. But blondes are something else. They are either virgins or tramps, with no room for middle ground. "I like to think of blondes as the knight in chess," blonde expert Courtney Love once explained to *Rolling Stone*. "It's the horsey-shape piece that moves in an L shape. It's what makes chess complicated. Without us, you cannot win, and you've got no one to blame for complicating everything."

Avril Lavigne, whose dirty blondness seems natural, scored her first hit when she was seventeen with an album titled *Let Go,* roping off musical territory sometimes called the Anti-Britney Zone. She kicked butt with her hard-rocking music, but she declined to show her butt—or anything else. Sometimes she talked tough, but it never lasted long, a product of her small-town Canadian upbringing.

If pressed, Avril invariably retreated into the vagaries of her virginal sweetness. Despite the sometimes ragged edge to her music, she was the first teen since Tiffany and Debbie Gibson to reject a sexual approach to her career. She wore oversized T-shirts and jeans, and she acted suitably shocked if randy reporters equated music and sex, as if the two were one in the same. She knew better—well, actually, she didn't know better, which made her naivete ever so endearing to devoted followers of the Virgin Blonde movement.

Hilary Duff, the fifteen-year-old blonde named "Teenager of the Year" by *Rolling Stone,* entered the music business through the Disney Channel's "Lizzie McGuire," one of the highest-rated cable shows for viewers between the ages of six and fourteen. When *The Lizzie McGuire Movie* was released in 2003, it grossed $42 million, and the accompanying soundtrack that featured songs performed by Hilary went Platinum. She followed that up with an album titled *Metamorphosis.*

Reporters loved to cover Hilary events because it invariably meant that they would get a blush out of her by saying something about her teen sex appeal or by asking her if the tabloid rumors about her boob job were true. Hilary looks older than her age and that can be confusing, until she pulls the plug on her dolled-up maturity, widens her eyes in little girl excitement, and utters her favorite phrase, "Oh, my God!"

Hilary once suggested that Avril Lavigne should appreciate her fans more by not criticizing them when they emulated her. When she read that, Avril's temper flared. In what could be described as the closest thing to a Virgin Blonde catfight, she told a *Newsweek* reporter that Hilary was "such a goody-goody, such a mommy's girl."

The reporter asked Avril if she had ever met Hilary.

"No," Avril confessed, slinking down on the couch to speak in a sugarcoated voice: "But I'm sure she's really nice and really sweet—I'm sure she's all smiles."

By the mid-2000s, the most famous Virgin Blonde on the planet was undoubtedly Texas-born temptress Jessica Simpson, who first got wind of her impending success at church camp when a minister told the campers that God had spoken to him and told him that one of them was going to use her voice to "touch the world."

Was he talking about me? Jessica wondered.

The following year, Jessica was among a group of students taken to the Dallas auditions for "The Mickey Mouse Club." She won the local competition with her rendition of "Amazing Grace," and went to Orlando to participate in the finals. Conspiracy theorists will find it interesting that her competition at the event consisted of Britney Spears, Christina Aguilera, and Justin Timberlake, all of whom dazzled the judges. Jessica choked and was sent back to Texas, where her father—a Baptist youth minister who worked with abused children—vowed to make her dreams come true.

That year her father gave her a purity ring—a silver band with a Christian cross—and promised to be her security and her support as the man in her life, until she grew up and found the man of her dreams. Put another way, he asked Jessica to stay a virgin until her wedding night. It was a bargain that Jessica readily accepted, partly because it came from her father, but mostly because she felt it came from God.

Growing up, Jessica took her responsibilities as a Christian seriously. She kept photographs of nearly two dozen missing children under her pillow, and she never went to sleep without praying for their safe return. At sixteen, she made an unsuccessful effort to adopt a Mexican baby that was found in a Dumpster. She was an activist Christian.

True to his word to make Jessica's dreams come true, her father was successful in landing her a recording deal with a local Christian label. Unfortunately, the label folded before her album could be released. Jessica's father took her recordings to every other Christian label in the country, but all passed with words that implied that she was simply too sexy to be accepted as a Christian performer. The rejections made Jessica feel bad about herself, for implicit in the pious criticisms were suggestions that she was somehow responsible for making men lust for her.

Luckily for Jessica, a Dallas talent scout for Columbia Records sent Jessica's demos to Sony Music chairman Tommy Mottola, who knew a thing or two about divas because he was married at the time to Mariah Carey. Mottola was impressed enough by her tapes to invite her to New York to audition for him in his office. Jessica sang a ballad and then she was told to sit down. Thinking she had choked again, as she had done at her Orlando audition, she was about to burst into tears, when she heard him say that he thought her music was going to "touch the world." Hallelujah—she had a record deal!

Oddly, Jessica signed her recording contract one week after Britney Spears signed hers, and one week before Christina Aguilera signed hers. It was as if the Virgin Blonde Grand Master had a plan afoot. Jessica started work on her album in 1997, but *Sweet Kisses* wasn't released until 1999, when Britney and Christina already had their albums out. It sold almost two million copies, a very good showing but far short of the multi-Platinum success enjoyed by Britney and Christina, whose music was all over the radio. Once again, Jessica came in third place. It was hard for her to take because, quite frankly, she has the best voice of the three, is arguably the most attractive—and, judging by family portraits with her mother and father, is a *real blonde*.

Early in her life, Jessica established a pattern of coming in third. That was probably because as a teen she did not drink, do drugs, or party with guys who were into the sex thing. "Well, I sure wasn't in the popular group, because I didn't party and do all that stuff," she told *Maxim*.

"Most girls hated me. They toilet-papered my house, egged my door, everything. It's funny, but it's almost always the case that those people end up working at Hooters, and the outsiders end up doing something really interesting with their lives."

Perhaps inspired by Britney and Christina's continuing success, Jessica dug in her heels and recorded a second album, *Irresistible*. They had time to release two singles before disaster struck—in the form of the September 11 attack against the World Trade Center in New York. After that the album simply stalled on the charts, as did many other albums, reflecting sales of less than 600,000 units. Heavily in debt, she returned to the studio to record another album, *In This Skin*. This time she planned to write all the songs herself, a departure from her previous albums, which had featured material hand-picked by hands-on label boss Mottola.

Meanwhile, Jessica married Nick Lachey, the man she had dated—without sex, she swears—since she was eighteen. When they met, it was love at first sight for Jessica, who felt that they were a heavenly match. They had more in common than physical attraction. Nick, like Jessica, had dreams of musical stardom: He was studying sports medicine at Miami University when he and a high-school friend formed a band named 98 Degrees. He left school and never looked back.

Shortly after getting married in October 2002, Jessica and Nick agreed to do a reality show for MTV titled "Newlyweds." The premise, a knockoff of the popular reality show, "The Osbournes," was simple: A camera crew would practically live with Jessica and Nick for four months, filming everything they did, except what happened in the bedroom, and the footage would be broken up into thirty-minute segments and aired on MTV.

At the time they agreed to do it, Jessica was working on *In This Skin* and Nick was working on his first solo album. They figured that the television exposure would help them promote their new albums. Doing it was a no-brainer. So what if they spent four months of their newlywed year with a camera crew invading their privacy? No big deal.

As it turned out, both albums performed poorly, but the television show was a huge success, making Jessica a media star. Viewers obsessed on her relationship with Nick and wondered how they would ever become an old married couple in view of the constant sparring that went on between them. Their adjustment to married life made for good television as they leaped into marriage with the entire world watching.

As entertaining as Jessica and Nick were as a married couple, it was Jessica's "dumb blonde" routine that made the show a success. For example: "Is this chicken—what I have—or is this fish? I know it's tuna, but it says chicken by the sea." Once, when asked if she wanted buffalo wings, she responded, "No, thanks, I don't eat buffalo." Then there was her reflection on aging: "Twenty-three is old. It's almost twenty-five, which is, like, almost mid-twenties."

Is Jessica as dumb as she sometimes seems? Don't bet on it. Dolly Parton once complained that it took a lot of money to look as tacky as she did. The same rationale applies to Virgin Blondes: It takes a lot of intelligence to appear dumb enough to be laughed at on a regular basis. In 2004, *People* magazine celebrated its thirtieth anniversary with a special star-packed issue that featured Jessica on the cover holding a pink birthday cake. Finally, she came in at first place, looking every bit the genius.

◆◇◆◇◆◇◆◇◆◇◆◇◆◇◆◇◆

Jessica Simpson's story offers two important lessons to would-be blondes in waiting for stardom: First, it takes more than being in the right place at the right time. Jessica was always in the right place at the right time, and still she lost out, time after time. Second, of all the ingredients necessary for success, the most important is always going to be publicity. You cannot be a celebrity without it.

The difference between a major star and a star wannabe is that the major star hounds publicity with a relentlessness that is sometimes frightening in its intensity, while the wannabe star runs away from publicity, often questioning its usefulness. It takes a certain amount of genius to understand all the nuances of fame.

Once, while working as a publicist, Pam Lewis had her job placed in perspective by singer/songwriter Vern Gosdin, who told her, "You are the only person in my life that I pay and I don't get anything back from."

"What do you mean?" she asked.

"Look at it this way," said Gosdin, a talented man but not a major star. "My time is valuable. I either go on a bus and they hand me a check at the end of the night. Or I write a song and I either cut it or someone else cuts it and I get a check—but I pay you. You make me talk to people I don't want to talk to—and you keep me away from working, which gives me a paycheck—or writing, which gives me a paycheck."

Pam thought about his short-sighted comments and concluded that it made perfect sense, at least from his perspective. "He said it kind of funny, but he said it meaning it, too," she says. "He would roll his eyes every time he had to do an interview because it meant he would have to sit there and answer some boring questions from journalists who sometimes didn't do their homework. I can see where it would get old."

Anyone inclined to give Jessica Simpson credit for genius would have to admire the way she took a media outlet—in this case MTV—and used it as if it were her own private publicity machine. She was able to obtain the fame she desired, not by virtue of hard work, or by presenting the world with the best singing voice it had ever heard, but rather by bombarding her audience with an unrelenting stream of entertaining publicity.

Jessica learned quickly what some artists take a lifetime to grasp. Apparently, it is a type of knowledge that is gender related. That may be why most publicists are women; it is the only part of the music business that has been female-dominated from the beginning. "The way I understand it," says Anita Mandell, who once headed up the publicity department at the now-defunct Decca Records, "it evolved from female groupies who headed the fan clubs—and from that, went into publicity."

Publicity may be the only facet of the music business where women have not encountered the level of gender-based hostility found in other departments. Sandy Neese, former head of publicity for Mercury Records, thinks that one reason for that may be that men are used to dealing with female publicists. The only time she has noticed problems has been when female publicists are given titles, such as vice president; it is the title that creates the confusion for some men, especially those who don't have titles, as if they aren't certain if they are supposed to show more respect to a woman who has a title.

"When they made me a vice president, I noticed I got spoken to by people who didn't bother with me before," she says. "People who I would have had to speak to first were now speaking to me first. So, it was very interesting to me to see how other peoples' perception of me changed. Once I was at a huge booking agency in Los Angeles with Mary Bailey and Shania—and this was after I had been a vice president maybe six months. We were having a film meeting and she was being introduced to some of the agents who dealt in films and this and that. I was just kind of sitting there quietly, you know—it wasn't my gig. I didn't really have much to say. So, this guy was acting like I was a piece of the wallpaper.

"Later, we were down in the lobby and he's standing there talking to Mary Bailey and I had gone over to use the phone. I saw her talking to him and then I saw him looking at me. Well, all of a sudden, he comes flying across the lobby. Can I get you a private phone? Can I get you something to drink? Can I get you this? Can I get you that? He did that because he found out I was a vice president. That's the way of the world—but it offended me."

◆◇◆◇◆◇◆◇◆◇◆◇◆◇◆◇◆◇◆◇◆

One of the most interesting developments of the New Millennium was the anti-Britney counterpoint that arose among a group of young women who took the country back to the early years of its musical development, largely with piano-based music that folded jazz and swing into country and pop to produce a refreshing body of work that attracted both critical and financial acclaim.

Performers such as Alicia Keys, Diana Krall, and Norah Jones went full circle, bringing back memories of Peggy Lee and Lil Hardin Armstrong and Billie Holiday. With the exception of Keys, who modestly bared her navel on occasion, the women rejected the shake-and-shimmy gymnastics of Britney and Christina in favor of a more laid-back glamour that projected their sex appeal almost entirely through their voices and faces. Their music was different in that while it had a retro sound and appeal, it drew not only from Lee and Holiday, but also from male performers such as Frank Sinatra. It was not androgynous, but it often projected sensibilities previously considered male.

Diana Krall was the trailblazer for this new movement. Born on the island of Nanaimo, British Columbia, she grew up dreaming of becoming an astronaut. A tomboy, she explored her neighborhood and dreamed of exploring outer space. She was sidetracked from that ambition by a household that made a big deal out of music. Her father played piano and her grandmother was an old-school singer who loved to belt out "Hard Hearted Hannah" just prior to bedtime.

Diana started performing at the age of fifteen and was considered precocious enough to win a scholarship to the Berklee College of Music. She didn't see it through, and left college to play professionally. She recorded two CDs, but neither attracted much attention. Then she put together a set of songs that better emphasized her sexy, whiskey voice and her abilities as a jazz pianist. *All for You,* recorded as a tribute to the Nat King Cole trio, went to the top of the jazz charts and stayed there an astonishing 82 weeks, establishing her as a player on the jazz scene.

By 2000, Diana was a major star. That year, she won her first Grammy for Best Jazz Vocal Performance, and she was considered a favorite to take home a Grammy for her album, *When I Look in Your Eyes,* until it became apparent that guitarist Carlos Santana would take home every award that year not firmly nailed down.

Diana seemed unlikely as a jazz musician. Tall and lean—and wouldn't you know it, pretty-girl blonde!—she had cover-girl looks and a sophisticated air about her, reminiscent of Peggy Lee, that generated an irresistible image notable for its cool confidence. She used pauses and sustained chords to draw the listener in and, once she had them where she wanted them, she finished them off with a voice lush enough to support a tropical garden. She was the opposite of Jessica Simpson, who sometimes became so animated during a performance, snapping her head and making overly dramatic facial gestures, that she sometimes made her audience uneasy. Diana learned early on that real musical power is derived from coolness, not heat. Small is bigger. Quiet is louder. Cool is hotter.

When Diana's 2001 album, *The Look of Love,* was released, *Entertainment Weekly* suggested that her "sensual cooing and luxuriously packaged high-glam image make her a worthy successor to the late Julie London, whom Krall honors [on this album] with an earthy rendition of London's hit, 'Cry Me a River.'" That was an odd comparison. Although their voices and singing styles are similar, London was never a consummate musician, territory that Diana lays claim to each time she takes the stage. A better comparison would be the 1950s' Rosemary Clooney, although before the singer died she insisted, "[Diana's] better than I was. I think she is of the caliber of Ella [Fitzgerald] and Peggy Lee. And she's a double threat, because she has what none of us did, being a brilliant pianist, too."

Alicia Keys is not a jazz pianist, but she incorporates elements of jazz into her unique blend of rhythm & blues, and hip hop. Born of Italian and African-American parents, she grew up in Harlem and began playing the piano at the age of five. While still in grammar school, she enrolled in the famous *Fame* school, the Performing Arts School of Manhattan, where she was given special attention by the teachers because of her obvious musical talent. Alicia didn't let all the attention go to her head, though, and she made an effort to keep her studies up, doing so well academically that she was able to graduate with honors from high school at the age of sixteen.

The next step was New York's Columbia University, where she enrolled as a music major. She was determined to get a college degree, but the lure of a recording contract with a major label was more than she could withstand, so she left school to turn professional, signing with Arista Records founder Clive Davis, who later took her with him to his new label, J Records. Her first album, *Songs in A Minor,* made her an instant star, when the single, "Fallin," went to the top of the charts. It is one of those romantic torch songs that gets down to the basics of what a woman feels when she is in a loving relationship. The song, delivered in a vocal style reminiscent of Stevie Wonder and Marvin Gaye, made such a splash that she walked away from the 2002 Grammys with five awards in hand.

Alicia is a striking woman who could have made it as a Dallas

Cowboys cheerleader or *Baywatch* babe if the singing gig hadn't worked out, but she has downplayed her beauty in an effort to garner more focus on her music. An *Entertainment Weekly* reporter once asked her where she felt the greatest pressure, in terms of people asking her to do things she really didn't want to do.

"For me, it really comes with being conscious of the image that I portray," she explained. "Because in a lot of different situations—with a lot of different male photographers, shall we go ahead and say—they see a young woman and they just want to see skin, they just want to see tits, ass, body, sex. That's been a big battle for me. When a person is constantly pushing that on you, it gets very wearing. You have to constantly be on the top-top-top of your game. Because they will catch you at a weak moment."

Norah Jones, a twenty-something torch singer whom *Rolling Stone* once proclaimed "The Good Girl," comes from that same place. Few photographers would have the guts to ask her to "take it off," because there's something about her doe-eyed innocence that suggests that a jail term might be in order if a photographer crossed the line with her. Besides, there is nothing overtly glamorous about Norah. She performs in the same jeans and T-shirts that she wears on the street. She can't see getting all gussied up just to play the piano and sing a few songs. She has a natural beauty that seems as timeless as her music.

The daughter of Indian sitar master Ravi Shankar, whom she seldom saw growing up, and a concert producer who had an extensive record collection, Norah started piano at an early age and ended up studying piano and music theory in the jazz program at the University of North Texas, near her hometown of Dallas. As so often happens, two years into the program, she tired of *talking* about music and struck out for New York, where she quickly landed work in the city's famous jazz rooms.

The day after her twenty-first birthday, Norah got an audition with Bruce Lundvall, the head of Blue Note Records, the jazz imprint of EMI Records. Lundvall recognized her talent immediately and arranged for two producers to work with her in the studio. When he heard the results, he suggested that it might be better if she was signed with the pop division. Norah would have none of that, insisting that she must stay with the smaller label, where she felt more comfortable. That presented a dilemma for Lundvall since her music, strictly speaking, was not jazz, but rather a hybrid of jazz, country, and pop. He told her that she would be happier with the pop division. She stood her ground. Finally, he said what the heck, and gave her what she wanted.

Shortly before the release of her first album, *Come Away With Me*,

Norah told friends that she hoped it would sell 10,000 copies, so that the record label would allow her to record a second album. It sold 10,000 copies the first week. When sales reached one million, she asked Lundvall if he would please stop selling the album, since she was frightened by all the attention it was receiving. Lundvall politely declined to stop sales—and the album ended up selling eight million copies worldwide.

"I know it was naive [to ask], but I was starting to panic," she explained to the *Los Angeles Times*. Not only did the album become the biggest-selling release in Blue Note's history, it garnered eight Grammy awards at the 2003 ceremonies—another panic time for the painfully shy singer, who had to take the stage to collect the trophies.

With the 2004 release of her second album, *Feels Like Home,* there was little doubt that Norah had even bigger things in her future. Wrote Tom Moon for *Rolling Stone:* "Where most creators of vocal pop music concentrate on crafting tight couplets and big-payoff refrains, Jones just sits at the piano and chases less obvious targets—ruminative moods and hushed-whisper atmospheres. And she's found, in two graceful albums, a whole different kind of mojo lurking inside the three-minute song." *People* critic Chuck Arnold notes that when Norah "achingly sings, 'It never rains when you want it to,' you'll be humbled by her graceful, unassuming talent."

What people seemed to like most about Norah was her ability to use her smoky voice to lure the listener into her world of laughing children, broken hearts, and shattered dreams that sometimes found a way to come back together by song's end. Along with performers like Diana Krall and Alicia Keys, she represented the hopes of the women who laid the groundwork for the women's revolution in music: The belief that music is an art form that does not require sexuality as a sales tool, unless sex is what you are selling.

There are no crystal balls capable of revealing the future of women in music, but it seems clear that whatever they do, whether the end result is uplifting or shocking, artistic or pedestrian, they will do it as equal partners from this point onward. For that, they can thank Lil Hardin Armstrong, Peggy Lee, Billie Holiday, Madonna, Alanis Morissette, Shania Twain—and all the others who gambled everything on the future.

Top Twenty Honor Roll

Women Who had Hits on Top Twenty Album Charts

1954-1959
Annette
Lavern Baker
Bobbettes
Teresa Brewer
Cathy Carr
Chordettes
Rosemary Clooney
Jill Corey
DeCastro Sisters
DeJohn Sisters
Doris Day
Toni Fisher
Fontane Sisters
Connie Francis
Ronnie Gaylord
Georgia Gibbs
Gogi Grant
Bonnie Guitar
Joni James
Kitty Kallen
Eartha Kitt
Peggy Lee
Kathy Linden
Laurie London
Denise Lor
Giselle Mackenzie
McGuire Sisters
Jaye P. Morgan
Patti Page
Playmates
Jane Powell
Della Reese
Debbie Reynolds
Jody Reynolds
Jo Stafford
Kay Starr

Dodie Stevens
Gale Storm
Caterina Valente
June Valli
Sarah Vaughan
Dinah Washington
Joan Weber

1960-1969
Jewel Akens
Angels
Annette
Barbara Lynn
Shirley Bassey
Jeanne Black
Marcie Blane
Jan Bradley
Anita Bryant
Vikki Carr
Cathy Jean &
Roommates
Cher
Claudine Clark
Dee Clark
Petula Clark
Patsy Cline
Judy Collins
Skeeter Davis
Dixiebelles
Patty Duke
Shirley Ellis
Shelley Fabares
Toni Fisher
Inez Foxx
Connie Francis
Gale Garnett
Bobbie Gentry

Barbara George
Gladys Knight &
the Pips
Lesley Gore
Eydie Gorme
Brenda Holloway
Mary Hopkins
Janis Ian
Brenda Lee
Barbara Lewis
Little Eva
Little Peggy March
Lolita
Mama Cass
Miriam Makeba
Martha & the
Vandellas
Barbara Mason
Hayley Mills
Patti Page
Paris Sisters
Ester Phillips
Sandy Posey
Della Reese
Diane Renay
Jeannie C. Riley
Julie Rogers
Rosie & the Originals
Merrilee Rush
Linda Scott
Shirelles
Nancy Sinatra
Singing Nun
Millie Small
Joanie Sommers
Dusty Springfield
Connie Stevens

Barbra Streisand
Supremes
Carla Thomas
Sue Thompson
Doris Troy
Dionne Warwick
Mary Wells
Nancy Wilson
Kathy Young

1970-1979
Lynn Anderson
Joan Baez
Blondie
Debby Boone
Beverly Bremmers
Alicia Bridges
Cher
Natalie Cole
Judy Collins
Rita Coolidge
Jessi Colter
Kiki Dee
Diana Ross &
Supremes
Carol Douglas
Yvonne Elliman
Donna Fargo
Roberta Flack
Aretha Franklin
Crystal Gayle
Gloria Gaynor
Gladys Knight & the
Pips
Heart
Thelma Houston
Janis Ian
Evelyn King
Carole King
Jean Knight
Rickie Lee Jones

Janis Joplin
Nicolette Larson
Vicki Lawrence
Cheryl Lynn
Mary MacGregor
Melissa Manchester
Maureen McGovern
Sister Janet Mead
Melanie
Bette Midler
Joni Mitchell
Dorothy Moore
Maria Muldaur
Anne Murray
Olivia Newton-John
Maxine Nightingale
Marie Osmond
Dolly Parton
Freda Payne
Pointer Sisters
Helen Reddy
Minnie Riperton
Vicki Sue Robinson
Linda Ronstadt
Carly Simon
Phoebe Snow
Barbra Streisand
Donna Summer
Sylvia
Bonnie Tyler
Anita Ward
Jennifer Warnes
Dionne Warwick
Betty Wright

1980-1989
Paula Abdul
Anita Baker
Bananarama
Bangles
Pat Benatar

Blondie
Laura Branigan
Edie Brickell
Irene Cara
Belinda Carlisle
Kim Carnes
Tracy Chapman
Charlene
Cher
Nenah Cherry
Natalie Cole
Taylor Dane
Sheila E
Sheena Easton
Gloria Estefan
Expose
Roberta Flack
Samatha Fox
Aretha Franklin
Debbie Gibson
Go-Go's
Heart
Whitney Houston
Janet Jackson
Joan Jett
Katrina & the Waves
Chaka Khan
Carole King
Gladys Knight
Cyndi Lauper
Madonna
Melissa Manchester
Teena Marie
Mary Jane Girls
Christine McVie
Bette Midler
Stephanie Mills
Anne Murray
Juice Newton
Olivia Newton-John
Stevie Nicks

208

Dolly Parton
Pointer Sisters
Stacey Q
Regina
Linda Ronstadt
Diana Ross
Sade
Carly Simon
Brenda K. Starr
Barbra Streisand
Donna Summer
Sylvia
Tiffany
T'Pau
Tina Turner
Bonnie Tyler
Tracey Ullman
Suzanne Vega
Dionne Warwick
Jody Watley
Karyn White
Jane Wiedin
Kim Wilde
Denice Williams
Vanessa Williams

1990-1999
Aaliyah
Paula Abdul
Tori Amos
Fiona Apple
Erykah Badu
Anita Baker
Mary J. Blige
Brandy
Toni Braxton
Mariah Carey
Mary Chapin
Carpenter
Deana Carter
Tracy Chapman

Natalie Cole
Sheryl Crow
Celine Dion
Missy Elliott
En Vogue
Gloria Estefan
Melissa Etheridge
Fleetwood Mac
Amy Grant
Indigo Girls
Heart
Whitney Houston
Janet Jackson
Jewel
Alison Krauss
K.D. Lang
Annie Lennox
Madonna
Reba McEntire
Sarah McLachlan
Natalie Merchant
Bette Midler
Alanis Morissette
Alannah Myles
No Doubt
Sinead O'Connor
Joan Osborne
Dolly Parton
Bonnie Raitt
Leann Rimes
Linda Ronstadt
Sade
Selena
Spice Girls
Lisa Stansfield
Barbra Streisand
Tina Turner
Shania Twain
Suzanne Vega
Vanessa Williams
Wilson Phillips

Wynonna
Trisha Yearwood

2000-
Aaliyah
Christina Aguilera
Ashanti
Beyonce
Mary J. Blige
Michelle Branch
Vanesse Carlton
Cher
Kelly Clarkson
Sheryl Crow
Dido
Celine Dion
Dixie Chicks
Hilary Duff
Missy Elliott
Melissa Etheridge
Faith Hill
Lauryn Hill
Janet Jackson
Jewel
Norah Jones
Alicia Keys
Avril Lavigne
Annie Lennox
Jennifer Lopez
Madonna
Sarah McLachlan
Monica
Mandy Moore
No Doubt
Pink
Lisa Marie Presley
Bonnie Raitt
Shakira
Jessica Simpson
Britney Spears
Shania Twain

Bibliography

Author Interviews

Marilyn Arthur
Estelle Axton
Mary Bailey
Renee Bell
Pat Benatar
Garth Brooks
Deana Carter
June Carter Cash
Tena Clark
Terri Clark
Rita Coolidge
Tracey Edmonds
Melissa Etheridge
Debe Fennell
Bobbie Gentry
Brenda Lee
Laurie Lewis
Pam Lewis
Anita Mandell
Kathy Mattea
Abra Moore
Sandy Neese
Tracy Nelson
Claire Parr
Vicki Peterson
Frances Preston
Bonnie Raitt
Mark Rothbaum
Shelia Shipley Biddy
Michael Steele
Doug Supernaw
Carla Thomas
Tiffany
Tanya Tucker
Shania Twain
Ann and Nancy Wilson
Tammy Wynette

All of the quotes in this book from the late Marion Keisker, not otherwise identified were taken from interviews in the Jerry Hopkins Collection at the University of Memphis; the interviews are part of the Mississippi Valley Collection at the university library.

Lil Hardin Armstrong's comments about Jelly Roll Morton were taken from a January 19, 1969, interview she did while in New Orleans. A transcript of the interview can be viewed at the Williams Research Center.

All chart information in this book was derived from information originally published by Billboard *and reprinted by* Rolling Stone *magazine. The information was tabulated and compiled by the author, who is responsible for its accuracy. The author first pointed out the women's 1996 revolution in music for the July 1997 issue of* Glamour *magazine.*

Books

Armstrong, Louis. *Louis Armstrong: In His Own Words.* New York: Oxford University Press, 1999.

Aquila, Richard. *That Old Time, Rock & Roll: A Chronicle of an Era.* New York: Schirmer Books, 1989.

Bego, Mark. *Linda Ronstadt: It's So Easy!* Austin, Texas: Eakin Press, 1990.

Bindas, Kenneth J. *All of This Music Belongs to the Nation.* Knoxville: University of Tennessee Press, 1995.

Bronson, Fred. *The Billboard Book of Number One Hits.* New York: Billboard, 1985.

Chase, Gilbert. *America's Music: From the Pilgrims to the Present.* New York: McGraw-Hill, 1955.

Cooper, Sarah (editor). *Girls! Girls! Girls! Essays on Women and Music.* New York: New York University Press, 1996.

Cusic, Don. *Reba McEntire: Country Music's Queen.* New York: St. Martin's Press, 1991.

Dannen, Fredric. *Hit Men: Power Brokers and Fast Money Inside the Music Business.* New York: Times Books, 1990.

Denisoff, R. Serge. *Inside MTV.* New Brunswick, NJ: Transaction Books, 1988.

Dickerson, James. *Goin' Back to Memphis: A Century of Blues, Rock & Roll, and Glorious Soul.* New York: Schirmer Books, 1996.

Dickerson, James. *Coming Home: 21 Conversations About Memphis Music.* Memphis: Scripps Howard, 1985.

Dickerson, James. *Just for a Thrill: Lil Hardin Armstrong, First Lady of Jazz.* New York: Cooper Square Press, 2002.

Dickerson, James. *Faith Hill: Piece of My Heart.* New York: St. Martin's Press, 2001.

Dickerson, James. *Dixie Chicks: Down-Home and Backstage*. Dallas: Taylor Trade Publishing, 2000.

Garon, Paul and Beth. *Woman With Guitar*. New York: Da Capo,1992.

Gruber, J. Richard. *Memphis 1948-1958*. Memphis: Memphis Brooks Museum of Art, 1986.

Gubernick, Lisa Rebecca. *Get Hot or Go Home*. New York: St. Martin's Press, 1993.

Hopkins, Jerry. *Festival: The Book of American Music Celebrations*. New York: Macmillan, 1970.

Leamer, Laurence. *Three Chords and the Truth*. New York: HarperCollins,1997.

Lee, Peggy. *Miss Peggy Lee: An Autobiography*. New York: Donald Fine, 1989.

Lynn, Loretta. *Loretta Lynn: Coal Miner's Daughter*. Chicago: Henry Regnery Company, 1976.

Morrison, Craig. *Go Cat Go!: Rockabilly Music and Its Makers*. Chicago: University of Illinois Press, 1996.

Muirhead, Bert. *The Record Producers File*. Dorset, England: Blandford Press, 1984.

McAleer, Dave. *The All Music Book of Hit Singles*. San Francisco: Miller Freeman Books, 1994.

Nash, Alanna. *Behind Closed Doors*. New York: Alfred A. Knopf, 1988.

Nite, Norm N. (with Ralph M. Newman). *Rock On: The Illustrated Encyclopedia of Rock & Roll*. New York: Thomas Y. Cromell, 1978.

Oermann, Robert K. and Mary A. Burwack. *Finding Her Voice: The Saga of Women in Country Music*. New York: Crown Publishers, (1993).

Parton, Dolly. *Dolly: My Life and Other Unfinished Business*. New York: HarperCollins, 1994.

Patoski, Joe Nick. *Selena: Como la Flor*. New York: Boulevard, 1997.

Reynolds, Debbie, and David Patrick Columbia. *Debbie: My Life*. New York: William Morrow and Co., 1988.

Reynolds, Simon, and Joy Press. *The Sex Revolts: Gender, Rebellion, and Rock & Roll*.
Cambridge, Massachusetts: Harvard University Press, 1995.

Shaw, Arnold. *Dictionary of American Pop/Rock*. New York: Schirmer Books, 1982.

Smith, Joe (edited by Mitchell Fink). *Off the Record: An Oral History of Popular Music*. New York: Warner Books, 1988.

Tarabororrelli, J. Randy. *Call Her Miss Ross*. New York: Carol Publishing Group, 1989.

Turner, Tina. *I, Tina*. New York: Avon, 1986.

Weinstein, Deena. *Heavy Metal: A Cultural Sociology*. New York: Lexington Books, 1991.

Weissman, Dick. *The Music Business: Career Opportunities and Self-Defense*. New York: Crown Publishers, 1979.

Wynette, Tammy, with Joan Dew. *Stand By Your Man*. New York: Simon and Schuster, 1979.

Articles

Aletti, Vince. "Whitney Plays It Safe." *Rolling Stone*, August 13, 1987.

Ali, Lorraine. "Backstage at Lilith." *Rolling Stone*, September 1997.

Andrews, Suzanna. "Changing Nashville's Tune." *Working Woman*, August 1995.

Arnold, Chuck. "Feels Like Home." *People*, February 23, 2004.

Axthelm, Pete. "Lookin' at Country With Loretta Lynn." *Newsweek*, June 18, 1973.

Baldwin, Dawn. "Aimee Mann Not Waiting 'Til Tuesday." *Nine-O-One Network*, Jan./Feb. 1987.

Binelli, Mark. "Teenager of the Year." *Rolling Stone*, September 18, 2003.

—. "The Accidental Superstar." *Rolling Stone*, March 18, 2004.

—. "Sometimes It's Hard to Be a Woman." *Rolling Stone*, October 2, 2003.

Browne, David. "Winging It." *Entertainment Weekly*, September 19, 1997.

Brown, Foxy. "Cyndi Lauper." *Interview*, May 1997.

Catlin, Roger. "McLachlan's Lilith Fair." *The Hartford Courant*, August 1997.

Clift, Eleanor. "Songs of Non-Liberation." *Newsweek*, August 2, 1971.

Cocks, Jay. "Madonna Draws a Line." *Time,* December 17, 1990.

Coker, Cheo Hodari. "Taking a Deep Breath, Again." *Los Angeles Times,* June 16, 1996.

Considine, J. D. "Luscious Jackson." *Entertainment Weekly,* October 1997.

Dickerson, James. "Memphis Women Rockers." *Nine-O-One Network,* January/February 1987.

——. "Tanya Tucker: Good Friends Make the Best Records." *Nine-O-One Network,* April 1988.

——. "Pop Music: Now a Woman's World." *Glamour,* July 1997.

——. "The Bangles." *Nine-O-One Network,* December 1987.

——. "Hard-Working Tanya Tucker Zooms Career Back Into Gear." *CoverStory,* August 1994.

——. "Carol Decker Puts 'Heart and Soul' Into This British Group's Music." *Nine-O-One Network,* December 1987.

——. "Chickasaw County Child." *Mississippi Magazine,* Winter 1968.

——. "Heart: You Can't Take Sex Out of Rock 'n' Roll." *Nine-O-One Network,* February 1988.

——. "A Taste of Pure Country." *CoverStory,* June 1994.

——. "Kathy Mattea: The Singer-Next-Door Who Won Nashville's Heart." *Nine-O-One Network,* April 1988.

Dunn, Jancee. "Cosmis Girl Jewel." *Rolling Stone,* May 1997.

——. "Christina." *Rolling Stone,* June 26, 2003.

Elder, Renee. "Reba May Hover Over Music Row." *Nashville Tennessean,* January 4, 1995.

Flick, Larry. "Is the World Ready for a Serious Cyndi Lauper?" *Billboard,* February 21, 1997.

Flynn, Brown Alan. "Petula Says Working Here Is Like Having a Party." *Memphis Press-Scimitar,* February 25, 1970.

Fong-Torres, Ben. "Linda Ronstadt: Heartbreak on Wheels." *Rolling Stone,* March 27, 1975.

Garratt, Sheryl. "Madonna." *The Face,* 1996.

Garvin, Glenn. "Bobbie Hopes Film Will Relaunch Recording Career." *Delta Democrat-Times,* June 6, 1976.

Gersten, Russell. "Records." *Rolling Stone,* March 28, 1974.

Grigoriadis, Vanessa. "Portrait of a Living Doll." *Rolling Stone,* November 27, 2003.

Hannaham, James. "Alanis in Wonderland." *Spin,* November 1995.

Heath, Chris. "Spice Girls." *Rolling Stone,* July 1997.

Heiman, Andrea. "Film Stars Decry Sex Harassing." *Los Angeles Times,* 1992.

——. "Facing Up to Sexual Harassment in Hollywood." *Los Angeles Times,* February 15, 1992.

Hesbacker, Peter, and Bruce Anderson. "Hit Singers' Careers Since 1940s: Have Women Advanced?" *Popular Music & Society* 1980.

Honick, Bruce. "Why Country's Getting Sexier." *Country Music,* July 1996.

Kahn, Sheryl. "Reba's Rules." *McCall's,* September 1996.

Keel, Beverly. "The House That Reba Built." *New Country,* June 1994.

Kelly, Jim "Alanis Morisette Interview." *Canadian Musician,* March 2002.

Kroll, Jack. "Wannabes Spice Girls." *Newsweek,* July 1997.

Ladouceur, Liisa. "Sarah McLachlan." *Pulse,* July 1997.

Laskow, Michael. "Nancy Brennan." *A&R Insider,* 1995.

Love, Courtney. "The Blonde Bombshell." *Rolling Stone,* May 15, 2003.

Lubenow, Gerald C. "The God of Grace." *Newsweek,* March 15, 1971.

Madden, Mike. "The Beat Is Latino." *Gannett News Service,* August 1997.

Meisel, Steven. "The Misfit." *Vanity Fair,* April 1991.

Michener, Charles. "The Divine Miss M." *Newsweek,* May 22, 1972.

Moon, Tom. "The Good Girl." *Rolling Stone,* March 4, 2004.

Noyer, Paul Du. "Music, Maestress,

Please!" *Q Magazine,* December 1994.

Oermann, Robert K. "Shania Twain: More Than Meets the Eye." *Nashville Tennessean,* February 28, 1996.

—. "Hunger Puts Janis Ian Back in the Spotlight." *Nashville Tennessean,* October 4, 1997.

Orlean, Susan. "California Girls." *Rolling Stone,* March 26, 1987.

Orth, Maureen, with Janet Huck. "No Fear of Flying." *Newsweek,* February 23, 1976.

Pareles, Jon. "Forget the Hard Rock: It's Support for Sisterhood." *The New York Times,* July 7, 1997.

Pener, Degen. "Butterflies Aren't Free." *Entertainment Weekly,* September 1997.

Phillips, Chuck. "Geffen Firm Said to Settle Case of Sex Harassment." *Los Angeles Times,* November 17, 1992.

—. "Anita Hill of Music Industry Talks." *Los Angeles Times,* 1992.

Randall, Nancy. "Sexual Harassment: Women by the Thousands are Fighting Back—And They Are Winning." *Nine-O-One Network,* February 1988.

Rapping, Elayne. "Empty vs. Mindless, Sure But Vicious Too." *The Guardian,* February 8, 1984.

"Rebirth of the Blues." *Newsweek,* May 26, 1969.

Robicheau, Paul. "Taking Aim at Ani DiFranco." *Boston Globe,* May 12, 1994.

Roland, Tom. "CMA Show Launch Pad for Twain." *Nashville Tennessean,* September 23, 1997.

Saal, Hubert. "Bonnie and Blue." *Newsweek,* November 6, 1972.

—. "Singing Is Better Than Any Dope." *Newsweek,* October 19, 1970.

—. "The Girls—Letting Go." *Newsweek,* July 14, 1969.

Schleier, Curt. "Nancy Sinatra." *The Detroit News,* November 8, 1995.

Schmitt, Brad. "Starstruck Trims Clients, Narrows Focus to Reba." *Nashville Tennessean,* May 29, 1997.

Schoemer, Karen. "Alternative Divas Luscious Jackson Break Out." *Newsweek,* March 31, 1997.

—. "The Malling of Shania." *Newsweek,* February 1996.

Schruers, Fred. "Sheryl: She Only Wants to Be With You." *Rolling Stone,* November 1996.

Smith, Danyel. "Janet Jackson." *Vibe,* 1994.

"The Spector of Payola '73." *Newsweek,* June 11, 1973.

Spurrier, Jeff. "The People's Courtney." *Details,* October 1995.

Svetkey, Benjamin."All Eyes on Britney." *Entertainment Weekly,* November 21, 2003.

Tannenbaum, Rob. "Liz Phair." *Details,* June 1994.

Verna, Paul. "Abra Moore's Profile Sprouts with 'Clover.'" *Billboard,* May 1997.

Waller, Don. "Sylvia Robinson: Godmother of Street Music." *Pulse,* October 1997.

"Where She Is and Where She's Going." *Time,* March 20, 1972.

Whittlesey, Kristin. "Fiona Apple." *Nashville Banner,* October 3, 1997.

Wild, David. "The Adventures of Miss Thing." *Rolling Stone,* November 2, 1995.

—. "Alanis Morissette." *Rolling Stone,* November 1995.

Will, Chris. "The Second Coming of Alanis." *Entertainment Weekly,* November 6, 1998.

Winegarner, Beth. "Cyndi Lauper." *San Francisco Chronicle,* March 30, 1997.

Yampert, Rick de. "Emmylou Sings the Praises of Women." *Nashville Tennessean,* August 3, 1997.

Young, Paul. "Jessica!" *Maxim,* January 2002.

Zollo, Paul. "Jewel: Songs of Hope for the Next Generation." *Acoustic Guitar,* July 1997.

Index